STUDY GUIDE

FOR

GARDNER'S

ART

THROUGH
THE
AGES

EIGHTH EDITION

STUDY GUIDE
FOR

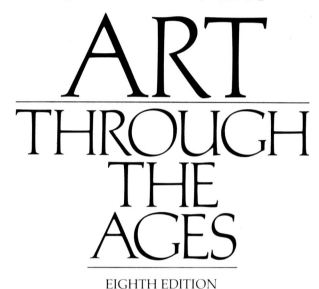

GARDNER'S
ART
THROUGH
THE
AGES

EIGHTH EDITION

Kathleen Cohen

San Jose State University

Horst de la Croix

With a Geographical Index of works
illustrated in the text, compiled
by Luraine Collins Tansey

HARCOURT BRACE JOVANOVICH, PUBLISHERS
San Diego   New York   Chicago   Atlanta   Washington, D.C.
London   Sydney   Toronto

PREFACE

This Study Guide to accompany Gardner's *Art through the Ages*, Eighth Edition, is intended to help students approach the vast amount of material encountered in a survey of art history. The guide provides them with a structure for their learning that both reinforces and supplements the structure implicit in the text.

The guide has been designed to ensure that upon completion of this course, students will be able to

1. Identify the time periods, geographical centers, and stylistic characteristics of major art movements from the prehistoric period to the present and name artists working in each movement
2. Discuss the work of major artists in terms of their artistic concerns and stylistic characteristics, the media they used, and the principal influences on them
3. Define and use common terms of art history
4. Recognize and discuss the iconography of specified works of art, as well as the iconography popular during various historical periods
5. Identify significant philosophical movements, religious concepts, and historical figures, events, and places and discuss their relation to works of art
6. Attribute unfamiliar works of art to an artist, a country and/or style, and a period

The questions in the first part of each unit call for short answers to be written in the guide. Studies have shown that the act of writing down an answer rather than merely reading it serves to imprint it more securely in the mind. Furthermore, reading through the text for specific answers helps students to concentrate effectively. These questions emphasize recognition of the stylistic characteristics of both artists and periods and the basic terminology of art history. The Glossary in the back of the text, as well as the text itself, can be used in completing many of these questions.

Each unit ends with a variety of discussion questions designed to engage students actively in assessing the significance of what they have learned. Some questions are of a general, philosophical nature, requiring reference to specific artists and styles. Some ask for interpretation of theories. Others involve the comparison of works, artists, and styles from different times and places, sometimes with reference to the students' daily experience. All are calculated to broaden the students' perspective by making them see familiar styles in unfamiliar contexts.

Summary charts throughout the guide cover the work of one or several chapters in the text. These are organized chronologically and contain sections for students to write in major artists, representative works, stylistic characteristics, and other relevant facts. Students should be urged to fill in these charts as much as possible from memory, using the text to complete any unanswered sections. The process will integrate the material into a coherent, condensed form that will help students understand important developments; the completed summary charts will be invaluable in reviewing for examinations.

Self-quizzes appear at the end of each of the five major divisions of the guide. Answers are given at the back, so that students can determine for themselves how well they are progressing.

The overall emphasis on stylistic characteristics is intended to give students the visual and intellectual tools to approach works of art they have never seen before with some degree of confidence. A feature of each of the five self-quizzes is a group of illustrations of works or details not shown in the main textbook, which students are asked to attribute to particular artists or periods, giving reasons for their answers. These exercises may be done as either closed- or open-book tests, at the discretion of the instructor.

Many of the questions in the guide will serve as excellent preparation for examinations. Instructors may wish to base some of their examination questions on the materials covered in the guide; they may even wish to establish with students at the beginning of the course that a specified percentage of the examination questions will be taken from the guide.

In the back of the guide is a Geographical Index, a listing of the locations (organized by country, city, and museum or site) of works illustrated in the main text. Compiled by art historian Luraine Collins Tansey, it is intended to encourage students' interest in seeing the actual works of art they have been studying—rather than reproductions—by helping them locate those works in their own regions and when they travel.

KATHLEEN COHEN
HORST DE LA CROIX

CONTENTS

Preface   v

Introduction   1

PART ONE: THE ANCIENT WORLD

Chapter One   The Birth of Art   3

Chapter Two   The Ancient Near East   7

Chapter Three   The Art of Egypt   16

Chapter Four   The Art of the Aegean   24

Chapter Five   The Art of Greece   32

    The Geometric and Archaic Periods   32

    The Fifth Century   37

    The Fourth Century and the Hellenistic Period   40

    Summary: The Art of Greece   45

Chapter Six   Etruscan and Roman Art   50

    The Etruscans and the Romans of the Republican Period   50

    The Early Empire and the Late Empire   56

    Summary: Etruscan and Roman Art   61

Chapter Seven   Early Christian, Byzantine, and Islamic Art   66

    Early Christian Art and Byzantine Art (at Ravenna)   66

    Byzantine and Islamic Art   72

Self-Quiz--Part One: The Ancient World   79

PART TWO: THE MIDDLE AGES

Introduction   87

Chapter Eight   Early Medieval Art   87

Chapter Nine   Romanesque Art   95

Chapter Ten Gothic Art   104
    Early and High Gothic Art   104
    Late and Non-French Gothic Art   110
    Summary: Gothic Art   113
Self-Quiz—Part Two: The Middle Ages   116

PART THREE: THE NON-EUROPEAN WORLD

    Introduction   123
Chapter Eleven   The Art of India   123
Chapter Twelve   The Art of China   132
Chapter Thirteen   The Art of Japan   138
Chapter Fourteen   The Native Arts of the Americas, Africa,
                 and the South Pacific   143
    Pre-Columbian Art   143
    North American Indian and Eskimo Art   148
    African Art   151
    Art of the South Pacific   154
    Summary: The Native Arts of the Americas, Africa,
           and the South Pacific   156
Self-Quiz—Part Three: The Non-European World   158

PART FOUR: THE RENAISSANCE AND THE BAROQUE AND ROCOCO

    Introduction   167
Chapter Fifteen   The "Proto-Renaissance" in Italy   167
Chapter Sixteen   Fifteenth-Century Italian Art   173
    The First Half of the Fifteenth Century   174
    The Second Half of the Fifteenth Century   178
Chapter Seventeen   Sixteenth-Century Italian Art   183
    Leonardo, Bramante, and Raphael   183
    Michelangelo, Andrea del Sarto, and Correggio and Mannerism   186
    Venice   190
    Summary: The Italian Renaissance   194
Chapter Eighteen   The Renaissance Outside of Italy   201
    The Fifteenth Century   201
    The Sixteenth Century   209
    Summary: The Renaissance Outside of Italy   216
Chapter Nineteen   Baroque Art   220
    The Seventeenth Century in Italy and Spain   220
    The Seventeenth Century in Flanders and Holland   225
    The Seventeenth Century in France and England   229
Chapter Twenty   The Eighteenth Century: Rococo and the Rise of Romanticism   233
    Late Baroque and Rococo   233
    The Rise of Romanticism   237

Summary: Seventeenth- and Eighteenth-Century Art   240
Summary: The Renaissance and the Baroque and Rococo   247
Self-Quiz—Part Four: The Renaissance and the Baroque and Rococo   248

PART FIVE: THE MODERN WORLD

Chapter Twenty-One   The Nineteenth Century: Pluralism of Style   259
The First Half of the Nineteenth Century   259
The Second Half of the Nineteenth Century   263
Summary: The Nineteenth Century   272
Chapter Twenty-Two   The Twentieth Century   278
Painting Before World War II   278
Sculpture and Architecture Before World War II   282
Painting, Sculpture, and Architecture After World War II   286
Summary: The Twentieth Century   294
Self-Quiz—Part Five: The Modern World   298

Answers for Self-Quizzes   308
Geographical Index   318

INTRODUCTION

1. According to the text, much of art historical research is based on the hypothesis that works produced at the same time and the same place will:

2. List three fundamental ways of classifying works of art as discussed on text pages 5-6.

   a.

   b.

   c.

3. To what type of space do the terms *plane* and *area* refer?

4. Define the following terms as used by art historians, using the text and Glossary as necessary:

   mass

   volume

   line

   perspective

   proportion

   value

   chiaroscuro

   hue

   texture

   contour

5.   What are the three primary colors?   the secondary colors?

a.   a.

b.   b.

c.   c.

6.   Define the following architectural terms:

plan

section

elevation

7.   Define the following sculptural terms:

high relief

low relief (bas-relief)

8.   Write down two types of material that could be used in creating *subtractive* sculpture.

_____   _____

Write down two types of material that could be used in creating *additive* sculpture.

_____   _____

DISCUSSION QUESTIONS

1.   Why is the establishment of a correct chronological sequence important to art historians?

2.   What is *iconography* and what are its functions in art-historical study?

3.   Discuss the difference between the *likeness* of an object and a *representation* of it.

4.   What is the difference between *conceptual* and *perceptual* approaches to art?

5.   What do you think T. S. Eliot meant when he said that "the past should be altered by the present as much as the present is directed by the past"?

PART ONE: THE ANCIENT WORLD

Chapter One
The Birth of Art

1. Define the following terms:

   dolmen

   corbeled vault

   menhir

   cromlech

   trilithon

   megalith

   tectiform

2. List four caves that contain Paleolithic paintings.

   a.   c.

   b.   d.

   What stylistic characteristics are shared by the paintings in these caves?

   a.

   b.

   c.

   d.

   What function are they believed to have served?

3. Abbé Breuil was one of the most important historians of Paleolithic art. Using the Bibliography in the back of the text, write down the name of his influencial work. _____
_____ .

4. What is carbon-14 dating, and what has been the overall effect of its use on art-historical studies of the Stone Age?

5. The figurine known as the *Venus of Willendorf* (FIG. 1-13) was probably used originally as:

6. What new type of subject matter became important in Mesolithic rock-shelter paintings?

   In what ways do these works differ from Paleolithic cave paintings?
   a.

   b.

   c.

7. Which two achievements of Neolithic man changed the economic basis of his life?
   a.

   b.

   Which two achievements changed his intellectual life?
   a.

   b.

8. In the simplified division of prehistory into the age of food-gathering and the age of food production, the Paleolithic period corresponds to _____ , while food production is thought to have begun in the _____ period.

9. Important Megalithic remains can be found in what three countries?
   a.   b.   c.

10. When is Stonehenge thought to have been erected?

    By what means has the dating been established?

DISCUSSION QUESTIONS

1. What is generally thought to have been the purpose of Paleolithic cave paintings such as the one in FIG. 1-1? What evidence supports this theory?

2. Compare the rendition of the human being depicted in FIG. 1-8 with the animal in the same scene and in FIG. 1-6. What might account for the differences in style?

3. Compare the style of the *Marching Warriors* in FIG. 1-14 with the human being depicted in FIG. 1-8. What do you think is represented in the two scenes?

4. Discuss the social and economic changes that took place in human development from the Paleolithic period through the Neolithic period and the ways in which art was affected by these changes.

5. What do archeologists generally consider Stonehenge's original purpose to have been? What evidence supports this belief?

Using the timeline at the beginning of Chapter 1 in the text, enter the appropriate dates for the following periods:

SUMMARY OF PREHISTORIC ART

a. The Later Old Stone Age, or the _____ period, is divided into three subperiods:

   Aurignacian–Gravettian–
   Upper Perigordian: _____ B.C. to _____ B.C.

   Solutrean: _____ B.C. to _____ B.C.

   Magdalenian: _____ B.C. to _____ B.C.

b. The Middle Stone Age, or the _____ period, is dated

   in the East Mediterranean _____ B.C. to _____ B.C.

   and in Spain and North Europe _____ B.C. to _____ B.C.

c. The New Stone Age, or the _____ period, is dated

   in the East Mediterranean _____ B.C. to _____ B.C.

   and in Spain and North Europe _____ B.C. to _____ B.C.

The great paintings of Lascaux and Altamira were painted during the _____ period.

The *Venus of Willendorf* was carved during the _____ period.

Fill in the chart below as much as you can from memory; then check your answers aginst the text and complete the chart.

	Typical Examples	Stylistic Characteristics	Significant Historical Events, Ideas, etc.
Paleolithic Painting			
Paleolithic Sculpture			
Mesolithic Painting			
Neolithic Structures			

Chapter Two
The Ancient Near East

1. Define the following terms:

   stele

   "spirit trap"

   intaglio

   megaron

   city-state

   apadana

   conventionalism

   formalization

   cylinder seal

   ziggurat

2. Recent archeological findings indicate that civilization did not originate in the Nile River valley of Egypt, as was earlier believed, but developed in grassy uplands in settlements like Jericho, located in _____ and dating from the _____ millennium B.C., and Çatal Hüyük, located in _____ .

3. The first known permanent stone fortifications were built at the site of _____ around _____ B.C.

4. What possible purpose might the head illustrated in FIG. 2-2 have served?

5. The extensive remains found in Çatal Hüyük, which flourished between _____ and _____ B.C., demonstrate the evolution of the economy from _____ to _____ .

6. Two advantages of the absence of streets in Çatal Hüyük were:

   a.

   b.

7. What subjects were portrayed in the wall paintings of Çatal Hüyük?

   a.

   b.

8. List three changes in artistic production that paralleled the shift from a food-gathering to a food-producing economy.

   a.

   b.

   c.

9. Using the quotation from Henri Frankfort that appears on page 45 of the text, complete the following table showing the different characteristics of Mesopotamian and Egyptian civilization.

	Mesopotamian	Egyptian
Type of Written Documents		
Subjects of Early Art		
Predominant Type of Monumental Architecture		
Political Structure		

10. List three characteristics of Sumerian religion.

    a.

    b.

    c.

11.   Three conventions found in Sumerian pictorial art are:

       a.

       b.

       c.

12.   What do scholars think the bull symbolized for the Sumerians?

13.   What do scholars think the struggle between animals and monsters symbolizes in Mesopotamian art?

14.   Who was Sargon?

           Naram-Sin?

           Gudea?

15.   List three stylistic characteristics of the *Victory Stele of Naram-Sin* (FIG. 2-21).

       a.

       b.

       c.

16.   The code of Hammurabi was:

17.   The Assyrian empire was located in _____ and dominated this area from approximately
       _____ to _____ B.C.

18.   The royal citadel of Sargon II was located in the city of _____ . It is thought that
       many of the rooms of this gigantic palace were covered by _____ vaults.

       What evidence is there for this hypothesis?

19. The doorway of the royal citadel of Sargon II was guarded by figures of _____

    List four stylistic features of these figures

    a.

    b.

    c.

    d.

20. The majority of Assyrian reliefs depict either scenes of _____ or _____
    List three characteristics of Assyrian relief sculpture that create an impression of violence and brutality.

    a.

    b.

    c.

21. Who was Nebuchadnezzar?

22. The Ishtar Gate (FIG. 2-33), which was built in the city of _____ , was decorated with representations of the _____ of Marduk and the _____ of Adad. All its surfaces were covered with _____ .

23. The Elamite culture flourished around _____ B.C. in the country now known as _____

24. List the Mesopotamian stylistic conventions found in the Elamite *Statue of Queen Niparasu* (FIG. 2-34).

    a.

    b.

    c.

25. The Persian dynasty founded by Cyrus in the sixth century B.C. was known as the _____
    dynasty. It came to an end with the death of Darius III after his defeat at Issus by _____

26. At its height in the fifth century B.C., the Persian empire extended from the _____
    River in the west to the _____ River in the east.

27. The great palace at Persepolis was erected in the _____ century under _____
    and _____ to symbolize Persian imperial power.

The architects created a powerful synthesis of architectural and sculptural elements drawn from the cultures of:

28. List four architectural features of the palace of Persepolis.

   a.

   b.

   c.

   d.

29. What subjects were depicted in the reliefs on the walls of the terrace and staircases of the palace at Persepolis?

   The following stylistic features can be found in these reliefs:

   a.

   b.

   c.

30. Locate the following sites or areas on the map on study guide page 15:

Çatal Hüyük	Ur	Persia
Jericho	Anatolia	Bogazköy
Khorsabad	Assyria	Nimrud
Babylon	Sumer	Nineveh
Persepolis	Luristan	

   Locate and label the Tigris and Euphrates rivers and the Mediterranean Sea.

DISCUSSION QUESTIONS

1. Discuss the social and economic changes that took place in the Ancient Near East that made possible the beginning of what we call civilization.

2. How did the religion practiced by Sumerians differ from that practiced by Paleolithic hunters? What was the relationship between religion and the state in Ancient Sumer?

3. Compare the *Seated Goddess* (FIG. 2-5) with the *Venus of Willendorf* (FIG. 1-13). In what ways are they similar and in what ways do they differ?

4. Compare the statuettes from the Abu Temple (FIG. 2-13) with the representations of Gudea (FIG. 2-22) and Queen Niparasu (FIG. 2-34). How might the media used have affected the style?

5. Compare the conventions used in depicting the figures in the relief from Persepolis (FIG. 2-39) with those used in earlier representations like the *Standard of Ur* (FIG. 2-15), the *Victory Stele of Naram-Sin* (FIG. 2-21), and the relief of Ashurnasirpal (FIG. 2-29). Consider changes in the proportions of the figures, the depiction of details, and the positioning of the head and shoulders in relation to the body.

6. Compare the layout and organization of the town of Çatal Hüyük (FIG. 2-3) with that of the citadel of Sargon II at Khorsabad (FIG. 2-25) and the palace complex at Persepolis (FIG. 2-36). What seemed to have been the major concerns of the creators of each complex? What materials and building techniuqes were utilized by each?

Using the timeline at the beginning of Chapter 2 in the text, enter the appropriate dates for the following periods. Fill in the charts as much as you can from memory; then check your answers against the text and complete the charts.

SUMMARY OF SUMERIAN ART

Early Dynastic Period: _____ B.C. to _____ B.C.

First Dynasty of Ur: _____ B.C. to _____ B.C.

Neo-Sumerian Period: _____ B.C. to _____ B.C.

	Typical Examples	Stylistic Characteristics	Historical Factors
Sumerian Architecture			Rulers: Principal Gods: Important Cities:
Sumerian Sculpture			Political Structure: Cultural Achievements:

SUMMARY OF AKKADIAN, BABYLONIAN, AND ASSYRIAN ART

Akkadian Dyansty: _____ B.C. to _____ B.C.

Babylonain Dynasty: _____ B.C. to _____ B.C.

Assyrian Empire: _____ B.C. to _____ B.C.

	Typical Examples	Stylistic Characteristics	Significant Historical People, Events, Ideas, etc.
Akkadian Sculpture			
Babylonian Sculpture			
Assyrian Architecture			
Assyrian Sculpture			

SUMMARY OF NEO-BABYLONIAN AND PERSIAN ART

Neo-Babylonian Kingdom: _____ B.C. to _____ B.C.

Persian Empire: _____ B.C. to _____ B.C.

	Typical Examples	Stylistic Characteristics	Significant Historical People, Events, Ideas, etc.
Neo-Babylonian Art			
Persian Architecture			
Persian Sculpture			
Persian Crafts			

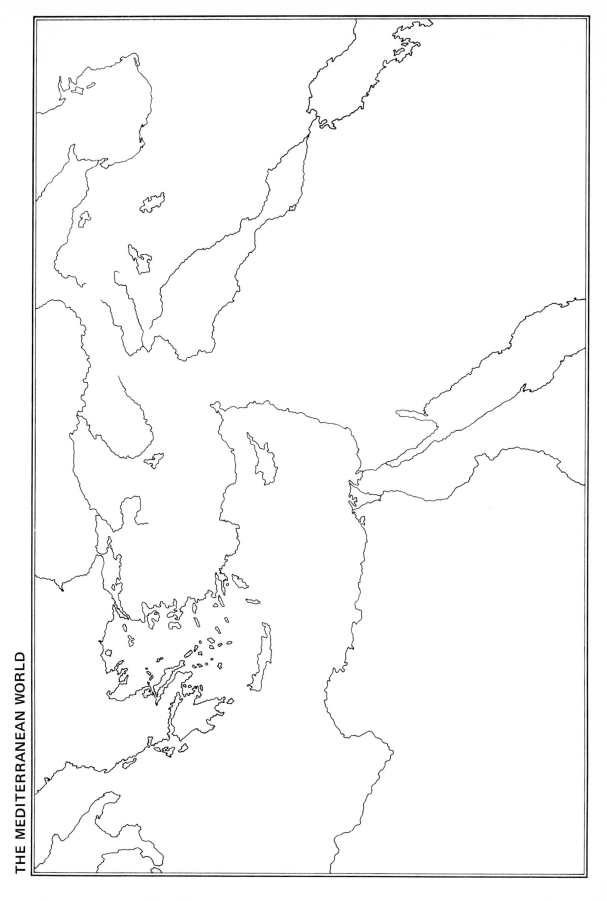

THE MEDITERRANEAN WORLD

Chapter Three
The Art of Egypt

Text Pages 70–101

1. Define the following terms:

necropolis

demotic writing

"reserve" head

reserve column

clerestory

fresco secco

hypostyle hall

canon of proportion

pylon

ben-ben

hieroglyphic writing

caryatid

"Book of the Dead"

2. Identify the following:

Flinders Petrie

Jean François Champollion

Menes

Imhotep

Khafre (Chephren)

Hyksos

Hatshepsut

Ramses II

Akhenaton

Nefertiti

Aton

Amen-Re

Amarna style

Tutankhamen

Osiris

Isis

3. Briefly describe the role played by the Nile in the development of Egyptian civilization.

4. What was the importance of the *Rosetta Stone*?

5. How did the belief in the life of the ka and its needs influence Egyptian art?

6. The *Palette of Narmer* (FIG. 3-2), which was created about 3000 B.C., is extremely important in Egyptian history and art for several reasons. Politically, it documents:

   Culturally, it records two important facts—

   a. about religion:

   b. about writing:

   Artistically, it embodies conventions that will dominate Egyptian official art to the end of the New Kingdom, namely:

   a.

   b.

   c.

7. Describe the function and basic structure of a mastaba.

8. Who was Re and what relationship was he supposed to have had to the Egyptian pharoahs?

9. In what way do the pyramids of Gizeh differ from King Zoser's pyramid at Saqqara?

10. Describe the post-and-lintel construction system.

11. What does the hawk symbolize in the statue of *Khafre* (FIG. 3-13)?

List four stylistic characteristics of the statue.

a.

b.

c.

d.

12. The pyramid tombs so popular in the Old Kingdom were replaced by _____ tombs in the Middle Kingdom.

The three basic units of Egyptian architecture seen in these tombs are:

a.

b.

c.

13. What did the Hyksos introduce to Egypt that revolutionized warfare?

14. List four major features of a typical pylon temple.

a.

b.

c.

d.

15. List two types of capitals used at Karnak.

a.   b.

16. In what century did Akhenaton proclaim the monotheistic religion of Aton and move his capital to Tel el-Amarna?

17. What was the major effect of the new Amarna style on figural representation?

18. What three new features can be seen in the painted relief of *King Smenkhkare and Meritaten* (FIG. 3-38)?

    a.

    b.

    c.

19. Although Ramses II lived after Akhenaton, the pillar statues that were carved for the interior of his temple (FIG. 3-35) ignore many of the stylistic features developed by the Amarna artists. Compare the figures from the Temple of Ramses II with the pillar statue of *Akhenaton* (FIG. 3-36); note particularly the differences in the proportions of the figures.

    Akhenaton   Ramses II

    What political factors might account for these differences?

20. The authors speculate that the freedom of the Amarna style may have been stimulated by artists from

    _____ .

21. Which stylistic features used in the decoration of the chest reproduced in FIG. 3-41 suggest that the chest could not have been created during the Old or Middle Kingdoms?

22. Locate the following on the map on study guide page 15:

Gizeh	Tel el-Amarna	Luxor
Saqqara	Karnak	Abu Simbel
Beni Hasan	Thebes	Hierakonpolis

    Locate the Nile River and the Red Sea.

DISCUSSION QUESTIONS

1. Discuss the use of convention and realism in Egyptian relief carving and painting. What types of subjects generally were treated more conventionally? Why? (Note particularly FIGS. 3-16, 3-17, 3-21, 3-33, 3-35, 3-38.)

2. Compare the portrait of *Sesostris III* (FIG. 3-22) with those of *Khafre* (FIG. 3-13) and of *Queen Nefertiti* (FIG. 3-37). What differences do you see, and how might these differences reflect changed social conditions?

3. Compare the Egyptian Pyramid of Zoser (FIG. 3-6) with the Ziggurat at Ur (FIGS. 2-10 and 2-11). In what ways are they similar? How do they differ? What was the function of each?

4. What do the Great Pyramids of Gizeh (FIGS. 3-7 and 3-9) and the palace at Persepolis (FIGS. 2-36 and 2-38) say about the major concerns of the men and the societies that commissioned them?

5. Compare the rock-cut tombs at Beni Hasan (FIGS. 3-18, 3-19, 3-20) with the mountain temples of Hatshepsut (FIG. 3-23) and Ramses II (FIGS. 3-24 and 3-25). In what ways are they similar? How do they differ? In what ways do all these tombs relate to temples such as the Temple of Amen-Re (FIG. 3-28)?

6. Compare the way the Egyptians depicted animals (FIGS. 3-17, 3-21, 3-33) with the way they were depicted by the artists of ancient Mesopotamia (FIGS. 2-16, 2-30, 2-31, 2-32) and those of Paleolithic Europe (FIGS. 1-1, 1-4 to 1-8, 1-10, 1-11). Which artists seem to portray them most naturally? What part does abstract pattern play in each? Which figures do you like best? Why?

7. After examining Egyptian works of art that were created during a span of more than two millennia, would you classify the overall outlook of the Egyptians as optimistic or pessimistic? Why?

Using the timeline at the beginning of Chapter 3 in the text, enter the appropriate dates for the following periods. Fill in the charts as much as you can from memory; then check your answers against the text and complete the charts.

SUMMARY OF EGYPTIAN ART—EARLY DYNASTIC AND OLD KINGDOM

Predynastic Period: _____ B.C. to _____ B.C.

Early Dynastic Period: _____ B.C. to _____ B.C. Dynasties _____

Old Kingdom: _____ B.C. to _____ B.C. Dynasties _____

	Typical Examples	Stylistic Characteristics	Significant Historical People, Events, Ideas, etc.
Early Dynastic Sculpture			Geographic Influences:
Old Kingdom Architecture			Gods: Rulers:
Old Kingdom Sculpture			Social Structure: Religious Beliefs:
Old Kingdom Painting & Relief			

SUMMARY OF EGYPTIAN ART—MIDDLE AND NEW KINGDOMS

Middle Kingdom: _____ B.C. to _____ B.C. Dynasties: _____

New Kingdom: _____ B.C. to _____ B.C. Dynasties: _____

Amarna Period: _____ B.C. to _____ B.C.

	Typical Examples	Stylistic Characteristics	Significant Historical People, Events, Ideas, Etc.
Middle Kingdom Art			
New Kingdom Architecture			
New Kingdom Painting & Sculpture			
Amarna Period Painting & Sculpture			

Chapter Four

The Art of the Aegean

1. Define the following terms:

   Linear B

   corbeled arch

   wet (or true) fresco

   Cyclopean walls

   tell

   pithoi

   dromos

   repoussé

   tholos

   in situ

   citadel

   bastion

   rhyton

2. Identify and briefly state the importance of the archeological work of each of the following:

Heinrich Schliemann

Arthur Evans

Using the Bibliography at the back of the text, write down the title and date of publication of one work by each of the following archeologists:

Schliemann: Evans:

3. Identify the following:

Minoan

Helladic

Cycladic

Mycenaean

Thera

4. Write down three characteristics that differentiate the culture of the ancient Aegean civilization from those of Egypt and Mesopotamia.

a.

b.

c.

5. What are potsherds? Why are they important for archeological research?

6. List three stylistic characteristics of the Early Bronze Age statuettes from the Cyclades.

a.

b.

c.

7. The "old" palaces of Crete are thought to have been built in the Middle _____ period, around the year _____ . They were destroyed around _____ .

   Give two possible reasons for the lack of fortification in Cretan palaces.

   a.

   b.

8. When did the potter's wheel come into use on Crete?

9. The "Golden Age" of Crete developed when the "new" palaces were built around _____ and lasted until they were destroyed, which was around _____ .

10. List four characteristics of the palace at Knossos.

    a.

    b.

    c.

    d.

11. In what way did the shape of a Minoan column differ from that of other columns?

12. In Minoan painting, human beings were most often represented in profile pose with a full-view eye, similar to conventions observed in Egypt and Mesopotamia, but they can be identified as Minoan because:

13. Which characteristics of Minoan ceramic decoration are apparent in *The Octopus Jar* (FIG. 4-17)?

    a.

    b.

    c.

14. What is particularly significant about the depiction of the human faces on *The Harvester Vase* (FIGS. 4-19 and 4-20)?

15. List three characteristics of Minoan sculpture as seen in the *Snake Goddess* (FIG. 4-21).

a.

b.

c.

16. Who was Pausanias?

17. What source seems to have influenced the composition of the Lion Gate of Mycenae?

18. Describe the structure of a beehive tomb.

19. Locate the following on the map on study guide page 31:

Aegean Sea   Tiryns
Crete   Vaphio
Cyclades   Troy (Ilium)
Knossos   Thera
Mycenae

DISCUSSION QUESTIONS

1. What are the current theories concerning the origin and demise of the Minoan culture and the relationship between Minoans and Mycenaeans?

2. Compare Minoan frescoes (FIGS. 4-12 and 4-13) with Egyptian examples (FIGS. 3-33 and 3-35). What differences do you see in the artists' approaches to composition and form, particularly in the depiction of motion and vitality?

3. In what ways does the palace at Knossos (FIGS. 4-5, 4-6, 4-9) differ from the palace of Sargon II at Khorsabad (FIGS. 2-25 and 2-26), from the palace of Darius at Persepolis (FIGS. 2-36 and 2-38), and from the citadel of Tiryns (FIGS. 4-23 and 4-24)? What do these differences seem to reflect about the major concerns of each civilization?

4. What explanation can you give for the obvious difference in style between *The Vaphio Cups* (FIGS. 4-30) and *The Warrior Vase* (FIGS. 4-31), which were all found in Mycenaean graves?

Using the timeline at the beginning of Chapter 4 in the text, enter the appropriate dates for the following periods. Fill in the charts as much as you can from memory, then check your answers against the text and complete the charts.

SUMMARY OF MINOAN ART

Early Minoan Period: _____ B.C. to _____ B.C.

Middle Minoan Period: _____ B.C. to _____ B.C.

Old Palace Period: _____ B.C. to _____ B.C.

New Palace Period: _____ B.C. to _____ B.C.

Late Minoan Period: _____ B.C. to _____ B.C.

	Typical Examples	Stylistic Characteristics	Significant Historical People, Events, etc.
Early Minoan Ceramics			
Middle Minoan Ceramics			
Late Minoan Ceramics			
Minoan Architecture			
Minoan Sculpture			
Minoan Painting			

SUMMARY OF CYCLADIC AND MYCENAEAN ART

Early Helladic _____ B.C. to _____ B.C.

Middle Helladic _____ B.C. to _____ B.C.

Late Helladic _____ B.C. to _____ B.C.

	Typical Examples	Stylistic Characteristics	Significant Historical People, Ideas, Events, etc.
Cycladic Sculpture			
Mycenaean Architecture			
Mycenaean Relief Sculpture			
Mycenaean Ceramics			
Mycenaean Crafts			

Using the timelines at the beginning of Chapters 2 through 4 in the text, fill in the dates for the various periods of Egyptian and Near Eastern art that are indicated below; then correlate the various periods of Minoan and Helladic art with them.

COMPARATIVE CHRONOLOGY

	Egypt	Near East	Crete	Greece
3500	Pre-dynastic (—)			
3000	Early Dynastic (—)	Sumerian (—)		
2500	Old Kingdom (—)			
		Akkadian (—) Neo-Sumerian		
2000	Middle Kingdom (—)	(—) First Dynasty of Babylon (—)		
1500	New Kingdom (—)			
1000	Late Period (—)	Assyrian (—)		
		Neo-Babylonian (—)		
500				
		Persian (—)		

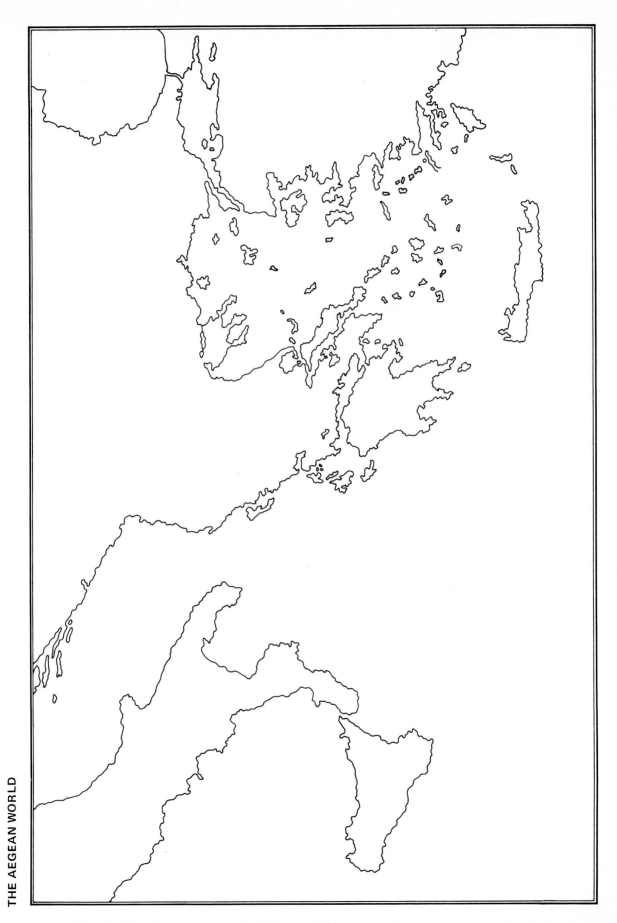

Chapter Five
The Art of Greece

THE GEOMETRIC AND ARCHAIC PERIODS   Text Pages 126–46

1. Define the following terms:

    contrapposto

    foreshortening

    engobe

    encaustic

    kouros

    kore

    entasis

    colonnade

    stylobate

    naos

2. For the Greeks, _____ was the "measure of all things."

3. In Greek philosophy, what set man apart from other creatures?

4. What form did the Greeks give to their gods?

5. Who were the Dorians?

    Ionians?

6. In what century did the various Greek-speaking states hold their first common ceremony?

    What was it?

7. Locate the following on the map on study guide page 31:

    Aegina   Ionia
    Argos   Paestum
    Attica   Peloponnesos
    Ilium (Troy)   Samos

8. Give the name for each vase shape shown below and briefly describe its function.

   Name:
                        Function:

   Name:
                        Function:

   Name:
                        Function:

   Name:
                        Function:

   Name:
                        Function:

   Name:
                        Function:

9. List three characteristics typical of vase decoration from the Geometric period.

    a.

    b.

    c.

10. What new subjects appeared on Greek vases of the Orientalizing period?

    a.   c.

    b.   d.

11. Describe the black-figure technique of pottery decoration.

    Describe the red-figure technique of pottery decoration.

    Name two black-figure painters.

    Name two red-figure painters.

    Who is generally given credit for the invention of the red-figure technique?

12. The Geometric Greek warrior shown in FIG. 5-12 is probably inspired by Syrian prototypes, but differs from Near Eastern representations by depicting the figure _____ .

13. Monumental free-standing sculpture first appeared in Greece around _____ in the _____ period.

14. What characteristics do sixth-century kouros figures share with Egyptian statues?

    In what respects do they differ from them?

15. Which parts of Greek statues were ordinarily painted?

16. What is the major significance of the *Kritios Boy* (FIG. 5-19)?

17. Draw simple diagrams of the following types of temples and identify the naos of each:

    a. temple in antis   c. prostyle temple

    b. amphiprostyle temple   d. peripteral temple

18. List four differences between the Doric and Ionic orders.

	Doric		Ionic
a.		a.	
b.		b.	
c.		c.	
d.		d.	

19.   Label the parts on the following diagram and indicate the architectural order for each half of the figure below.

shaft	volute	pediment
capital	entablature	triglyph
abacus	architrave	metope
echinus	cornice	frieze

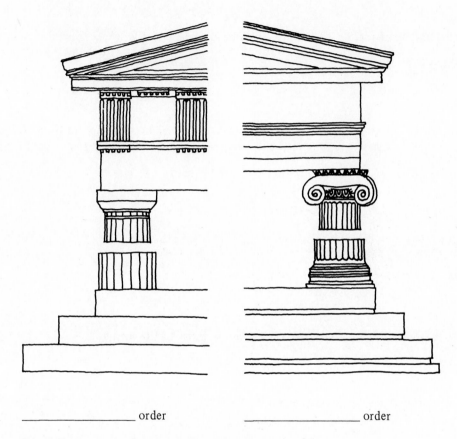

_____ order   _____ order

20.   On what parts of a Greek temple was sculptural decoration commonly used?

21.   What features of the façade of the Treasury of the Siphnians at Delphi (FIG. 5-27) identify it as an Ionic building?

22.   What are the main compositional problems of pedimental sculpture? How were they solved in the Temple of Aphaia at Aegina (FIG. 5-30)?

DISCUSSION QUESTIONS

1. Consider the ethnic, geographic, climatic, and political factors that shaped Greek life. How did they set Greece apart from earlier cultures? Do you agree with the authors that these factors might account for the creative energy of the Greeks?

2. For the Greeks, what was the definition of the good life? How was Greek humanistic education related to achieving that ideal? To what degree did Greek society achieve the ideal? What was the place of women in that society?

3. Compare the conception of the individual human being in Greek society and in the earlier societies of the Ancient Near East. What effect did these beliefs have on the art produced and the way each culture perceived its gods?

4. Considering both techniques and motifs utilized, discuss the changes in vase decoration from early Minoan times through the fifth century in Greece.

5. Compare the structure and function of Egyptian temples, such as the Temple of Horus at Edfu (FIG. 3-27), with those of Greek temples, such as the Temple of Hera at Paestum (FIGS. 5-25 and 5-26). Name the various parts of each structure.

THE FIFTH CENTURY   Text Pages 146–63

1. The Persians sacked Athens in the year _____ .

2. What was the significance of the Battle of Salamis?

3. What technique was used to cast *The Riace Bronzes* (FIGS. 5-33 to 5-36)?

4. Briefly describe the *cire perdue* method of casting bronze.

5. Locate the following on the map on study guide page 31:

   Athens   Olympia
   Delphi   Salamis
   Epidaurus   Sparta

6. The *Discobolos* (FIG. 5-38) was created by the sculptor _____ about _____ B.C. What are its "transitional" characteristics?

7. The sculptures of the west pediment of the Temple of Zeus at Olympia represent what mythological subject?

By means of this mythological guise, what seems to be symbolized by the sculptures?

a.

b.

c.

How do the authors explain the neutral facial expression of Hippodameia?

8. What was the Delian League?

9. Who was Pericles?

10. Two Ionic elements used in the Parthenon are:

a.   b.

What was the main purpose of the building?

Who were its architects?

Who designed its sculptural decorations?

11. What are the Elgin marbles?

12. In what ways do the figures from the east pediment of the Parthenon (FIGS. 5-47 and 5-48) differ from those of the east pediment of the Temple of Aphaia at Aegina (FIGS. 5-30, 5-31, 5-32)?

a.

b.

c.

13. What do the metopes of the Parthenon depict?

14. What is represented on the Parthenon's inner frieze?

    List four pairs of opposites that are balanced in the carving of the frieze.

    a.

    b.

    c.

    d.

15. What is the Propylaea?

16. Two Ionic buildings on the Athenian Acropolis are:
    a.   b.

17. Why is the Erechtheum an unusual building?

    What explanations have been given for its unusual features?

18. List three stylistic features that characterize the relief of *Nike Fastening Her Sandal* (FIG. 5-59).
    a.

    b.

    c.

19. What was the Canon of Polykleitos?

    Why do the authors equate the *Doryphoros* (FIG. 5-61) with the Doric order?

20. The vase decoration of the Niobid Painter is thought to reflect the style of the mural painter _____

    _____ .

    In what way did his style break with the traditional decorative style?

21. The use of the white-ground technique was most popular on vases known as _____ .

    What were its advantages over the black-figure or red-figure techniques?

    What were its disadvantages?

DISCUSSION QUESTIONS

1. What is meant by "the problem of the corner triglyph" in Doric architecture? Why do the authors feel that it was a constant irritation to Greek architects?

2. What are the so-called structural refinements of the Parthenon (and other Greek temples)? What may have been their purpose? Which of the several interpretations given by the authors makes the most sense to you? Why?

3. Compare the caryatids of the Treasury of the Siphnians at Delphi (FIG. 5-27) with those of the Erechtheum on the Acropolis (FIG. 5-57). How do they express the characteristics of the Archaic and the Classical styles of Greek sculpture?

4. By comparing the *Mantiklos "Apollo"* (FIG. 5-13), the kouros from Tenea (FIG. 5-15), the *Kroisos* (FIG. 5-16), the *Kritios Boy* (FIG. 5-19), the *Apollo* from the Temple of Zeus at Olympia (FIG. 5-40), and the *Doryphoros* (FIG. 5-61), discuss the development of the standing male nude in Greek sculpture. Note particularly the changing proportions, the depiction of motion, and the conception of the figure in space.

5. Since most of the works of the Great Masters of Greek sculpture are known to us only through Roman copies, how has it been possible to attribute works to specific artists? What are some of the problems faced by a copyist? How closely can a marble copy resemble a bronze original?

THE FOURTH CENTURY AND THE HELLENISTIC PERIOD   Text Pages 163-81

1. Who fought against whom in the Peloponnesian War? Who won?

2. How did Greek political and social life change after the Peloponnesian War?

    a.

    b.

    c.

3. Who was Plato?

        Aristotle?

        Philip of Macedon?

        Alexander?

4. In what major ways did fourth-century Greek sculpture differ from that of the fifth century?

        Point out some qualities of Praxiteles' *Hermes and Dionysos* (FIGS. 5-65 and 5-66) that express these differences.

        a.

        b.

        c.

        d.

5. The original *Aphrodite of Cnidos*, one of the first Greek female nudes, was carved by _____

    in the _____ century.

6. A quality not generally found in fifth-century sculpture appears in the work of Scopas. What is it?

7. What innovations did Lysippos make in figure sculpture?

        a.

        b.

8. The main advantage of a Corinthian over an Ionic capital was:

9. How do the meanings of the terms "Helladic," "Hellenic," and "Hellenistic" differ?

10. List five countries conquered by Alexander the Great.

    a.   c.   e.

    b.   d.

    What effect did his conquest have on them?

11. Three Hellenistic centers of culture were:

    a.   b.   c.

12. Note four stylistic characteristics that identify the *Nike of Samothrace* (FIG. 5-76) as a Hellenistic sculpture.

    a.

    b.

    c.

    d.

13. The subject depicted in the frieze on the Altar of Zeus and Athena from Pergamon (FIGS. 5-78 and 5-79) was:

    What devices were used to emphasize the anguish and drama of the theme?

    a.

    b.

    c.

14. Who was Laocoön?

15. List two works created by the Rhodian sculptors Agesander, Athendorus, and Polydorus.

a.   b.

16. Write down three of the major concerns of Hellenistic artists that set them apart from earlier Greek artists.

a.

b.

c.

17. What did the sculptural group of *Eros and Psyche* (FIG. 5-85) symbolize?

18. The Temple of Apollo at Didyma (FIG. 5-88) is called a _____ temple because it has two colonnades surrounding the naos. It it also a hypaethral temple because:

How did the use of space differ from that found in earlier Greek temple complexes?

19. What were the functions of the following features of the theater at Epidaurus (FIGS. 5-89 and 5-90)?

orchestra

proscenium

skene

parodos

20. The grid pattern or "checkerboard" plan, which was used in many Hellenistic cities, is generally associated with the architect _____ .

21. Define the following terms:

stoa

agora

bouleuterion

peristyle

tesserae

smalto

22. In what year did the Romans sack the Greek city of Corinth, thereby completing the absorption of the Greek city-states into the Roman empire?

23. Locate the following on the map on study guide page 31.

Corinth	Pella	Samothrace
Macedonia	Priene	Halicarnassus
Miletus	Pergamon	

DISCUSSION QUESTIONS

1. Compare the social and political conditions of the Hellenistic period with those found in fifth-century Athens. In what ways did the art produced during each period reflect these conditions?

2. Comapre the *Fallen Warrior* from Aegina (FIG. 5-31) with the *Dionysos* (*Herakles*?) from the Parthenon (FIG. 5-47) and the *Dying Gaul* from Pergamon (FIG. 5-77); note the various stylistic conventions used in each. Also, discuss how each figure reflects the social conditions of the period in which it was made.

3. Discuss the development of the female figure in Greek sculpture as seen in the *Peplos Kore* (FIG. 5-17), the figures from the Parthenon frieze (FIG. 5-52), *Nike Fastening Her Sandal* (FIG. 5-59), *the Statuette of a Young Woman* (FIG. 5-60), the *Nike of Samothrace* (FIG. 5-76), *Aphrodite of Cyrene* (FIG. 5-67), and the *Old Market Woman* (FIG. 5-84). Pay particular attention to the amount of motion given to the figures, the degree of realism, and the means used by the sculptors to achieve these effects. How do these figures reflect the changing styles and concerns from the Archaic through the Hellenistic periods?

4. Compare the scale, the use of space, and the structural elements in the Hellenistic Temple of Apollo at Didyma (FIGS. 5-20f and 5-88) and the Parthenon (FIGS. 5-43 and 5-45). In what ways does the Temple of Apollo foreshadow later Roman practice?

5. Why do you suppose Greek Archaic and Early Classical sculptors were fascinated by the male nude rather than the nude female figure?

SUMMARY: THE ART OF GREECE   Text Pages 124–81

Identify briefly the following gods, goddesses, heroes, etc.:

Aphrodite

Apollo

Artemis

Athena

Centaur

Dionysos

Gorgons

Hera

Herakles

Hermes

Laocoön

Lapith

Nike

Zeus

Using the timeline at the beginning of Chapter 5 in the text, enter the appropriate dates for the following periods. Fill in the charts as much as you can from memory; then check your answers against the text and complete the charts.

CHRONOLOGY OF GREEK ART

Proto-Geometric Period:	_____ B.C. to	_____ B.C.
Geometric Period:	_____ B.C. to	_____ B.C.
Archaic Period:	_____ B.C. to	_____ B.C.
Classical Period:	_____ B.C. to	_____ B.C.
Transitional:	_____ B.C. to	_____ B.C.
Early Classical:	_____ B.C. to	_____ B.C.
Late Classical:	_____ B.C. to	_____ B.C.
Hellenistic Period:	_____ B.C. to	_____ B.C.

	Political Leaders & Events	Cultural & Scientific Developments
Geometric & Archaic Periods		
Classical Period		
Hellenistic Period		

SUMMARY OF GREEK VASE PAINTING AND MOSAICS

	Typical Examples	Stylistic Characteristics	Artists
Geometric Vase Painting			
Archaic Vase Painting			
Classical Vase Painting			
Hellenistic Mosaics			

SUMMARY OF GREEK ARCHITECTURE

	Typical Examples	Stylistic Characteristics & Order
Archaic		
Classical		
Hellenistic		

SUMMARY OF GREEK SCULPTURE

	Typical Examples	Stylistic Characteristics	Artists
Geometric			
Archaic			
Transitional			
Early Classical			
Late Classical			
Hellenistic			

Chapter Six

Etruscan and Roman Art

Text Pages 182–245

THE ETRUSCANS AND THE ROMANS OF THE REPUBLICAN PERIOD   Text Pages 184–214

1. The so-called compromise theory regarding the origin of the Etruscans maintains that they came from

   _____ and intermixed with the native populations to form the early Italic culture

   known as _____ .

2. The development of Etruscan art was strongly influenced by the Greek colonization of Italy in the

   _____ and _____ centuries B.C.

3. Four important Etruscan settlements were located at:

   a.   c.

   b.   d.

4. Our knowledge of early Etruscan houses is principally derived from:

   a.

   b.

5. What is an atrium?

6. Who was Vitruvius?

7. List five architectural characteristics of Etruscan temples that distinguish them from Greek temples.

   Etruscan temple   Greek temple

   a.   a.

   b.   b.

   c.   c.

   d.   d.

   e.   e.

8. In what way was the Etruscans' rise and fall from power reflected in the decoration of their tombs?

9. Define the following terms:

    necropolis

    tufa

    tumulus

    canopic urn

    acroterium figure

10. One subject commonly painted in early Etruscan tomb interiors was:

11. List three stylistic characteristics of the *Apollo* from Veii (FIG. 6-8) that distinguish it as Etruscan.

    a.

    b.

    c.

12. What were the favorite materials of Etruscan sculptors?

    a.   b.

13. Why is the Etruscan *She-Wolf of the Capitol* (FIG. 6-10) so famous?

14. What is a chimera?

15. The Etruscans practiced divination. What is it?

16.   Describe the medium and technique used for decorating *The Ficoroni Cist* (FIG. 6-13).

17.   The two cultures whose art most strongly influenced that of Rome were _____

and _____ .

18.   In which of the visual arts did Roman artists make major and innovative contributions?

19.   What major characteristic of Roman Republican portraits differentiates them from Greek examples?

20.   Define the following terms:

pseudoperipteral

bucrania

21.   List four non-Greek features of the Temple of the "Sibyl" ("Vesta?") at Tivoli (FIG. 6-17).

a.

b.

c.

d.

22.   How does the Sanctuary of Fortuna Primigenia (FIG. 6-18) manifest the "Roman Imperial spirit"?

23.   What enabled the Romans to create an "architecture of space rather than of sheer mass"?

24.   Two ancient cities that were buried when Mount Vesuvius erupted in A.D. 79 were _____

and _____ .

25. What was the basis for the *castrum* type of city plan?

26. The chief functions of the forum of a Roman city were:

a.

b.

c.

27. Briefly describe the plan of a Roman atrium house; note how it differs from that of the Greek house at Priene (FIG. 5-94).

28. What, in the authors' opinion, may have been the particular Roman contribution to painting?

29. Four pictorial devices used by Roman painters to suggest recession in depth are:

a.

b.

c.

d.

30. Describe the "Arcadian spirit."

31. List three Greek characteristics that are apparent in the mosaic of *The Battle of Issus* (FIG. 6-38).

a.

b.

c.

What feature seems to be more Roman?

32.   The technique used to create the Faiyum portrait (FIG. 6-41) is known as _____ .

What seems most remarkable about the portrait, and how does the artist achieve these effects?

33.   Locate the following on the map on study guide page 55:

Vulci   Roma
Tarquinii   Pompeii
Praeneste   Herculaneum
Faiyum

DISCUSSION QUESTIONS

1.   Compare the *Apollo* from Veii (FIG. 6-8) with the *Apollo* from Olympia (FIG. 5-40). Explain how the typical Etruscan features of the former contrast with the typical Greek features of the latter. How are these influences combined in the *Mars from Todi* (FIG. 6-9)?

2.   How do the style, color, subject matter, and mood of an Etruscan fresco (FIG. 6-4) compare with those of a Greek vase painting (FIG. 5-64)?

3.   What did Horace mean by the statement "Conquered Greece led her proud conqueror captive"?

4.   What different building techniques were used and what esthetic effects were achieved by the architects of the Sanctuary of Fortuna Primigenia (FIG. 6-18), the Mortuary Temple of Hatshepsut (FIG. 3-23), and the Ziggurat at Ur (FIG. 2-10)?

5.   What is meant by the term illusionism? How is it used in Roman painting?

6.   If the Greek genius expressed itself in art, science, and philosophy, in what fields did the more practical Romans excel? How are these differing concerns reflected in the surviving monuments of the two cultures?

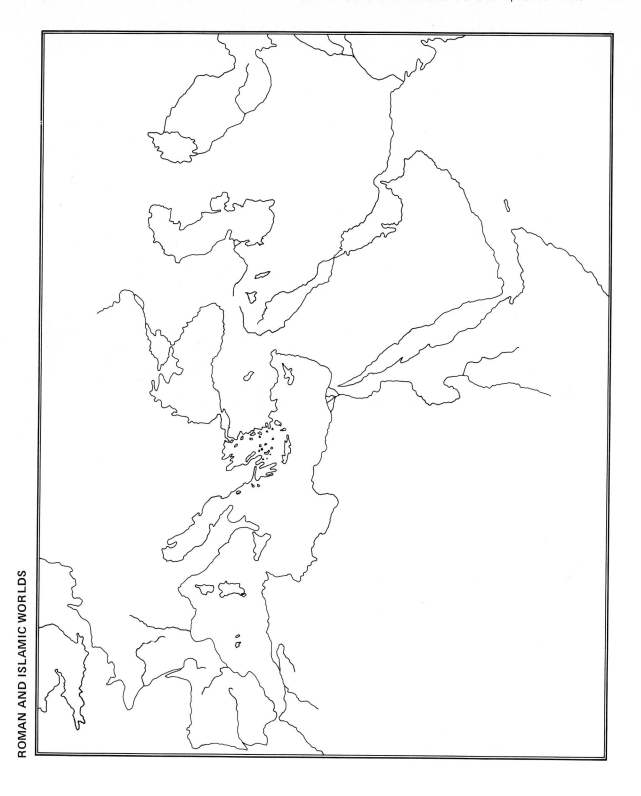

ROMAN AND ISLAMIC WORLDS

THE EARLY EMPIRE AND THE LATE EMPIRE   Text Pages 214-45

1. Who was Octavian Caesar?

2. What was the "Pax Romana"?

3. What is an insula?

4. What was the function of the Pont du Gard near Nemausus?

5. The town plan of Thamugadis is based on the layout of _____ , which

    had the form of a _____ divided into _____ by

    two main traffic arteries, the _____ and the _____ .

6. The Roman Colosseum was used for:

    While the core of the Colosseum is concrete, its exterior shell is constructed in _____ .

    Why is the Colosseum in danger of collapsing?

7. Describe the Roman arch order.

    In what sequence, from the ground up, were the Greek orders used for the decoration of multi-storied Roman
    buildings?
    a.   b.   c.

    On what esthetic considerations was this sequence based?

8. What was the function of a Roman basilica?

   Describe the plan of the Basilica Ulpia (FIG. 6-48):

9. Where and for whom was the Domus Aurea built?

   How did the architect use concrete in its construction?

10. Which revolutionary architectural concept finds its fullest expression in the Roman Pantheon (FIGS. 6-51, 6-52, 6-53)?

    Who is believed to have been its possible designer?

    The center of its dome is pierced by a circular opening called _____ .

11. What functions, other than sanitary ones, did the Roman baths fulfill?

    What were Seneca's complaints concerning them?

12. Define the following terms:
    barrel vault

    centering

    groin vault

    coffering

13. Much of the art produced under Augustus was strongly influenced by the art of _____ , which existed side by side with work created in the realistic Republican tradition.

14. In what respects do the reliefs from the Ara Pacis Augustae (FIGS. 6-59 and 6-60) resemble the Parthenon frieze (FIG. 5-52)?

    a.

    b.

    c.

    How do they differ from it?

    a.

    b.

    c.

15. The subjects depicted in the reliefs on the Arch of Titus are:

    a.

    b.

16. How do the reliefs on the Column of Trajan (FIGS. 6-64 and 6-65) differ from those on the Ara Pacis Augustae (FIGS. 6-59 and 6-60) and the Arch of Titus (FIGS. 6-62 and 6-63)?

    a.

    b.

    c.

    In what respects do they seem to forecast the art of the Middle Ages?

17. Roman portrait sculpture shows a fluctuation between two opposite artistic tendencies. What are they?

    a.

    b.

18. Which emperors, other than Augustus, commissioned art that showed strong Greek influence?

    a.

    b.

19. One of the very few equestrian portraits of a Roman emperor to survive the Middle Ages is that of

   _____ .

   It appears to owe its survival to:

20. Two factors that contributed to the decline of Roman Imperial power in the third century were:

    a.

    b.

21. How does the portrait of *Philip the Arab* (FIG. 6-74) express the uncertainties and unrest of his time?

    a.

    b.

    c.

22. Who was Diocletian?

    Constantine?

23. Diocletian built an important fortified palace at _____ in what is now country of

   _____ .

   What feature of the peristyle court of the palace was to be of great importance to the development of
   Medieval architecture?

24. What might have been the source for the "baroque" character of the so-called "Treasury" at Petra?

25. Where was the Porta Nigra built? What was its function?

26. List five themes common to Late Roman art that were depicted in the mosaics of the Piazza Armerina:

    a.   c.   e.

    b.   d.

27. What type of vaulting was used to construct the Basilica of Constantine?

28. List four characteristics of fourth-century Roman sculpture that are illustrated by *The Tetrarchs* (FIG. 6-88).

    a.

    b.

    c.

    d.

29. Why do the authors feel that the Arch of Constantine is a monument to the decline of Roman creative power?

30. Locate the following on the map on study guide page 55:

    Nemausus (Nîmes)   Augusta Trevirorum (Trier)
    Gallia   Germania
    Spalatum (Split)

    Using a colored pencil or pen, lightly color in the area covered by the Roman empire in the second century A.D.

DISCUSSION QUESTIONS

1. How did the Romans and the Greeks differ in their conception of architectural space? Include the Greek Parthenon (FIGS. 5-44 and 5-45), the Roman Pantheon (FIGS. 6-51, 6-52, 6-53), the Baths of Caracalla (FIGS. 6-55 and 6-56), and the Piazza Armerina (FIG. 6-82) in your discussion. How did the building techniques used by each determine the types of spaces that could be constructed?

2. How were both realistic and Greek idealizing characteristics incorporated in the Ara Pacis Augustae (FIGS. 5-58, 5-59, 5-60)? What was the purpose of the work? How did its iconography reflect that purpose?

3. In what ways does the *Augustus of Primaporta* (FIG. 6-57) resemble the Greek *Doryphoros* (FiG. 5-61)? In what ways is the figure closer to that of the Etruscan *Mars from Todi* (FIG. 6-9)?

4. Discuss the development of Roman portraits by comparing and contrasting the heads of a Republican Roman (FIG. 6-14), Augustus (FIG. 6-67), Vespasian (FIG. 6-69), Hadrian (FIG. 6-71), Caracalla (FIG. 6-73), Philip the Arab (FIG. 6-74), Constantine (FIG. 6-87), and Maximin Daia (FIG. 6-92).

5. Analyze the stylistic differences between the reliefs from the Arch of Constantine (FIGS. 6-90 and 6-91), the Arch of Titus (FIGS. 6-62 and 6-63), and the Parthenon (FIGS. 5-51 and 5-52). In what ways do the style and the subject matter of these reliefs reflect the social, religious, and political concerns of the society for which each was made?

SUMMARY: ETRUSCAN AND ROMAN ART Text Pages 182–245

Using the timeline at the beginning of Chapter 6, enter the appropriate dates for the following periods. Fill in the charts as much as possible from memory; then check your answers against the text and complete the charts.

SUMMARY OF ETRUSCAN ART

Period of Etruscan domination: _____ B.C. to _____ B.C.

Decline of Etruscan power: _____ B.C. to _____ B.C.

	Typical Examples	Stylistic Characteristics	Significant Historical People, Events, etc.
Architecture			
Painting			
Sculpture			

SUMMARY OF ROMAN HISTORICAL AND CULTURAL BACKGROUND

Roman Republican Period: _____ B.C. to _____ B.C.

Early Imperial Period: _____ B.C. to A.D. _____

Late Imperial Period: A.D. _____ to _____

Division of Empire: A.D. _____

	Significant People	Political and Historical Events	Cultural Factors and Influences
Republican Period			
Early Imperial Period			
Late Imperial Period			
Fifth Century Western Empire			

SUMMARY OF ROMAN PAINTING

	Typical Examples	Stylistic Characteristics
First Style or _____ Style		
Second Style or _____ Style		
Third Style or _____ Style		
Fourth Style or _____ Style		

SUMMARY OF ROMAN ARCHITECTURE

	Typical Examples	Stylistic Characteristics
Republican Period		
Early Imperial Period		
Late Imperial Period		

SUMMARY OF ROMAN SCULPTURE

	Typical Examples	Stylistic Characteristics
Republican Period		
Early Imperial Period		
Late Imperial Period		

Chapter Seven

Early Christian, Byzantine, and Islamic Art

Text Pages 246–309

EARLY CHRISTIAN ART AND BYZANTINE ART (AT RAVENNA)   Text Pages 248-78

1. Define the following terms:

    mystery cults

    catacomb

    loculi

    cubicula

    orans figure

    narthex

    nave

    apse

    ambulatory

    transept

    codex

    vellum

66   Copyright © 1986 by Harcourt Brace Jovanovich, Inc. All rights reserved.

parchment

hieratic

mausoleum

2. The Roman emperor _____ recognized Christianity in the year _____,
    and the Emperor _____ made it the official religion of the Empire.

3. Who were the Goths?

4. In what century did the Islamic religion sweep through much of the Near East?

5. What is the primary distinction between Early Christian and Late Roman works of art?

6. What did the story of Jonah symbolize for Early Christians?

7. How was Christ most often represented during the Period of Persecution?
    a.   b.

    List three attributes he acquired during the Period of Recognition.
    a.   b.   c.

    From what source were these attributes taken?

    What was their purpose?

8. Three architectural sources for the Early Christian Basilica of Old St. Peter's in Rome were:
    a.   b.   c.

How did Early Christian builders modify the plan of the Roman pagan basilica in order to convert it to Christian use?

9. The type of Roman plan, adapted by Early Christian builders, that became most popular with Byzantine architects was:

10. How does the Church of Santa Costanza differ from basilican churches?

What may have been its original purpose?

11. In what ways, other than subject matter, can Early Christian mosaics be distinguished from earlier Roman examples?

a.

b.

What qualities of the mosaic medium made it the favorite of Early Christian and Byzantine artists?

12. Identify Sol Invictus and explain his appearance in Christian art.

13. List the Imperial attributes assimilated by Christ that are illustrated in the mosaic from Santa Pudenziana in Rome (FIG. 7-11).

a.   c.

b.

Identify the name of each of the Four Evangelists as associated with the following symbolic creatures:

Winged man: Lion:

Ox: Eagle:

14. The Roman illusionistic elements that were retained in the Early Christian mosaic *The Parting of Lot and Abraham* (FIG. 7-12) were:

What new formal elements that point toward later Medieval art appear in this mosaic?

What was their purpose?

15. The style of the *Vatican Vergil* (FIG. 7-14) is reminiscent of that used in _____, while the repetition of figures in the *Vienna Genesis* (FIG. 7-15) is closer to the technique used in

_____ .

16. List three stylistic features of the *Ludovisi Battle Sarcophagus* (FIG. 7-17) that are not illusionistic and that point toward an emerging Medieval style.

a.   c.

b.

17. What is the meaning of the cupids and grapes on *The Good Shepherd Sarcophagus* (FIG. 7-18)?

18. Explain the lack of interest in monumental sculpture from the fourth to the twelfth century:

19. In what ways does the ivory *St. Michael the Archangel* (FIG. 7-20) reflect Classical prototypes?

What new compositional devices are used?

20. Explain the symbolism of the *chi-rho* monogram on the *Sarcophagus of Archbishop Theodore* (FIG. 7-22).

21. List three stylistic characteristics of the murals at Dura-Europos that do not conform with the Greco-Roman pictorial tradition.

    a.   c.

    b.

22. Ravenna became the capital of the western empire in the _____ century.

23. Who was Galla Placidia?

    Theodoric?

    Justinian?

    Theodora?

24. What type of plan was used in the mausoleum of Galla Placidia (FIGS. 7-24 and 7-25)?

25. The three-aisled basilica erected in Ravenna's seaport by Theodoric in the sixth century is now known as

    _____ .

26. Write down two remnants of Roman illusionism that can be found in the mosaic *Christ as the Good Shepherd* in the mausoleum of Galla Placidia (FIG. 7-26).

    a.   b.

27. Name two architectural features that distinguish Ravennese from Roman basilicas.

    a.   b.

28. Explain the meaning of the following symbols from the apse mosaic of Sant' Apollinare in Classe (FIG. 7-30):

    Jeweled cross

    Three sheep below the cross

    Twelve sheep

Compare the mosaic with that from the mausoleum of Galla Placidia (FIG. 7-26), and describe the stylistic changes that have occurred:

a.

b.

c.

29. Briefly describe the plan and structure of San Vitale at Ravenna.

What was the function of the gallery?

30. What is the subject of the mosaics of Justinian and Theodora (FIGS. 7-36 and 7-37) in the apse of San Vitale?

What does Justinian's halo signify?

What explanation is given for the curious overlapping of Justinian and Maximianus?

31. Who built the fortress monastery of St. Catherine on Mt. Sinai? When?

What is the subject of the apse mosaic?

List three stylistic features of the mosaic.

a.

b.

c.

DISCUSSION QUESTIONS

1. Compare the basilica of Old St. Peter's (FIGS. 7-4 and 7-6) with the reconstruction of the Basilica Ulpia (FIG. 6-48). What similarities and what differences do you see in the plans, elevations, and building materials used? How did the purposes of the varying parts of the two buildings differ? How was the more "spiritual" purpose of the Christian building reflected in the structure?

2. What is meant by the "denaturing" of art during the Late Roman and Early Medieval periods?

3. Compare the ivory carving *St. Michael the Archangel* (FIG. 7-20) with the *Diptych of Anastasius* (FIG. 7-21); note the features of each that reflect the Classical naturalistic tradition and those that look forward to the style of the Middle Ages.

4. Noting changes in style and content from the *Idyllic Landscape* (FIG. 6-37) and the *Allegory of Africa* (FIG. 6-83) through *Christ Enthroned in Majesty, with Saints* (FIG. 7-11), *The Parting of Lot and Abraham* (FIG. 7-12), *Saint Onesiphorus and Saint Porphyrius* (FIG. 7-13), *Christ as the Good Shepherd* (FIG. 7-26), *The Miracle of the Loaves and the Fishes* (FIG. 7-28), and *Justinian and Maximianus* (FIG. 7-39) to the mosaic of Sant' Apollinare in Classe (FIG. 7-30), discuss the development of pictorial form from Roman illusionism to Byzantine pattern and symbolism.

5. The apse mosaics of San Vitale have been said to embody the Byzantine ideal of "sacred kingship." What iconographic features of the mosaics illustrate this concept?

BYZANTINE AND ISLAMIC ART   Text Pages 278–309

1. The church of Hagia Sophia was built in Constantinople by the architects _____ and _____ between A.D. _____ and _____ , during the reign of Emperor _____ .

Briefly describe the plan and structure of Hagia Sophia.

What eastern and western elements are combined in the plan to make the building a "unique hybrid"?

2. Define *pendentive*, and explain the advantage of pendentive construction.

3. The Second Byzantine Golden Age took place between the _____ and _____ centuries.

When was the First Byzantine Golden Age?

4. List three characteristics typical of Late Byzantine churches.

   a.

   b.

   c.

5. What is a *squinch*? How was it used?

6. Describe the features that identify St. Mark's in Venice as a Byzantine building.

   a.   c.

   b.   d.

7. Religious architecture of "holy" Russia was most strongly influenced by the architecture of _____

   _____ .

   What feature of these churches is most distinctly Russian?

8. What are the dates of the Iconoclastic Controversy?

   What was its effect on the visual arts?

9. Describe the style of the murals of Santa Maria de Castelseprio (FIG. 7-54).

   When are they thought to have been painted?

10. The range of style during the Second Byzantine Golden Age is seen in a comparison of the mosaics of Daphne (FIG. 7-55) and the frescoes of Nerezi (FIG. 7-56). Briefly describe the style of each.

    Daphne:

    Nerezi:

11. What does the rainbow symbolize in the mosaics of St. Mark's in Venice (FIG. 7-58)?

12. List the three Theological Virtues.

    a.   b.   c.

The four Cardinal Virtues.

a.   b.   c.   d.

13.   When was the Third Golden Age of Byzantine art?

14.   What is the theme of the fresco from the side chapel of the Mosque of the Ka'riye in Istanbul (FIG. 7-60)?

How does the style differ from that of the mosaics of Justinian and Theodora from Ravenna. (FIGS. 7-36 and 7-37)?

15.   What earlier style was revived in the so-called *Paris Psalter* (FIG. 7-61)?

16.   In what countries, other than Turkey, can important examples of Byzantine art be found?

a.   b.   c.

17.   What Byzantine characteristics are apparent in the icon called *The Vladimir Madonna* (FIG. 7-62)?

a.   c.

b.

18.   Define the following terms:

pantocrator

icon

iconostasis

19.   The style of carving of the *Veroli casket* (FIG. 7-64) shows the influence of _____.
It dates from the _____ century.

20.   What was the "Hegira"?

21.   List five countries conquered by the Islamic soldiers in the seventh century.

a.   c.   e.

b.   d.

22. Mohammedan power in Spain continued from the _____ century until _____ , when Granada fell to Ferdinand and Isabella. In spite of continued pressure, Constantinople did not fall to the Mohammedans until _____ .

23. Point out two basic differences between the Islamic and Christian faiths.

   a.

   b.

24. Where and when did the following Islamic dynasties rule:

   Umayyads

   Abbasids

   Fatimids

25. What reasons can be given for the great size of early Islamic mosques?

   a.

   b.

26. Define the following terms:

   qiblah

   mihrab

   minbar

   minaret

   iman

   muezzin

   caliph

27. The Great Mosque at Samarra covers approximately _____ acres.

28. Briefly describe the early Moslem hypostyle system of construction.

What seems to have been the purpose and function of early Moslem palaces?

29. Islamic ornament is characterized by:

a.

b.

c.

d.

30. Why were stucco reliefs popular with Islamic builders?

Some of the very richest examples of stucco decoration are found in the _____ ; they date from the _____ century.

31. What is a *madrasah*?

How does it differ architecturally from the hypostyle mosque?

32. The most famous of all Islamic mausoleums is the _____ at _____ , which was built in the _____ century.

33. Who were the Ottoman Turks?

What new type of mosque did they develop? How did it differ from the hypostyle mosques favored in other Islamic countries?

34. What did the circle set in the square symbolize for Islamic architects?

35. Who was Sinan the Great?

36. What is important about the structure of the Selimiye Cami (FIGS. 7-83 to 7-86)?

37. Why were textiles so highly valued in the Islamic world?

38. Why were monumental sculpture, mural painting, and panel painting so rare in early Islamic art?

39. The earliest Islamic illuminated manuscripts are dated about _____ .

Many of the finest manuscripts were created for the rulers of _____ .

What orthodox Islamic restriction apparently did not affect the illustration of secular books?

40. List three stylistic characteristics of Islamic illumination as seen in FIG. 7-88.

a.

b.

c.

41. Locate the following on the map on study guide page 55:

Alexandria	Mshatta
Constantinople	Cordoba
Mecca	Granada
Baghdad	Toledo
Jerusalem	Ravenna
Damascus	

Using a pencil or pen of a different color than that used to outline the Roman Empire, indicate on the map the areas under Moslem control by the tenth century.

DISCUSSION QUESTIONS

1. Compare the building techniques used and the effects achieved in San Vitale (FIGS. 7-32, 7-33, 7-34), Hagia Sophia (FIGS. 7-41 to 7-44), the Mosque at Cordoba (FIG. 7-68), the Selimiye Cami (FIG. 7-86), the Basilica of Constantine (FIGS. 6-85 and 6-86), and the Pantheon (FIGS. 6-51, 6-52, 6-53). Note particularly the lighting effects created by each.

2. Compare the scenes from the *Paris Psalter* (FIG. 7-61) and Rublëv's *Old Testament Trinity* (FIG. 7-63) with the Classical painting *Herakles and Telephos* (FIG. 6-36) and the *Idyllic Landscape* (FIG. 6-37). What similarities and differences do you see?

3. Compare the interplay of architectural mass and decoration found in the Alhambra (FIGS. 7-78 and 7-79), the mausoleum of Sultan Hasan (FIGS. 7-80 and 7-81), the Taj Mahal (FIG. 7-82), and the Mosque of Selim II (FIGS. 7-83 to 7-86).

4. Compare the treatment of volume and space in the illumination of *Laila and Majnun* (FIG. 7-88) with the one from the *Paris Psalter* (FIG. 7-61). In what ways does the Persian miniature differ from the Byzantine one? What factors might account for the differences?

5. What reasons do the authors give for including Islamic art in the chapter with Early Christian and Byzantine art? After having read the chapter, do you feel that the essential qualities of Islamic art distinguish it from or relate it to Western art? How?

Self-Quiz

PART ONE: THE ANCIENT WORLD

I. **Matching.** Choose the culture or period in the right column that best corresponds to the monument or site in the left column and enter the appropriate letter in the space provided.

_____ 1. *Stele of Hammurabi*

_____ 2. Colosseum

_____ 3. Basilica of Old St. Peter's

_____ 4. Lascaux

_____ 5. Palaces of Xerxes and Darius

_____ 6. Palace at Knossos

_____ 7. "Treasury of Atreus"

_____ 8. Erechtheum

_____ 9. Palace at Mshatta

_____ 10. Temple of Hera at Paestum

_____ 11. Stonehenge

_____ 12. Tel el-Amarna

_____ 13. Baths of Caracalla

_____ 14. Mortuary Temple of Hatshepsut

_____ 15. *Standard of Ur*

_____ 16. Pyramid of Khafre

_____ 17. Tombs at Caere

_____ 18. Sant' Apollinare Nuovo

_____ 19. Ziggurat at Ur

_____ 20. Hagia Sophia

_____ 21. Fortifications at Tiryns

_____ 22. Taj Mahal

_____ 23. Rock-cut tombs of Beni Hasan

_____ 24. Basilica Ulpia

_____ 25. Town plan of Priene

_____ 26. Altar of Zeus and Athena at Pergamon

_____ 27. Ishtar Gate

_____ 28. Dipylon Cemetery

_____ 29. *Victory Stele of Naram-Sin*

_____ 30. *Harvester Vase*

a. Paleolithic
b. Neolithic
c. Egyptian, Old Kingdom
d. Egyptian, Middle Kingdom
e. Egyptian, New Kingdom
f. Sumerian
g. Assyrian
h. Babylonian
i. Persian
j. Akkadian
k. Minoan
l. Mycenaean
m. Greek Geometric
n. Greek Archaic
o. Greek Classical
p. Greek Hellenistic
q. Etruscan
r. Roman
s. Early Christian
t. Byzantine
u. Islamic

II. **Matching.** Choose the name in the right column that best corresponds to the art work in the left column (artist matched to work, patron matched to work, etc.) and enter the appropriate letter in the space provided.

_____ 31. Ara Pacis Augustae

_____ 32. Stepped Pyramid of King Zoser

_____ 33. *Hermes and Dionysos*

_____ 34. *Dionysos in a Sailboat* (kylix)

_____ 35. Bronze equestrian statue from the Capitoline Hill

_____ 36. San Vitale

_____ 37. *Discobolos*

_____ 38. Sculpture from Parthenon

_____ 39. Hagia Sophia

_____ 40. Amarna style

_____ 41. *Doryphoros*

_____ 42. Palace at Persepolis

_____ 43. Column with narrative reliefs

_____ 44. Fourth-century basilica in Rome

_____ 45. Palace at Spalatum (Split)

_____ 46. Mosque of Selim II

_____ 47. Temple at Abu Simbel

_____ 48. Mausoleum in the shape of a cross

_____ 49. Sant' Apollinare Nuovo

_____ 50. *Apoxyomenos*

_____ 51. *Seated Boxer*

_____ 52. Parthenon

_____ 53. Propylaea

_____ 54. Citadel at Khorsabad

_____ 55. Reliefs from Nimrud

a. Praxiteles
b. Constantine
c. Lysippos
d. Iktinos and Kallikrates
e. Polykleitos
f. Marcus Aurelius
g. Darius
h. Imhotep
i. Justinian
j. Trajan
k. Anthemius of Tralles and Isidorus of Miletus
l. Exekias
m. Myron
n. Augustus
o. Phidias
p. Apollonius
q. Akhenaton
r. Ashurnasirpal II
s. Theodoric
t. Galla Placidia
u. Mnesikles
v. Diocletian
w. Sinan the Great
x. Ramses II
y. Sargon II

III. **Multiple Choice.** Circle the most appropriate answer.

56. Mycenae and Troy were excavated by   a. Wolley   b. Champollion   c. Evans   d. Akhenaton   e. Schliemann

57. Figurines of priestesses or goddesses holding snakes would most likely be found in   a. Nimrud   b. Knossos   c. Mycenae   d. Khorsabad   e. Dier el-Bahri

58. The Ishtar Gate was built under   a. Ashurbanipal   b. Sargon   c. Nebuchadnezzar   d. Akhenaton   e. Hammurabi

59. The Persians took over the use of large, winged bull-man guardian figures from the   a. Sumerians   b. Minoans   c. Greeks   d. Egyptians   e. Assyrians

60. The Mycenaean civilization went into a marked decline either because of climatic changes or invasions from the north about   a. 1500 B.C.   b. 1200 B.C.   c. 1000 B.C.   d. 800 B.C.   e. 600 B.C.

61. Ka figures were important in the art of   a. Egypt   b. Paleolithic Europe   c. Archaic Greece   d. Sumer   e. Crete

62. Statuettes from the Abu Temple at Tell Asmar date from   a. the Babylonian period under Hammurabi   b. the Early Dynastic period of Sumerian domination   c. the Assyrian period   d. the New Babylonian period   e. the Persian period

63. Mastaba was the name applied to   a. a Mesopotamian ziggurat   b. a type of Old Kingdom Egyptian tomb   c. a megalithic tomb   d. an Egyptian grave statue that served as a home for the soul   e. a tomb shaped like the "Treasury of Atreus"

64. A megalithic stone circle was erected at   a. Knossos   b. Saqqara   c. Khorsabad   d. Ur   e. Stonehenge

65. A Neolithic skull modeled in plaster to form the features of the deceased was found at   a. Lascaux   b. Memphis   c. Çatal Hüyük   d. Jericho   e. Nimrud

66. An important Magdalenian site is   a. Lascaux   b. Nineveh   c. Catal Hüyük   d. Persepolis   e. Abu Simbel

67. A "palace-style" vase would most likely be found   a. in the Royal Cemetery at Ur   b. at Amarna   c. in a ziggurat   d. in an Egyptian tomb   e. on the island of Crete

68. A Mycenaean architectural feature that is thought to have formed the basis for the structural plan of later Greek temples is the   a. pylon   b. megaron   c. tholos   d. atrium   e. echinus

69. A Greek temple with a single row of columns around the exterior is known as   a. a temple *in antis*   b. a prostyle temple   c. an amphiprostyle temple   d. a peripteral temple   e. a dipteral temple

70. During the Period of Persecution, Christ was most often represented   a. as Ruler of the World   b. with a halo   c. as the Good Shepherd   d. on the cross   e. as an infant

71. The Propylaea was   a. a Roman temple   b. an Etruscan fortification   c. the entrance gate to the Acropolis   d. part of the Forum of Trajan   e. an Islamic mosque

72. A relief showing the *Spoils from the Temple in Jerusalem* is carved on the Arch of   a. Constantine   b. Titus   c. Septimus Severus   d. Trajan   e. Diocletian

73. Pompeiian wall paintings of the Second Style were characterized by   a. fantastic architecture based on the theater   b. mere copies of inlaid stone materials   c. the wall seemingly opened out into an illusionistic space   d. the wall divided into various sections, some sections being painted decoratively and others containing what seem to be panel paintings hung on the wall   e. bas-relief panel

74. The courtyard in front of Old St. Peter's was called the   a. atrium   b. narthex   c. nave   d. bema   e. pendentive

75. The subterranean burial grounds of the Early Christians were called   a. megarons   b. entablatures   c. catacombs   d. basilicas   e. mandorlas

76. One of the favorite subjects of Greek Archaic sculptors was the standing, nude male figure that was called a   a. kori   b. tholos   c. kylix   d. kouros   e. ka

77. The triangular section on top of a Greek temple is called the   a. pediment   b. echinus   c. cornice   d. stylobate   e. acroterion

78. An amphiprostyle temple is characterized by   a. a row of columns all around the exterior   b. two columns in front plus pilasters formed by the extension of the side walls   c. a row of columns across the front and back   d. a double row of columns around the exterior

79.   The *Aphrodite of Cnidos* was carved by   a. Phidias   b. Praxiteles   c. Lysippos   d. Polykleitos
      e. Polydoros

80.   The plan of Hagia Sophia at Constantinople was based on   a. a central dome with two adjoining half-
      domes   b. a hypostyle hall   c. a Greek cross with barrel vaults   d. a flat-roofed nave with two aisles
      e. a latin-cross plan with rib vaults

IV.   Identification.

81.   Compare the following reliefs, attributing each to a culture and an approximate date. Give the reasons for
      your attributions, citing stylistic characteristics of similar works you have studied.

A.

Culture: _____

Date: _____

B.

Culture: _____

Date: _____

Reasons:

82.   What group built the building illustrated below? Approximately when was it erected? Give the reasons for your attributions, citing stylistic characteristics of similar buildings you have studied.

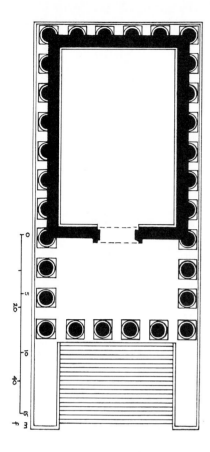

Culture: _____

Date: _____

Reasons:

83. Compare the following heads, attributing each to a culture and an approximate date. Give the reasons for your attributions.

A. Culture: _____

     Date: _____

B. Culture: _____

     Date: _____

Reasons:

84.   Attribute the following relief to a culture, period, and approximate date. Give the reasons for your attributions. What do you think this relief symbolizes?

Culture: _____ Period: _____

Approximate date:_____

Reasons:

85. Compare the two works below, attributing each to a culture and an approximate date. Give the reasons for your attributions.

A. Culture:_____ Date: _____   B. Culture: _____ Date: _____

Reasons:

PART TWO: THE MIDDLE AGES

INTRODUCTION   Text Pages 310–13

1. What years are generally encompassed within the period called Medieval?

2. How has the attitude of historians toward this period changed since the eighteenth century?

3. Name three major interrelated elements that formed the basis of Medieval civilization.

    a.

    b.

    c.

Chapter Eight

Early Medieval Art

Text Pages 314–39

1. According to the map on page 314 of the text, where did the following barbarian tribes settle?

    Saxons: Franks:

    Ostrogoths: Burgundians:

    Visigoths: Lombards:

    Vandals: Avars:

2. In what century did the Huns invade Europe?

3. Catholicism became firmly established in Western Europe with the conversion of the Frankish king

    _____ in the late _____ century and with the success of Augustine's mission

    to _____ in the _____ century.

4. Define the following terms:

    fibula

    zoomorphic

    stave church

    cloisonné

    interlace

    prototype

    bay

    module

    westwork

    pier

    manuscript illumination

5. The decoration of Early Germanic fibulae can be characterized as:

6. What was found at Sutton Hoo, and what was its importance?

7. Who were the Vikings?

8. Monasticism was founded by _____ in the _____ century in the eastern
    Christian world and by _____ in the _____ century in the West.

9. The Celts of Ireland were converted to Christianity in the _____ century. What two factors best account for the independent development of their art?

   a.

   b.

10. What is meant by Hiberno-Saxon?

11. List three characteristics of the style utilized on the ornamental page from the *Book of Lindisfarne* (FIG. 8-6).

    a.

    b.

    c.

12. In comparison with the illumination of Hiberno–Saxon manuscripts, those produced by the monastic orders that accepted Roman orthodoxy are apt to be characterized by:

13. During the Middle Ages, why did illuminators of manuscripts copy earlier examples rather than work directly from nature?

14. When was Charlemagne crowned as head of the Holy Roman Empire?

    Where was his capital city?

15. Name one important result of Charlemagne's project to retrieve the true text of the Bible.

16. List three ways in which the artist of the *Gospel Book of Archbishop Ebbo of Reims* (FIG. 8-10) has modified the style found in the *Gospel Book of Charlemagne* (FIG. 8-9).

    a.

    b.

    c.

17. The text of the *Utrecht Psalter* (FIG. 8-10) reproduces _____ , and the illustrations are done in a style similar to that of _____. A related style is seen in the metalwork on the cover of the _____.

18. What was the major art form of the Avars?

19. What was the function of the *Paliotto* at Sant' Ambrogio in Milan?

    Who was its designer?

20. The basic building material of the Germanic tribes was _____.

21. The Palatine Chapel of Charlemagne resembles the church of _____ in Ravenna, but is distinguished by:

    a.

    b.

22. What was the function of the Torhalle of Lorsch?

    What was its form based on?

23. What religious institution played a central role in the revival of learning?

24. Although the church of the monastery of St. Gall is a three-aisled basilica, it differs from its Early Christian prototypes in the following ways:

    a.

    b.

    c.

25. What feature found at St. Riquier, but not at St. Gall, was common to most Carolingian churches?

26. How did the Ottonian period derive its name?

    Its geographical center was the modern country of _____.

27. A major Ottonian building is the Abbey church of _____ at _____
It retains the following Carolingian features:

a.   b.   c.

28. Describe the alternate-support system.

What was its function?

Why did it appeal to northern builders?

29. Who was Bishop Bernward?

30. The style of the figures on the bronze doors at St. Michael's at Hildesheim (FIG. 8-25) probably derives
from manuscript illumination of the _____ period. In what major way does it differ
from its prototypes?

31. What two stylistic features seen in the *Gospel Book of Otto III* (FIG. 8-28) were not apparent in earlier
Carolingian illumination?

a.

b.

32. Locate the following on the map on study guide 94:

Lindisfarne   Hildesheim
Sutton Hoo   Centula
St. Gall   Tours
Aachen   Reichenau
Oseberg   Lorsch
Milan

DISCUSSION QUESTIONS

1. What factors do the authors believe inclined the Germanic tribes to adopt the animal style? What was its origin? By what means was it transmitted to them?

2. Compare the abstract decorative art of the Early Middle Ages in Europe as seen in the ornamental page from the *Book of Lindisfarne* (FIG. 8-6) with the Islamic decorative style as seen in the Ardebil carpet (FIG. 7-87). In what ways do they resemble each other? What is distinctive about each?

3. Discuss the interaction of the Roman illusionist tradition with the barbarian tradition of linear decoration in manuscript illumination of the Early Middle Ages. Compare FIGS. 8-6 to 8-11 and FIGS. 8-27 and 8-28.

4. In what ways can the plan of St. Gall (FIG. 8-19) and the church of St. Michael's at Hildesheim (FIG. 8-23) be related to the Germanic sense of design as manifested in Frankish ornaments (FIG. 8-1) and to the Medieval way of thinking? What importance do these buildings have for the development of Romanesque architecture in northern Europe?

5. Discuss the historical and political factors represented by the image of the enthroned Otto III from his gospel book (FIG. 8-28). In what ways is this image related to the changing political and religious situation in Western Europe?

6. Compare the style and the technique used to create the *Paliotto* from Sant' Ambrogio in Milan (FIG. 8-13) with those of the doors of St. Michael's at Hildesheim (FIG. 8-25). What might have been the stylistic sources for each?

Using the timeline at the beginning of Chapter 8 in the text, enter the appropriate dates for the following periods. Fill in the chart as much as you can from memory; then check your answers against the text and complete the chart.

SUMMARY OF EARLY MEDIEVAL ART

Migration Period and Germanic Kingdoms: _____ to _____

Celtic Culture in Ireland: _____ to _____

Carolingian Period: _____ to _____

Ottonian Period: _____ to _____

	Typical Examples	Stylistic Characteristics	Significant Historical People, Events, etc.
Migration Period Crafts			
Early Manuscripts			
Carolingian Manuscripts			
Ottonian Manuscripts			
Carolingian Architecture			
Ottonian Architecture			

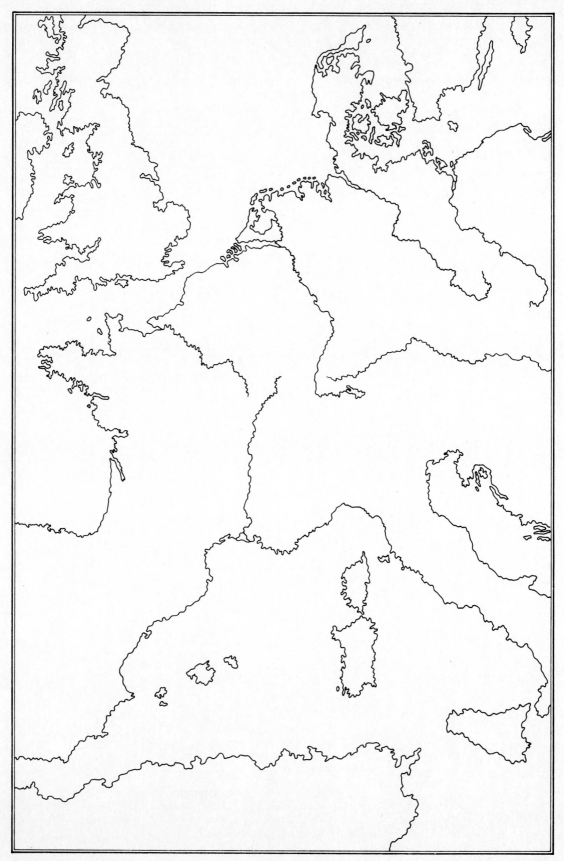

EUROPE

Chapter Nine
Romanesque Art

1. Briefly describe the political and economic system known as feudalism.

2. Two important monastic orders during the Romanesque period were _____

   and _____. Which of the orders most encouraged the development of art?

3. Two important, immediate effects of the Crusades were:

   a.

   b.

   A third effect, perhaps less immediate but even more significant in the long run, was:

4. Define the following terms:

   château fort

   choir

   tribune

   pilaster

   corbel

   diaphragm arch

compound pier

buttress

crossing

square schematism

groin vault

rib vault

sexpartite vault

radiating chapel

5. What common experience made the use of stone vaults so important to Romanesque builders?

6. List four types of vaults used at St. Philibert in Tournus.

a.   c.

b.   d.

What was the importance of the ambulatory at St. Philibert?

7. List three characteristics of Romanesque buildings as seen in the church of St. Sernin at Toulouse.

a.

b.

c.

8. Why were so many Romanesque churches of such great size, even though they were frequently located in isolated places?

9. What was the purpose of the ambulatory with radiating chapels, found in so many Romanesque churches?

10. The main drawback of barrel vaulting was:

11. Label the following parts on the plan below: ambulatory, apse, bay, buttress, crossing, nave, transept, radiating chapel, aisles, choir.

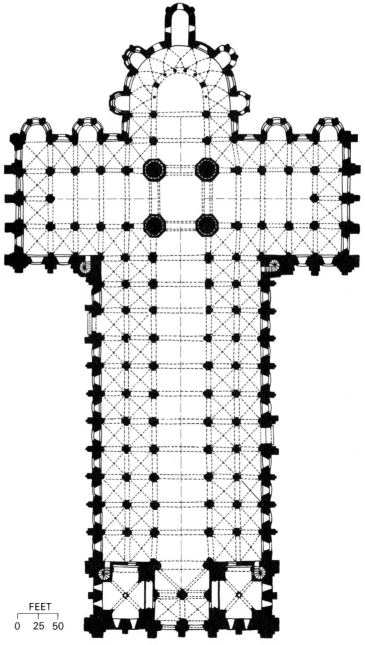

FEET
0   25   50

12. Name the two areas that demonstrate the greatest development of masonry vaulting during the Romanesque period.

    a.   b.

13. It is generally thought that the German cathedral of _____ may be one of the earliest, fully vaulted Romanesque churches in Europe.

14. The "master model of Norman Romanesque architecture" is the church of _____

    at _____. It was built between _____ and _____.

    Among the progressive features of the building, which look ahead to later Gothic architecture, are:

    a.

    b.

    c.

    d.

15. William of Normandy conquered England in the year _____.

16. Two key elements of Gothic architecture were combined for the first time in the vaults of Durham Cathedral. What are they?

    a.

    b.

17. List three features that Pisa Cathedral shares with its Early Christian prototypes.

    a.

    b.

    c.

    List four features that distinguish it from them.

    a.

    b.

    c.

    d.

18.   What is the structural advantage of the sequence of domes used to cover the naves of Aquitainian churches?

19.   Identify the following individuals:

Wiligelmus

Gislebertus

Bishop Odo

Master Hugo

Beatus of Liébana

20.   The prototype of the stone carving of *Christ in Majesty* from St. Sernin at Toulouse (FIG. 9-24) most likely was _____.

21.   Label the following parts of a Romanesque portal on the diagram below: lintel, tympanum, archivolts, voussoir, trumeau, jambs.

22.   The subject carved on the tympanum at Moissac is _____.

Typical Romanesque conventions seen in the figures of Moissac are:

a.

b.

c.

23. The subject of the west tympanum of St. Lazare at Autun is _____;
the tympanum of the central portal of the narthex of La Madeleine at Vézelay shows:

Why can it be said that the iconography of the tympanum of Vézelay was influenced by the Crusades?

24. List three characteristics that distinguish the style of the portal sculpture of St. Trophime at Arles from the styles of those at Vézelay and at Autun.

a.

b.

c.

To what influences can these differences be attributed?

25. What is depicted on the Bayeux tapestry?

What technique was used to create it?

26. What stylistic features are shared by the Tahull fresco (FIG. 9-36) and the manuscripts from Saint-Omer (FIG. 9-37) and Citeaux (FIG. 9-38)?

a.

b.

c.

27. How has the Romanesque style as seen in the Bury Bible (FIG. 9-39) been modified from earlier examples?

a.

b.

28. Describe the theme of Christ's second coming as illustrated in the typanum at Moissac (FIG. 9-27) and the *Apocalypse of Saint-Sever* (FIG. 9-40).

What is the source of this imagery?

29. Locate the following on the map on study guide page 94:

Durham	Caen	Speyer
Paris	Vézelay	Autun
Cluny	Angouléme	Moissac
Toulouse	Tahull	Florence
Arles	Pisa	Modena
Tournus	Bayeux	

DISCUSSION QUESTIONS

1. What are the distinguishing features of the Romanesque style seen in the church of St. Sernin at Toulouse (FIGS. 9-4, 9-5, 9-6) compared with those in Old St. Peter's in Rome (FIGS. 7-4 and 7-6)?

2. Describe the various evolutionary steps, in both plan and elevation, that led from the Carolingian to the Romanesque style in northern European churches.

3. What evidence do you see that the *Christ in Majesty* from St. Sernin (FIG. 9-24) was derived from a metal prototype such as the scene from the cover of the *Codex Aureus of St. Emmeram* (FIG. 8-12)?

4. Compare the carvings from St. Trophime at Arles (FIG. 9-34) with the portal sculpture from Moissac (FIG. 9-27), Autun (FIG. 9-30), and Vézelay (FIG. 9-32). What is the subject of each portal. How do they differ stylistically? Can you see any relationships to earlier Medieval or Classical styles?

5. What features indicate the common stylistic derivation of the fresco from Santa Maria at Tahull (FIG. 9-36) and the apse mosaic from Monreale (FIG. 7-57)? What changes do you see?

6. What portents of change appear in the illumination depicting the scribe Eadwine from the *Canterbury Psalter* (FIG. 9-41)? Compare the treatment of the drapery and body of Eadwine with that in the illustrations from the *Gospel Book of Charlemagne* (FIG. 8-9), the *Gospel Book of Archbishop Ebbo of Reims* (FIG. 8-10), and *The Life and Miracles of St. Audomarus* (FIG. 9-37).

7. Why do you think Bernard of Clairvaux was so disturbed by the sumptuous art of the churches? Do you agree with him?

Using the timeline at the beginning of Chapter 9 in the text, enter the appropriate dates for the following period. Fill in the charts as much as you can from memory; then check your answers against the text and complete the charts.

SUMMARY OF ROMANESQUE ARCHITECTURE

Romanesque Period: _____ to _____

	Typical Examples	Stylistic Characteristics
Languedoc-Burgundy		
Germany-Lombardy		
Normandy-England		
Tuscany		
Aquitaine		

SUMMARY OF ROMANESQUE SCULPTURE AND PAINTING

	Typical Examples	Stylistic Characteristics	Significant Historical People, Events, etc.
Sculpture			
Painting			
Manuscript Illumination			

Chapter Ten
Gothic Art

EARLY AND HIGH GOTHIC ART   Text Pages 372–98

1. List some of the ways in which the social and economic structure of the Gothic period differed from that of the Romanesque.

    a.

    b.

    c.

    d.

2. What was "courtly love"?

3. What was the primary historical importance of the Franciscan movement?

4. Indentify the following:

    Albigensian crusade

    Scholasticism

    Eleanor of Aquitaine

    St. Dominic

    St. Thomas Aquinas

    Pope Innocent III

    St. Denis

Bernard of Clairvaux

Abbot Suger

5. Where is the Île-de-France?

6. List three of the features of the new choir at St. Denis as described by Abbot Suger that are characteristic of the new Gothic style.

    a.

    b.

    c.

7. List the three structural and/or design features that characterize a Gothic vault.

    a.

    b.

    c.

    What are the advantages of the pointed arch over the round arch?

8. Describe the difference between Medieval *scientia* and *ars*.

9. List three Romanesque features retained in Laon Cathedral.

    a.

    b.

    c.

List three new Gothic features found in the cathedral.

a.

b.

c.

10. Describe the modification made in the nave elevation of Notre Dame of Paris that changed it from Early to High Gothic.

What was the purpose of the change?

11. The figures from the Royal Portals of Chartres Cathedral, the earliest and most complete surviving Early Gothic portals, were carved between _____ and _____. The following scenes are represented on the tympana:

Right: Left: Central:

The figures carved on the jambs represent:

In what ways do these jamb figures differ significantly from Romanesque figures?

a.

b.

c.

12. Define the following terms:

chevet

triforium

rectangular-bay system

crossing spire

embrasure

mullion

soffit

13. What was the function of the flying buttress?

Why was it an essential element of the Gothic architectural vocabulary?

14. Label the following parts of a Gothic church on the diagram below: clerestory, flying buttress, nave arcade, triforium, vaults.

Is this an Early Gothic or High Gothic church?

15. How does the plan of Bourges Cathedral (FIG. 10-20) differ from that of Chartres (FIG. 10-16)?

    Which design was more influential?

16. What are the similarities in the façades of Notre Dame in Paris (FIG. 10-9) and Amiens Cathedral (FIG. 10-22)?

    a.

    b.

    What are the differences?

    a.

    b.

17. The rayonnant style developed in the second half of the _____ century and was associated with the court of _____.

18. Who was the Jean de Chelles?

19. What was the purpose of the Sainte Chapelle in Paris?

    How did its structure reflect that purpose?

20. Which of the great French cathedrals had the highest vaults? What happened to them?

21. According to Émile Mâle, what was the source of the iconographic programs of many of the great Gothic cathedrals?

22. What changes can you see in the figures of *St. Martin and St. Jerome* from the Porch of the Confessors (FIG. 10-31) when compared with the jamb figures from the Royal Portals of Chartres Cathedral (FIG. 10-14)?

    a.

b.

c.

23. The jamb figures from the central portal of the west façade of Reims Cathedral are tied to the architecture by the following devices:

    a.   b.

    The sculptor of the *Visitation* group was strongly influenced by the style of _____.

    The elegant, courtly style that is associated with rayonnant architecture is seen in the figure of

    _____ from the _____ group.

24. In what way did Hugh of St. Victor liken stained-glass windows to the Holy Scriptures?

25. How did the armatures supporting stained-glass windows change from the twelfth to the thirteenth century?

26. Who was Villard de Honnecourt?

    What did Villard use as the basis for drawing many of his figures?

27. What influences are seen in the illuminations of the *Psalter of St. Louis* (FIG. 10-37)?

    a.

    b.

    c.

DISCUSSION QUESTIONS

1. Discuss the change in the role of women during the Gothic period and how it relates to the cult of the Virgin Mary. What effect did these changes have on art?

2. Comparing St. Étienne at Caen (FIGS. 9-14 and 9-15), Laon Cathedral (FIGS. 10-5 to 10-8), Notre Dame of Paris (FIGS. 10-9 to 10-12), and Chartres Cathedral (FIGS. 10-13 to 10-18), discuss the evolution of architectural form from Romanesque through Early Gothic to High Gothic. Consider changes in plan, elevation, and construction methods.

3. What effect did the changing philosophical conception of the relation between the soul and the body have on Gothic sculpture?

4. Trace the development of Medieval architectural sculpture in relation to its structural setting from St. Sernin at Toulouse (FIG. 9-24) through St. Pierre at Moissac (FIG. 9-28) and the Royal Portals (FIG. 10-14) and Porch of the Confessors (FIG. 10-31) at Chartres to the figures from Reims Cathedral (FIG. 10-33).

5. What contribution might the writings of "pseudo-Dionysus the Areopagite" have made to the development of Gothic architecture?

6. In what ways does Erwin Panofsky believe that the methods used by the Scholastic philosophers were similar to those used by Gothic architects?

LATE AND NON-FRENCH GOTHIC ART   Text Pages 398–411

1. During what century did the High Gothic style flourish, and when did the Late Gothic period begin?

2. What feature of *The Virgin of Paris* (FIG. 10-38) was typical of much Late Gothic sculpture?

3. From what did the Late Gothic flamboyant style derive its name?

4. Why did architectural production decline in the Île-de-France during the fourteenth and fifteenth centuries?

5. An important example of French flamboyant Gothic architecture is the church of _____ in Rouen, the capital of _____ .

6. Who were William of Sens and William the Englishman?

7. The "decorated" style of English Gothic architecture flourished in the _____ century.

8. The last English Gothic style, seen at Gloucester, is called _____ . It is characterized by the following features:

    a.

    b.

9. Describe fan vaulting.

10.   The German cathedral of _____ was finished in the nineteenth century when the original thirteenth-century plan was discovered.

Describe its "curtain walls."

11.   The church of St. Elizabeth at Marburg is an early example of a favorite German type of Gothic structure known as a _____. It differs from the standard basilican type of church in the following respects:

a.

b.

12.   Briefly describe the style used in the depiction of the *Death of the Virgin* on Strasbourg Cathedral.

13.   Who were Ekkehard and Uta?

What is significant about their appearance in a cathedral?

14.   What features does the *Bamberg Rider* (FIG. 10-55) share with the figures from the Reims portal (FIG. 10-33)?

15.   Identify those features of Florence Cathedral that differentiate it from northern Gothic churches.

16.   Why do the authors feel that the design of the Florentine campanile forecasts the ideals of Renaissance architecture?

17.   How is the façade of Orvieto Cathedral related to those of French Gothic churches?

In what major way does it differ?

18. Why were Italian Medieval town halls like the one at Siena constructed with heavy walls and battlements?

Why, by contrast, could the Doge's Palace at Venice be constructed without fortifications?

19. Locate the following on the map on study guide page 94.

Chartres	Salisbury	Cologne
Laon	Gloucester	Bamberg
St. Denis	Wells	Naumburg
Reims	London	Venice
Amiens	Marburg	Siena
Rouens	Strasbourg	Orvieto

DISCUSSION QUESTIONS

1. What similarity do you see between the S-curve of *The Virgin of Paris* (FIG. 10-38) and that used by Praxiteles for the *Hermes* (FIG. 5-65)? In what ways are the two figures different?

2. In what ways has the classic French High Gothic structure as typified by Amiens Cathedral (FIGS. 10-22 to 10-25) been modified in the English and Italian buildings like Salisbury Cathedral (FIGS. 10-42 to 10-45) and Florence Cathedral (FIGS. 10-58, 10-59, 10-60)?

3. Compare the figures of *Ekkehard and Uta* from Naumburg (FIG. 10-54) with the figures from Reims (FIG. 10-33). How are the German figures related to the French prototypes? How do they differ?

4. The equestrian figure of the *Bamberg Rider* (FIG. 10-55) is reminiscent of that of the Roman emperor Marcus Aurelius (FIG. 6-72). Compare the stylistic treatment of horse and rider as well as the relation of each figure to the space surrounding it.

5. How did the representations of Christ change from Early Christian times the through the Gothic period? Consider representations in an early catacomb fresco (FIG. 7-3), at San Vitale (FIG. 7-38), at Monreale (FIG. 7-57), at Moissac (FIG. 9-27), and at Cologne (FIG. 10-56). What historical factors do you think might have contributed to these different representations?

SUMMARY: GOTHIC ART   Text Pages **370-411**

Using the timeline at the beginning of Chapter 10 in the text, center the appropriate dates for the following periods. Fill in the charts as much as possible from memory; then check your answers against the text and complete the charts.

HISTORICAL SUMMARY OF GOTHIC PERIOD

Early Gothic Period: _____ to _____

High Gothic Period: _____ to _____

Late Gothic Period: _____ to _____

Significant Religious Leaders and Events	Significant Political Leaders and Events	Cultural Developments

SUMMARY OF GOTHIC ARCHITECTURE

	Typical Examples	Stylistic Characteristics
French Early Gothic		
French High Gothic		
French Rayonnant		
French Late Gothic		
English		
German		
Italian		

SUMMARY OF GOTHIC SCULPTURE AND STAINED GLASS

	Typical Examples	Stylistic Characteristics
French Early Gothic Sculpture		
French High Gothic Sculpture		
German Gothic Sculpture		
Stained Glass		

Self-Quiz

PART TWO: THE MIDDLE AGES

I. **Matching.** Choose the style or period in the right column that best corresponds to the art work or site in the left column and enter the appropriate letter in the space provided.

_____	1. Gloucester Cathedral
_____	2. Amiens Cathedral
_____	3. Sutton Hoo treasure
_____	4. *Utrecht Psalter*
_____	5. St. Sernin at Toulouse
_____	6. Speyer Cathedral
_____	7. St. Denis ambulatory
_____	8. St. Michael's at Hildesheim
_____	9. *Book of Lindisfarne*
_____	10. *Gospel Book of Archbishop Ebbo*
_____	11. *Gospel Book of Otto III*
_____	12. Laon Cathedral
_____	13. Salisbury Cathedral
_____	14. Royal Portals at Chartres Cathedral
_____	15. Palatine Chapel at Aachen
_____	16. Portal sculpture at Reims Cathedral
_____	17. St. Maclou at Rouen
_____	18. Chapel of Henry VIII in London
_____	19. Doge's Palace in Venice
_____	20. Chartres Cathedral
_____	21. San Miniato al Monte in Florence
_____	22. Durham Cathedral
_____	23. Notre Dame in Paris
_____	24. St. Étienne at Caen
_____	25. Monastery at St. Gall
_____	26. Oseberg ship burial
_____	27. St. Pierre at Angouléme
_____	28. Milan Cathedral
_____	29. Sainte-Chapelle in Paris
_____	30. Beauvais Cathedral

a. Migration period & Irish Christian
b. Carolingian
c. Ottonian
d. Languedoc-Burgundian Romanesque
e. German-Lombard Romanesque
f. Norman-English Romanesque
g. Tuscan Romanesque
h. Aquitanian Romanesque
i. Early Gothic
j. High Gothic
k. Gothic rayonnant style
l. Late Gothic

II. Matching. Choose the identification in the right column that best corresponds to the name or term in the left column and enter the appropriate letter in the space provided.

_____ 31. Charlemagne	a.	Carolingian church and monastery
_____ 32. Villard de Honnecourt	b.	sculptor of tympanum at Autun
_____ 33. Gislebertus	c.	conquered England in 1066
_____ 34. fibula	d.	large primitive safety pin
_____ 35. choir	e.	the gallery between the arcade and clerestory
_____ 36. archivolt	f.	crowned Holy Roman Emperor in A.D. 800
_____ 37. pier	g.	combined Irish and Anglo–Saxon style
_____ 38. cloisonné	h.	austere leader of Cistercian order
_____ 39. westwork	i.	a multi-storied mass with façade and towers on the western end of a Medieval church
_____ 40. Hiberno–Saxon	j.	section of church reserved for the clergy
_____ 41. St. Gall	k.	one of a series of concentric moldings in a Gothic or Romanesque portal
_____ 42. psalter	l.	knob-like ornament on a pinnacle
_____ 43. Bishop Bernward	m.	book containing the Psalms of the Bible
_____ 44. St. Louis	n.	a vertical, unattached masonry support
_____ 45. triforium	o.	Bishop of Hildesheim
_____ 46. William of Normandy	p.	Gothic architect and draftsman
_____ 47. Bernard of Clairvaux	q.	thirteenth-century French king
_____ 48. Abbot Suger	r.	cleric who built St. Denis
_____ 49. chevet	s.	a pillar in the center of a Romanesque or Gothic portal
_____ 50. Wiligelmus	t.	the eastern end of a church including choir, ambulatory, and radiating chapels
	u.	a process of enamelling using cells made of metal wire
	v.	a beam used to span an opening
	w.	fourteenth-century German king
	x.	sculptor of Modena Cathedral portal

III. Multiple Choice. Circle the most appropriate answer.

51. A trumeau would most likely be found   a. on an Ionic temple   b. as part of the doorway of a Medieval cathedral   c. as part of the support system of a beehive tomb   d. as part of an Etruscan tomb   e. in a Medieval wall elevation above the arcade

52. The Palace Chapel at Aachen was built around   a. 500   b. 650   c. 800   d. 1000   e. 1150

53. The *Book of Lindisfarne* is   a. done in the Hiberno–Saxon style   b. part of the Sutton Hoo find   c. a Carolingian psalter   d. a gospel book dating from around 800   e. a Byzantine manuscript

54. The west tympanum of St. Lazare at Autun contains an illustration of   a. the emperor and the empress presenting gifts to Christ   b. the Last Judgment   c. Christ and the twenty-eight elders of the Apocalypse   d. the Madonna holding the Child   e. the Last Supper

55. During the Carolingian period, Reims was most famous for   a. its manuscripts   b. its mosaic decoration   c. its interlace carving   d. its architecture   e. its sarcophagi

56. A Gothic church is often distinguished from an Early Christian basilica by   a. the use of transepts   b. the use of nave and aisles   c. the use of bays   d. the use of a clerestory   e. the use of an apse

57. Monumental sculpture first appeared on the façades of churches in   a. seventh-century Italy   b. eighth-century England   c. ninth-century Spain   d. eleventh-century Germany   e. eleventh-century France

58. The animal interlace style was most popular among   a. the Sumerians   b. Irish monks   c. the Carolingians   d. the Ottonians   e. the thirteenth-century French

59. Triforium is the term used to describe   a. the area where the nave intercepts the transept   b. the arch thrown across a barrel vault from one pier to the next   c. an anteroom where sacred vestments are kept   d. a blind arcade below the clerestory in Gothic nave walls   e. an entrance porch where the unbaptized must stay during services

60. The original home of the Goths was   a. Asia Minor   b. the Pontic region above the Black Sea   c. the Baltic region   d. France   e. Italy

61. Curtain walls would most likely be found in association with   a. domes set on pendentives   b. barrel vaults   c. groin vaults   d. corbeled vaults   e. pointed rib vaults and flying buttresses

62. The earliest jamb or column statues that you have studied are found on the west portal of   a. St. Michael's at Hildesheim   b. St. Pierre at Moissac   c. Chartres Cathedral   d. Amiens Cathedral   e. Reims Cathedral

63. The centuries from about 350 to 750 are generally referred to as the   a. Hellenistic period   b. Middle Ages   c. Migration period   d. Carolingian period   e. Ottonian period

64. The Gothic style of architecture developed in the region that is called   a. the Rhineland   b. Normandy   c. Tuscany   d. Languedoc   e. Île-de-France

65. Which element of Gothic architecture is not found in some Romanesque examples?   a. pointed arch   b. rib vault   c. towers   d. flying buttresses   e. latin-cross plan

66. Sutton Hoo is famous   a. for its magnificent twelfth-century cathedral   b. as the site of a battle in which the Normans conquered England   c. as the site of a ship burial   d. for its rock-cut tombs   e. for its production of Medieval manuscripts

67. Which of the following is *not* a Romanesque church: a. Durham Cathedral   b. Notre Dame in Paris   c. St. Étienne at Caen   d. Sant'Ambrogio in Milan   e. St. Sernin at Toulouse

68. The Portal of the Kings from the west façade of Chartres Cathedral dates from about   a. 950   b. 1050   c. 1150   d. 1250   e. 1450

69. The Sutton Hoo treasure was found in   a. England   b. France   c. eastern Germany   d. the Pontic region of Russia   e. Italy

70. The Medieval church discussed that was highest in proportion to its width was   a. Sant'Apollinare Nuovo   b. Salisbury   c. Amiens   d. Hildesheim   e. Beauvais

71. A sexpartite rib vault was typical of buildings in which style?   a. Romanesque   b. Early Gothic   c. High Gothic   d. Ottonian   e. Carolingian

72. The sculptures of the tympanum at Moissac represent   a. the Last Judgment   b. Christ and the twenty-four Elders of the Apocalypse   c. the Miracles of St. Firmin   d. the Life of the Virgin   e. the Mission of the Apostles

73. The windowed section on the nave wall above the aisle roofs of a church is known as the   a. clerestory   b. gallery   c. triforium   d. trumeau   e. archivolt

74. The square east end is a distinguishing feature of the cathedral of   a. Hildesheim   b. Chartres   c. Salisbury   d. Amiens   e. St. Sernin

75. The portal sculpture of St. Trophime at Arles was carved in which century?   a. tenth   b. eleventh   c. twelfth   d. thirteenth   e. fourteenth

76. The primary medium used to decorate the apse of the church of Santa Maria at Tahull was   a. mosaic   b. sculpture   c. fresco   d. stained glass   e. gold and enamel

77. The art of stained glass was most highly developed during which period?   a. Migration   b. Carolingian   c. Ottonian   d. Romanesque   e. Gothic

78. The greatest tendency toward realism is seen in which of the following Medieval sculptures: a. tympanum of St. Lazare at Autun   b. trumeau figures from St. Pierre at Moissac   c. figures from the Porch of the Confessors at Chartres Cathedral   d. the *Annuciation* group at Reims Cathedral   e. *Ekkehard and Uta* from Naumburg Cathedral

79. The greatest emphasis on the horizontal elements is found in the Gothic cathedral of   a. Chartres   b. Amiens   c. Cologne   d. Florence   e. Beauvais

80. Which of the following is a hall church?   a. Orvieto Cathedral   b. St. Sernin at Toulouse   c. St. Elizabeth at Marburg   d. Salisbury Cathedral   e. Speyer Cathedral

IV.   Identification.

81. Compare the following manuscript pages, attributing each to a particular cultural period and approximate date. Give the reasons for your attributions.

A. Period: _____

   Date: _____

B. Period: _____

   Date: _____

Reasons:

82. Compare the two sculptures below, attributing each to a particular period and approximate date. Give the reasons for your attributions.

A. Period: _____

Date: _____

B. Period: _____

Date: _____

Reasons:

83. In what period, style, and century was the church below erected? To what group of churches is it related? What features demonstrate this relationship?

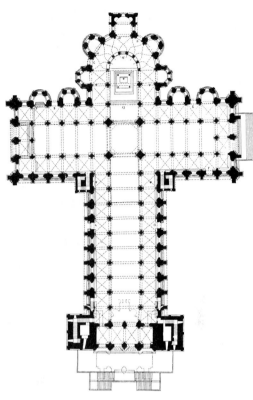

Period: _____

Century: _____

Stylistic affiliations:

84. Label as many parts of the Medieval church illustrated below as you can. Identify and date the building. It contains features of two architectural styles; what are they?

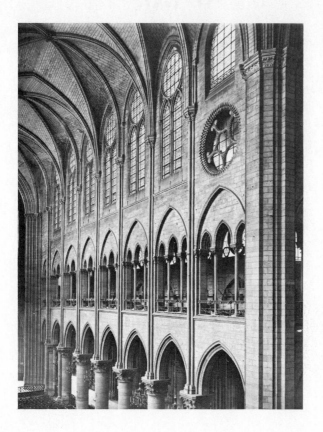
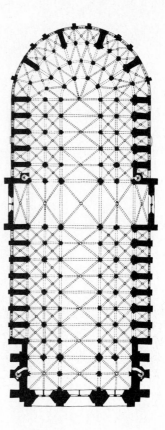

Name: _____   Date: _____   Styles: _____ & _____

Describe the architectural features that are characteristic of each style used in this building.

PART THREE: THE NON-EUROPEAN WORLD

INTRODUCTION   Text Pages 412–15

1. What qualities of non-European art seem to relate it more closely to the prehistoric and Medieval than to the later developments in Western art?

2. Give four examples of early contacts between Europe and non-Western cultures.

   a.

   b.

   c.

   d.

   What effects did these early contacts have on Western art?

   When and why did non-Western art begin to have a serious impact on European art?

Chapter Eleven

The Art of India   Text Pages 418–37

1. Identify/define the following:

   Upanishads

   yakshas

   yakshis

stupa

ushnisha

urna

torana

chaitya

mandala

mudra

Bhagavad-Gita

jataka

chandi

rathas

sutra

2. During what millennium did the first great flowering of Indian art occur?
    Two important sites from this period are:
    a.

    b.

3. List two characteristics of Indian sculpture.

    a.

    b.

4. What type of subjects were most commonly represented on the intaglio steatite seals of Mohenjo-Daro?

5. At what date did the Aryan invasions of India begin?

    What religion did they bring?

6. Name two religions that developed in India in the sixth century B.C.

    a.

    b.

7. Who was Siddhartha?

        Asoka?

8. Briefly give the Buddhist meaning for the following symbols:
    Lotus

    Wheel

9. Where is the Great Stupa located?

    Describe at least two functions of the stupa.

10. Name four objects that are commonly used to symbolize the Buddha.

    a.   c.

    b.   d.

11.   List two stylistic characteristics of the carving that decorates the toranas of the Great Stupa (FIG. 11-6).

a.

b.

12.   What two stylistic features distinguish the chaitya hall at Karli (FIG. 11-7, 11-8, 11-9)?

a.

b.

13.   Briefly describe the difference between Hinayana and Mahayana Buddhism.

14.   Which culture provided artistic models for the images of the *Seated Buddha* from Gandhara (FIG. 11-10)?

15.   List three stylistic characteristics of the Mathura Buddha (FIG. 11-11).

a.

b.

c.

16.   By what century had Hinduism regained supremacy in India?

17.   Who was Siva?

18.   What is the meaning of the three-headed figure of Siva at Elephanta (FIG. 11-15)?

19.   The function of Siva's dance was:

20.   The primary function of a Hindu temple is:

21.   What particular art form produced under the Chola kingdom of south India was most outstanding?

22.   What brought about the decline of Hindu sculpture and architecture in the seventeenth century?

23.   List three characteristics of Gupta art that are apparent in the paintings at Ajanta (FIG. 11-23).

   a.

   b.

   c.

24.   How was Indian painting affected by the Moslem conquests?

25.   Name two countries that adopted Mahayana Buddhism.

   a.   b.

   Name one country that adopted Hinayana Buddhism.

26.   In what country is the stupa of Borobudur located?

   In what century was it built?

   What is symbolized by the base and the four rectilinear tiers?

            by the upper four circular tiers?

            by the stupa on the uppermost terrace?

27.   The *Ramayana* is an epic sacred to:

28.   List three characteristics of the Early Khmer figure created in the seventh century (FIG. 11-28).

a.

b.

c.

29.   Why is the Bayon at Angkor Thom (FIG. 11-32 and 11-33) considered to be the culmination of Indian temple architecture?

30.   Locate the following on the map on study guide page 131:

India and Pakistan
    Mohenjo-Daro
    Gandhara
    Sanchi
    Karli
    Elephanta
    Ajanta
    Khajuraho
Sri Lanka (Ceylon)
    Polonnaruwa

Thailand
Java
    Borobudur
Kampuchea (Cambodia)
    Angkor Wat

Indus River
Himalayas

DISCUSSION QUESTIONS

1.   Compare the Buddha from Gandhara (FIG. 11-10) and the Siva from Elephanta (FIG. 11-15) with the Roman figures from the Ara Pacis Augustae (FIG. 6-60), the *Apollo* from Olympia (FIG. 5-40), the figures of *St. Martin and St. Jerome* from Chartres (FIG. 10-31), the *Amorous Couple* from the chaitya hall at Karli (FIG. 11-9), and the relief from the Pergamon Altar of Zeus and Athena (FIG. 5-79). Which figures seem to be the most spiritual? What stylistic features do you think achieve this quality? Discuss the use of open and closed form and the use of rigid, static poses over diagonal motion.

2.   In what way does the function of a temple as residence of the god rather than as a hall for congregational worship affect the style of the architecture of Hindu and Greek temples? Compare the Hindu temples in Chapter 11 with a Greek temple (FIG. 5-45) and Christian examples (FIGS. 7-41, 7-42, 10-10, 10-11, 10-12). What function does light play in each type of building? How is sculpture used in each?

3.   What Greek and Medieval Christian figures can you think of that share the monumental calm and sense of timelessness of the Early Khmer figure of *Harihara* (FIG. 11-28)? What stylistic features do they have in common?

4.   What different metaphysical views are represented by the image of Siva dancing (FIG. 11-22) and the Seated Buddha (FIG. 11-12)?

5.   Discuss the iconography of Buddhism as seen in the stupa of Borobudur in Java (FIG. 11-26).

6.   What was the relationship between kings and temples in Angkor Wat? What did the temples of Angkor Wat symbolize?

Using the timeline at the beginning of Chapter 11 in the text, enter the appropriate dates for the following periods. Fill in the charts as much as you can from memory; then check your answers against the text and complete the charts.

SUMMARY OF INDIAN ART

Indus Valley Civilization	_____ B.C. to	_____ B.C.
Maurya (Asoka) Period	_____ B.C. to	_____ B.C.
Sunga Period	_____ B.C. to	_____ B.C.
Andhra Period	_____ B.C. to	_____ B.C.
Kushan Period	A.D. _____ to	_____
Gupta Period	A.D. _____ to	_____
Later Hindu Dynasties	A.D. _____ to	_____
Moslem Dynasties	A.D. _____ to	_____

	Typical Examples	Stylistic Characteristics	Significant Historical People, Events, etc.
Indus Valley Civilization			
Maurya (Asoka) Period			
Sunga Period			
Andhra Period			
Kushan Period			

SUMMARY OF INDIAN ART (continued)

Gupta Period			
Later Hindu Dynasties			
Moslem Dynasties			

SUMMARY OF JAVANESE AND CAMBODIAN ART

	Typical Examples	Stylistic Characteristics	Significant Historical People, Events, etc.
Java			
Cambodia			

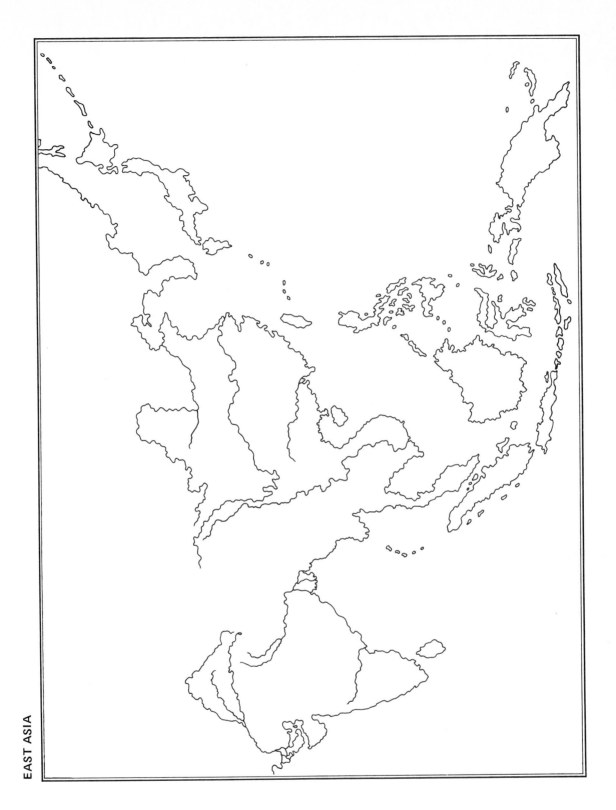

EAST ASIA

Chapter Twelve
The Art of China

Text Pages 438–61

1. Although the languages spoken in various parts of China are different, a common _____ has made possible the sharing of a common heritage.

2. The major art form during the Shang dynasty was:

3. List two adjectives that characterize the silhouette of Shang and Chou bronzes and two phrases that characterize the decoration of each.

	Shang	Chou
Silhouette:	_____	_____
	_____	_____
Decoration:	_____	_____
	_____	_____

4. Name one material other than bronze that was very popular for jewelry and ritual objects in the Late Chou period.

5. What was found in the tomb of Emperor Shih Huang Ti at Shensi?

6. What were the primary sources of the subject matter of the art of the Han dynasty?

   a.

   b.

7. List three stylistic characteristics of Han reliefs.

   a.

   b.

   c.

8. What power did the Han Chinese attribute to Jade?

9. Briefly state why Buddhism was adopted in China during the Three Kingdoms period.

10. Describe three stylistic features, derived from Indian prototypes, that occur in the earliest Chinese images of Buddha.

   a.

   b.

   c.

11. What three features do the Chinese figures from the Yunkang caves share with figures from sixth-century Greece and early-twelfth-century France?

   a.

   b.

   c.

12. How did the popularity of the Paradise Sects of Buddhism affect Buddhist art in China?

13. By what century had the landscape scroll apparently been developed?

14. What did the critic Hsieh Ho mean by "spirit-consonance engendering movement"?

15. What effects did the new wave of Indian influence have on Chinese Buddhist art of the T'ang period?

   a.

   b.

16. Describe the similarities you see between the poses of the Chinese *Bodhisattva* (FIG. 12-13) and *The Virgin of Paris* (FIG. 10-38).

17.   What kind of perspective was used in the Chinese painting of the *Paradise of Amitabha* (FIG. 12-16)?

18.   Many ceramic figures were made for burial in tombs during the _____ dynasty.

19.   Write down Ching Hao's criteria for the classification of "divine" painting.

What does he place in the lowest category of painting?

20.   Describe the stylistic characteristic that the following Sung painters had in Common: Tung Yuan, Chu-jan, Fan K'uan, and Kuo Hsi.

21.   Name the three elements that are typical of Southern Sung landscape painting.

a.

b.

c.

22.   How did the beliefs of the Zen sect of Buddhism influence art?

23.   The technique of incised designs showing through a colored slip (*T'zu-chou*) was developed by potters of the _____ dynasty.

24. How did the invasions of Kublai Khan influence the Chinese approach to landscape painting?

a.

b.

25. Briefly describe the position of amateur artists during the Ming period.

26. List three types of glazes that were developed by Ming potters.

a.

b.

c.

27. Who was Kuan-yin?

28. What artistic style is favored by the People's Republic of China?

29. Name three essential elements of Chinese architecture.

a.

b.

c.

30. From what form did the Chinese pagoda develop?

31. Locate the following on the map on study guide page 131:

China   Hunan
Peking   Lungmen
Shantung   T'ien-lung Shan
Szechwan   Pien-ching
Tunhwang   Hangchow
Yunkang   Shensi

DISCUSSION QUESTIONS

1. Compare a bronze kuang from the Shang period (FIG. 12-1) with the roughly contemporary Mycenaean *Vaphio Cups* (FIG. 4-30). How does each artist relate the form of the vessel with the form of the animal? Can you think of another period in Western art when animal patterns were closer to those expressed in the Chinese bronze?

2. Compare a Han relief (FIG. 12-6) with a Sumerian relief (FIG. 2-18) and a Mycenaean dagger (FIG. 4-28). In each case consider the type of line used, the relationship of the figures to the space, and the formal conventions for depicting the figures.

3. Discuss the differences in portraying equine motion and balance in a Chinese bronze horse from the Han dynasty (FIG. 12-7), Greek horses from the Parthenon (FIG. 5-51), the Medieval rider from Bamberg (FIG. 10-55), Donatello's *Gattamelata* (FIG. 16-13), Verrocchio's *Colleoni* (FIG. 16-53), and Géricault's *Mounted Officer of the Imperial Guard* (FIG. 21-16). Which of these Western representations comes closest to the Chinese depiction? What stylistic features do they have in common? How are they different?

4. Discuss the development of the representation of the Buddha in Eastern art. Note the treatment of the figure and the drapery of a Chinese Buddha (FIG. 12-11) and that of an Indian Buddha (FIG. 11-11).

5. Discuss the effects of political and religious changes on Chinese artists of the sixteenth century. Cite specific works to illustrate your discussion.

6. What is the major difference between Chinese and Western attitudes toward nature? How have these attitudes been reflected in art?

7. Compare the warriors from the tomb of Emperor Shih Huang Ti (FIGS. 12-4 and 12-5) with the Greek warriors from Aegina (FIGS. 5-31 and 5-32), the Roman soldiers from the Arch of Titus (FIGS. 6-62 and 6-63), the Avar horseman from the Nagy-szent-miklós treasure (FIG. 8-14), and the *Bamberg Rider* (FIG. 10-55). What can the placement of the figures tell us about the cultures that produced them?

Using the timeline at the beginning of Chapter 12 in the text, enter the appropriate dates for the following periods. Fill in the chart as much as you can from memory; then check your answers against the text and complete the chart.

SUMMARY OF CHINESE ART

Shang Dynasty	_____ B.C. to	_____ B.C.
Chou Dynasty	_____ B.C. to	_____ B.C.
Han Dynasty	_____ B.C. to A.D.	_____
T'ang Dynasty	A.D. _____ to	_____
Northern Sung Dynasty	A.D. _____ to	_____
Southern Sung Dynasty	A.D. _____ to	_____
Yüan Dynasty	A.D. _____ to	_____
Ming Dynasty	A.D. _____ to	_____
Ch'ing Dynasty	A.D. _____ to	_____

	Typical Examples	Stylistic Characteristics	Significant Historical People, Events, etc.
Shang			
Chou			
Han			
T'ang			
Northern Sung			
Southern Sung			
Yüan			
Ming and Ch'ing			

Chapter Thirteen

The Art of Japan

1. Define the following terms:

   haniwa

   apsara

   Shinto

   Yamato-e

   makimono

   samurai

   tokonoma

   Kabuki

   Ukiyo-e

   tatami

2. Briefly describe the process of creating lacquer figures.

   What are the advantages of this technique?

3. What was the main art form of the Jomon culture?

4. In what century was Buddhism introduced into Japan?

5. Identify the qualities of the statue of *Miroku* (FIG. 13-3) that are Japanese rather than Chinese.

    a.

    b.

6. Which Chinese style most strongly influenced Japanese art of the Late Nara and Early Heian periods?

7. Name two examples of Japanese painting of the seventh and eighth centuries that show strong Chinese influence.

    a.

    b.

8. Name the largest and most important Shinto shrine in Japan.

    To what century does the style of the main building of that shrine date?

    What Japanese custom assures us that the present building looks pretty much like the first and original one?

9. Describe the type of image that was introduced during the Heian period that reflected the influence of Esoteric Buddhism.

10. What Chinese compositional device was adopted by Japanese painters at the very end of the Fujiwara period?

11. List three characteristics of the Yamato-e style as seen in the Genji scrolls.

    a.

    b.

    c.

12. In contrast with the art supported by the Fujiwaras, the art preferred by the rulers of the Kamukura period emphasized:

    a.

    b.

13. The fifteenth-century Japanese painter who adopted the monochrome landscape style of Chinese masters of the Sung period was:

    How did his style differ from that of the Sung masters?

14. Name the religious sect that influenced the development of the Japanese tea ceremony.

    Briefly explain the purpose of the tea ceremony.

15. List three characteristics of the style of painting favored by the Momoyama rulers.

    a.

    b.

    c.

    How does the contemporary style of Hasegawa Tohaku differ from this style?

16. The simplicity and elegance of Japanese teahouses is thought to have influenced the design of the seventeenth century palace at _____.

    Briefly describe the gardens of the palace.

17.   What is the purpose of a Zen rock garden?

18.   Which Chinese school influenced the Japanese Nanga "southern" painters?

How did the Nanga painters transform the technique of their Chinese models?

a.

b.

19.   Who was Hishikawa Moronobu?

20.   Name two nineteenth-century Japanese artists who specialized in printmaking.

a.   b.

21.   What structural system was used in Japanese domestic architecture?

What aspect of Japanese architecture has had the most effect on Western architectural theory?

22.   Locate the following on the map on study guide page 131:

Korea	Kyoto (Heian-kyo)	Ashikaga
Japan	Nara	Momoyama
Ise	Kamakura	Tokyo (Edo)

DISCUSSION QUESTIONS

1.   Compare the architectural style and building technique of the Kondo (Golden Hall) of Horyu-ji (FIG. 13-6) with that of the Shoden of the Ise Shrine (FIG. 13-7). In what way does the Kondo reflect Chinese proto-types?

2.   Compare the treatment of the animals in the Japanese scroll attributed to Toba Sojo (FIG. 13-11) with the page from Villard de Honnecourt's notebook (FIG. 10-36). What type of drawing style has each artist used? How does each relate to the dominant religion of its time?

3.   In what way does the Japanese tea ceremony relate to the style of the painting illustrated in FIG. 13-21?

4.   Compare a Harunobu print (FIG. 21-60) with Degas' *Ballet Rehearsal* (FIG. 21-59). In what ways does Degas' composition resemble that of the Japanese print?

5.   Discuss briefly the interaction of native traditions and Chinese influence in the art of Japan from the fifth through the fifteenth century. What characteristics can be identified as native Japanese? What features can be considered as imported from China?

6.   How do Japanese gardens reflect the attitude of the Japanese toward nature? How do they differ from gardens you have seen?

Using the timeline at the beginning of Chapter 13 in the text, enter the appropriate dates for the following periods. Fill in the chart as much as you can from memory; then check your answers against the text and complete the chart.

SUMMARY OF JAPANESE ART

Period	Dates
Jomon Culture	_____ B.C. to A.D. _____
Archaic Period	A.D. _____ to _____
Nara Period	A.D. _____ to _____
Fujiwara Period	A.D. _____ to _____
Heian Period	A.D. _____ to _____
Kamakura Period	A.D. _____ to _____
Ashikaga Period	A.D. _____ to _____
Momoyama Period	A.D. _____ to _____
Tokugawa (Edo) Period	A.D. _____ to _____

	Typical Examples	Stylistic Characteristics	Significant Historical People, Events, etc.
Jomon/Archaic			
Nara			
Heian/Fujiwara			
Kamakura			
Ashikaga			
Momoyama			
Tokugawa (Edo)			

Chapter Fourteen

The Native Arts of the Americas, Africa, and the South Pacific Text Pages 484–519

PRE-COLUMBIAN ART   Text Pages 486–95

1. Define the following terms:

   pre-Columbian

   Meso-American

   corbeled vault

   roof comb

   stirrup spout

2. Which Meso-American culture is often referred to as the "mother culture" of that region?

   Where was its heartland?

   When, approximately, did it flourish?

   What type of art objects did it produce?

   Among these, what seem to have been the artists' favorite subjects?

   What distinguishes their style from that of the Maya?

3. What medium was most favored by the artists of the West Mexico areas of Jalisco, Nayarit, and Colima?

   What subjects figured prominently in the art of that region?

What quality is characteristic of the Colima figures?

4. In what area did the Maya culture flourish?

    What dates include the "classic period" of Maya culture?

5. Describe the stylistic feature that is most characteristic of Maya sculpture.

6. What scenes are depicted in the Bonampak murals?

    What subjects are depicted in the art of Rio Azul?

7. Identify the following:
    Teotihuacán

    Quetzalcóatl

    Tláloc

8. Where did the Aztec establish their capital?

    What explanation is given for the Aztec practice of human sacrifice?

9. Describe the major characteristic of Aztec sculpture.

10. What was Chavín?

11. What is shown on the Raimondi stone?

12. The two cultures that coexisted in the coastal region of Peru from about 200 B.C. to A.D. 600 were:

    a.   b.

    What are the most characteristic products of these cultures?

    What are the distinctive features that permit us to identify the products as belonging to one or the other culture?

13. Name two important art forms of the Tiahuanaco people.

    a.

    b.

14. When did the Inca begin their imperialistic expansion?

15. The southern capital of the Inca empire was _____.

16. Inca architecture is most famous for:

17. Locate the following on the map on study guide page 147:

    La Venta   Tikal   Chavín de Huantár
    Jalisco   Copán   Moche
    Nayarit   Chichén-Itzá   Nasca
    Colima   Teotihuacán   Tiahuanaco
    Palenque   Mexico City   Cuzco
    Bonampak

Enter the appropriate dates for the following cultures and fill in the chart as much as possible from memory; then check your answers against the text and complete the table and chart.

SUMMARY OF PRE-COLUMBIAN ART

Mexico:

Olmec	_____ B.C. to _____ B.C.
West Mexico (shaft-tomb relics)	A.D. _____
Classic Maya (Teotihuacán)	A.D. _____ to _____
Aztec (Tenochtitlán founded)	A.D. _____

South America:

Chavín	_____ B.C.
Mochica/Nasca	_____ B.C. to A.D. _____
Tiahuanaco	to A.D. _____
Inca (beginning of expansion)	A.D. _____

	Typical Examples	Stylistic Characteristics	Significant Historical People, Events, etc.
Olmec			
West Mexico			
Maya			
Teotihuacán			
Aztec			
Chavín			
Mochica			
Nasca			
Tiahuanaco			
Inca			

THE AMERICAS

NORTH AMERICAN INDIAN AND ESKIMO ART Text Pages 495–504

1. List two stylistic characteristics of Eskimo art.

   a.

   b.

2. In what state is the Serpent Mound located?

   How long is the mound?

3. List two sites in North America where rock paintings or engravings have been found.

   a.   b.

4. Name three major art forms of the North American Indian.

   a.

   b.

   c.

5. List two characteristics of prehistoric Southwest Indian pottery.

   a.

   b.

   What method was used to make this pottery?

6. What is most significant about Pueblo Bonito?

7. Describe a kiva.

8. What was the purpose of Navajo sand painting?

9. In addition to their spiritual uses, art objects created by the Indians of the Northwest Coast were often expressions of _____.

10. List some recurrent characteristics of the style of the Indians of the Northwest Coast.

    a.

    b.

    c.

    d.

11. Describe the changes in design and materials that occurred in the art of the Indians of the Great Plains about 1830.

12. What was the False Face Society of the Iroquois?

13. Locate on the map on study guide page 147 the areas settled by the following North American Indian tribes/cultures:

    Mesa Verde   Arapaho
    Navajo   Iroquois
    Tlingit

Fill in the chart as much as possible from memory; then check your answers against the text and complete the chart.

SUMMARY OF NORTH AMERICAN INDIAN AND ESKIMO ART

	Tribes	Stylistic Characteristics	Cultural Factors
Eskimo			
Southwest Area			
Northwest Coast			
Great Plains			
Eastern Woodlands			

AFRICAN ART   Text Pages 504–12

1. What dates have been established for African Nok sculpture?

    Write down two characteristics of these works.

    a.

    b.

2. What is Ife?

3. In what historical period was the African kingdom of Benin predominant?

4. To what does the term *cire perdue* pertain?

5. Give two stylistic characteristics of Benin art.

    a.

    b.

6. Identify the following:

    Yoruba

    Gelede

    mbari

7. What was the purpose of African ancestral figures like those illustrated in FIGS. 14-50 and 14-51?

8. How did the artist treat the human body in the Dogon carvings illustrated in FIG. 14-55?

9. Locate the homelands of the following tribes on the map on study guide page 153:

Tassili	Ashanti
Nok	Kongo
Yoruba	Dan
Dogon	Benin
Bangwa	Ife

Fill in the chart as much as possible from memory; then check your answers against the text and complete the chart.

SUMMARY OF AFRICAN ART

	Typical Examples	Stylistic Characteristics	Cultural Factors
Tassili			
Nok			
Yoruba			
Bangwa			
Dogon			
Ashanti			
Kongo			
Dan			
Benin			

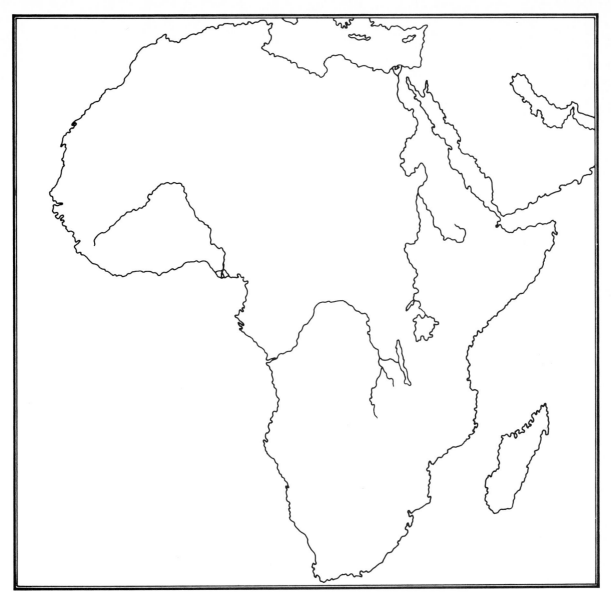

AFRICA

ART OF THE SOUTH PACIFIC   Text Pages 512–19

1. Name the three cultural areas of Oceania.

   a.   b.   c.

2. Define the following terms:

   mana

   tapa

   malanggan

   Asmat pole

3. List three characteristics of Polynesian art as seen in the image of Kukailimoku (FIG. 14-57):

   a.

   b.

   c.

4. What stylistic tendency of Polynesian art is represented by tattoo patterns?

5. Describe the characteristics of Polynesian art that are merged in the art of the Maori peoples of New Zealand.

   a.

   b.

6. In what ways does Melanesian art differ from that of Polynesia?

   a.

   b.

   c.

7. What was the purpose of the decorated skull from New Guinea shown in FIG. 14-68?

8. What was the importance of "Dream Time" in the lives of native Australians?

9. Who were the Djanggawul sisters and brothers?

10. Describe the "X-ray" style of painting from the area in Arnhem Land called Oenpelli.

Fill in the chart as much as possible from memory; then check your answers against the text and complete the chart.

SUMMARY OF THE ARTS OF OCEANIA

	Typical Examples	Stylistic Characteristics	Cultural Factors
Polynesia			
Melanesia			
Australia			

SUMMARY: THE NATIVE ARTS OF THE AMERICAS, AFRICA, AND THE SOUTH PACIFIC   Text Pages 484–519

DISCUSSION QUESTIONS

1. Compare the sculptural style of Central Mexico as seen in the Temple of Quetzalcóatl at Teotihuacán (FIG. 14-9) and the Aztec figure of *Coatlicue* (FIG. 14-10) with Maya work as seen in the *Great Dragon* (FIG. 14-6) and the *Maize God* (FIG. 14-7). What similarities and what differences do you see?

2. Compare the Raimondi stone from the Chavín cult (FIG. 14-11) with the examples of Mexican relief carving cited in the preceding question. Is the Raimondi stone closer to the Maya style or to that of Central Mexico? in what ways?

3. How do the pyramids of pre-Columbian America compare in structure and function with those of Egypt and Ancient Near East?

4. What similarities can you find between the social structures of pre-Columbian America and those of Egypt and the Ancient Near East? In what ways do you think the art forms of the various cultures were influenced by their social structures?

5. Discuss the different building techniques and architectural decoration used by the Maya and Peruvian architects. What features would enable you to distinguish between a Maya and a Peruvian building?

6. Compare the prehistoric Indian Serpent Mound (FIG. 14-22) with Smithson's *Spiral Jetty* (FIG. 22-84). What do they have in common? How do they differ? What do you think was the purpose of each?

7. Compare the style and organization of Navajo sand painting (FIG. 14-29) with that of the animal paintings from Lascaux (FIG. 1-1) and with Mantegna's fresco from the *Camera degli sposi* (FIG. 16-65). What type of pictorial organization is used in each? Which type does the sand painting resemble most closely?

8. Compare the artistic and political effect and the symbolic meanings of the costumes of the Indian warrior (FIG. 14-37), the African dancer (FIG. 14-46), the Ife king (FIG. 14-42), the French king (FIG. 20-1), the Byzantine emperor (FIG. 7-39), and the Egyptian pharoah (FIG. 3-36). What does the clothing that leaders wear in our society say about the way they see their role?

9. How do the roles of art and the artist differ in African tribes as compared with those in European and Oriental cultures?

10. Describe briefly the function of masks in the cultures of Africa, Oceania, and the North American Indian.

COMPARATIVE CHRONOLOGY

Enter the appropriate time spans in the appropriate spaces on the following chronological chart for the periods listed below.

India: Indus valley civilization; Maurya, Sunga, Andhra, Kushan, and Gupta periods; Moslem invasions

China: Shang, Chou, and Han dynasties; Three Kingdoms; T'ang, Northern and Southern Sung, Yüan, and Ming dynasties

Japan: Jomon culture; Asuka, Nara, Fujiwara, Heian, Kamakura, Ashikaga, Momoyama, and Tokugawa (Edo) periods

Pre-Columbian America: Chavín, Olmec, Mochica, Nasca, Classic Maya, Teotihuacán, Tiahuanaco, Aztec, Inca, and Mesa Verde cultures

Europe and the Near East: Sumerian, Egyptian Old Kingdom, Egyptian New Kingdom, Assyrian, Greek, Roman, Early Byzantine, Carolingian, Romanesque, Gothic, Renaissance, and Rococo periods; Romanticism and Impressionism (as new styles)

	India	China	Japan	Pre-Columbian America	Europe and the Near East
3000 B.C.					
2500 B.C.					
2000 B.C.					
1500 B.C.					
1000 B.C.					
500 B.C.					
B.C. A.D.					
A.D. 500					
A.D. 1000					
A.D. 1500					
A.D. 2000					

Self-Quiz

PART THREE: THE NON-EUROPEAN WORLD

I.   **Matching.** Choose the identification in the right column that best corresponds to the name or term in the
left column and enter the appropriate letter in the space provided.

_____ 1. sutra

_____ 2. mandala

_____ 3. stupa

_____ 4. Kuan-yin

_____ 5. Siddhartha

_____ 6. makimono

_____ 7. bodhisattva

_____ 8. Ukiyo-e

_____ 9. ushnisha

_____ 10. Moronobu

_____ 11. Kamakura

_____ 12. roof comb

_____ 13. stele

_____ 14. Chavín

_____ 15. kiva

_____ 16. Yoruba

_____ 17. tapa

_____ 18. malanggan

_____ 19. chaitya

_____ 20. kuang

a. Buddhist goddess of compassion
b. an account of a sermon or dialogue involving the Buddha
c. a large mound-shaped Buddhist shrine
d. a person who is a potential Buddha
e. a Japanese horizontal scroll
f. Eskimo ceremonial object
g. a magical, geometric symbol of the cosmos
h. the man who became Buddha Sakyamuni
i. protuberance of the Buddha's forehead
j. pre-Columbian culture in South America
k. one of the first Japanese artists to use the woodblock technique to illustrate everyday subjects
l. a form of Japanese genre painting ("pictures of the floating world")
m. decoration on Maya temples
n. African tribe
o. Buddhist assembly hall
p. intricately carved Melanesian ceremonial masks
q. carved stone slab or pillar, often used as a marker
r. cloth made from hammered bark
s. covered libation vessel from China
t. circular ceremonial center in a pueblo
u. Japanese city and period named after thirteenth- and fourteenth-century rulers

II. **Matching.** Choose the geographical location in the right column that best corresponds to the culture or period in the left column and enter the appropriate letter in the space provided.

_____ 21. Han

_____ 22. Indus valley civilization

_____ 23. Dan

_____ 24. Maya

_____ 25. Dogon

_____ 26. Gupta

_____ 27. Shang

_____ 28. Inca

_____ 29. Heian

_____ 30. Kushan

_____ 31. Mimbre

_____ 32. Benin

_____ 33. Nok

_____ 34. Olmec

_____ 35. Nara

_____ 36. T'ang

_____ 37. Aztec

_____ 38. Ashanti

_____ 39. Nasca

_____ 40. Tokugawa

_____ 41. Sung

_____ 42. Jomon

_____ 43. Mochica

_____ 44. Maurya

_____ 45. Melanesian

a. India
b. China
c. Japan
d. North America
e. South America
f. Africa
g. Oceania
h. Mexico and Central America

III. **Multiple Choice.** Circle the most appropriate answer.

46. Ceramic portrait jars with stirrup spouts were the most famous works produced by the   a. Aztec   b. Hopi   c. Mochica   d. Inca   e. Maya

47. Japanese painting of the Nanga School was most strongly influenced by   a. Indian miniatures   b. Momoyama screens   c. Ukiyo-e prints   d. Chinese "literary" school painting   e. a revival of forms from the Jomon period

48. The most striking characteristics of art of the Kamakura period were   a. grace and delicacy   b. strength and realism   c. esoteric symbolism and religious significance   d. decorative forms and rich gold work   e. primitive power and awkward forms

49. Buddhism entered China in the period known as   a. Shang   b. Chou   c. Han   d. Sung   e. Ming

50. One of the most important early Buddhist shrines, the Great Stupa, is located in   a. Sanchi   b. Khajuraho   c. Ajanta   d. Tunhwang   e. Nara

51. The Shang period is most famous for its   a. painted scrolls   b. bronzes   c. representations of the Buddha   d. ceramic haniwas   e. jade burial suits

52. Important cliff dwellings were found at   a. La Venta   b. Mesa Verde   c. Tlingit   d. Teotihuacán   e. Colima

53. Many Neolithic rock paintings were found in Africa in the region of   a. Ivory Coast   b. Congo   c. Liberia   d. Tessili   e. Angola

54. An important Maya site was   a. Teotihuacán   b. Cuzco   c. Quito   d. Tikal   e. Chavín de Hauntár

55. During the Heian period a new type of image was brought into Japan that   a. was very delicate with graceful folds   b. was decorated with complicated interlace patterns   c. was heavier with multiple arms   d. was markedly realistic   e. showed a strong influence of Greco–Roman imagery

56. An important site in the early Indus valley civilization was   a. Mohenjo-Daro   b. Sanchi   c. Borobudur   d. Horyu-ji   e. Ajanta

57. Sixth-century Chinese artistic representations created under the influence of the Buddhist Paradise Sects, in contrast to those done for the Esoteric Sects, tended to stress   a. more complex symbolism   b. greater pomp   c. increasing naturalism and grace   d. stiffer, more formal compositions   e. strange, awkward postures

58. The artistic traditions of Greece and Rome influenced those of Buddhism through contact in the region of   a. Karli   b. Sanchi   c. Gandahara   d. Elephanta   e. Mohenjo-Daro

59. One of the most important Buddhist monuments of Southeast Asia was erected in the eighth century at   a. Borobudur   b. Bali   c. Sanchi   d. Angkor Thom   e. Laradjhonggrang

60. The shrines of Angkor Wat and Angkor Thom are located in   a. Thailand   b. Kampuchea   c. Ceylon   d. Burma   e. Vietnam

61. A triple-headed image of Siva as incarnation of the forces of creation, preservation, and destruction is an important image of which religious faith?   a. Zen Buddhism   b. Hinduism   c. Islam   d. Shinto   e. Esoteric Buddhism

62. One of the earliest Buddhist temples in Japan was constructed during the seventh century near Nara and is known as the   a. Yunkang   b. Ise shrine   c. Horyu-ji   d. Toyokuni shrine   e. Lomas Rishi

63. The murals at the Ajanta caves best illustrate the characteristics of Gupta art, which are   a. grace and delicacy   b. exaggerated realism and power   c. strong emotion and motion   d. clairity, dignity, and serenity   e. complicated symbolism and mannerist exaggeration

64. An important artistic form during the Jomon period was the creation of   a. clay haniwa figures   b. Buddhist images with many arms   c. painted makimono   d. bronze vessels   e. figures of Siva dancing

65. Two funeral suits made of pieces of jade sewn with gold wire were unearthed in a tomb in   a. pre-Columbian Mexico   b. pre-Columbian Peru   c. Japan   d. China   e. India

66. An important fifteenth-century Japanese painter was   a. Sesshu   b. Hokusai   c. Fan K'uan   d. Ma Yuan   e. Harunobu

67. The pre-Columbian peoples of West Mexico from the areas of Jalisco, Colima, and Nayarit are most famous for their   a. stone sculpture   b. weaving   c. ceramics   d. stone pyramids   e. earth mounds

68. Which of the following features was least typical of Maya architecture?   a. flying façades   b. roof combs   c. corbeled vaults   d. stone construction   e. flying buttresses

69. Pre-Columbian art was most highly developed in South America   a. in the Central Andes region   b. in the Amazon region   c. near Tierra del Fuego   d. in the highland region of Brazil   e. in what is now Argentina

70. Fine bronze work was done by the tribe known as   a. Dogon   b. Benin   c. Nok   d. Bangwa   e. Dan

71. A large mound approximately 1,400 feet long, known as the Serpent Mound, was constructed by the Indians of   a. the American Southwest   b. the Woodlands region above the Ohio River   c. the Northwest Coast   d. the Plains region   e. California

72. As opposed to Indians of other regions, those of the Northwest Coast of America placed much greater emphasis on art as an expression of   a. fertility rituals   b. social status   c. initiation rituals   d. death rituals   e. military might

73. In contrast to the style of Polynesian art, that of Melanesia is more   a. restrained   b. colorful and flamboyant   c. simplified   d. compact   e. solid

74. Which of the following cultures made *least* use of masks?   a. Melanesia   b. Iroquois   c. Polynesia   d. Northwest Coast of America   e. Dan

75. Some of the most realistic representations in African art were done of the kings of   a. Nok   b. Ife   c. Dan   d. Tassili   e. Kuba

76. Some beautiful Maya murals were found at   a. Teotihuacán   b. Tenochtitlán   c. Bonampak   d. Quiriguá   e. Veracruz

77. Giant stone heads were found in La Venta that are thought to have been done by the   a. Colima   b. Olmec   c. Aztec   d. Inca   e. Mochica

78. The capital of the Inca empire was located at   a. Tiahuanaco   b. Teotihuacán   c. Tikal   d. Cuzco   e. Quito

79. Temple-topped pyramids where human sacrifice took place were important in the religious rituals of the   a. Olmec   b. Inca   c. Aztec   d. Tlingit   e. Adena

80. Masterful use of the dry-masonry technique of an outstanding feature of the architecture of the   a. Aztec   b. Mochica   c. Inca   d. Nasca   e. Olmec

IV. Identification.

81. Below are two images of warriors. Attribute each of them to a country, a culture or period within that country, and an approximate date. Give the reasons for your attributions.

A. Country: _____

  Culture or Period: _____

  Date: _____

Reasons:

B. Country _____

  Culture or Period: _____

  Date: _____

82.   Compare the two landscapes below, attributing each to a country, period, and approximate date. Give the reasons for your attributions.

A.   Country: _____

　　Period: _____

　　Date: _____

B.   Country: _____

　　Period: _____

　　Date: _____

Reasons:

83. Discuss the relief below, attributing it to a country, group or period, and an approximate date. Give the reasons for your attributions. What is the subject? How does it reflect the society that produced it?

Country: _____ Date: _____

Group or Period: _____

Reasons:

84. Discuss the animal represented below, attributing it to a country, group or period, and an approximate date. Give the reasons for your attributions.

Country: _____ Date: _____

Group or Period: _____

Reasons:

85. Compare the two figures of women shown below, attributing each to a country, period, and approximate date. Give the reasons for your attributions.

A. Country: _____   B. Country: _____

Period: _____   Period: _____

Date: _____   Date: _____

Reasons:

PART FOUR: THE RENAISSANCE AND THE BAROQUE AND ROCOCO

INTRODUCTION   Text Pages 520–27

1. List five social and historical developments that are associated with the transition from the Middle Ages to the Renaissance.

    a.

    b.

    c.

    d.

    e.

2. What was a Renaissance "Humanist"?

3. Define *l'uomo universale*.

Chapter Fifteen

The "Proto-Renaissance" in Italy

Text Pages 528–47

1. During what centuries did the "proto-Renaissance" take place in Italy?

2. What social class rose to prominence in Italy's communes and became a major patron of the arts during the Renaissance?

3. List some of the social upheavals that followed the outbreak of the "Black Death" in 1348.

   a.

   b.

   c.

4. What is meant by the term "Great Schism"?

5. Name two English philosophers who stressed the importance of personal experience and intuition in acquiring knowledge.

   a.

   b.

6. What is meant by the "humanization of religion"?

   Who was at least partially responsible for it?

7. List four elements of Franciscan "radicalism" that influenced the development of "proto-Renaissance" art.

   a.

   b.

   c.

   d.

8. Identify two trends shown in the works of Nicola and Giovanni Pisano that later become significant in the development of Renaissance art.

   a.

   b.

9. Which style dominated Medieval Italian painting?

Describe some of its stylistic characteristics.

a.

b.

c.

How did Duccio modify this traditional style?

Name three changes made by him.

a.

b.

c.

10. Describe briefly the fresco technique.

11. Name the two locations where Giotto's best surviving frescoes can be found.

a.

b.

12. What seem to have been the artistic traditions that influenced Giotto and contributed to the shaping of his style?

a.

b.

c.

13. List four characteristics of Giotto's style as seen by comparing his *Madonna Enthroned* (FIG. 15-12) with Cimabue's version of the same subject (FIG. 15-11).

a.

b.

c.

d.

14.   How did Simone Martini help to form the so-called International style?

List four characteristics of that style.

a.

b.

c.

d.

15.   What was a *condottiere*?

16.   In what respect is Simone Martini's fresco of *Guidoriccio da Fogliano* an innovation?

What information about this fresco makes us aware of the provisional nature of art-historical knowledge?

17.   Panoramic views of the city of Siena and its surrounding countryside were painted by _____ in the Palazzo Pubblico in Siena as part of a fresco known as _____.

What revolutionary aspects are found in this fresco (FIGS. 15-22, 15-23, 15-24)?

a.

b.

18.   What historical event seems to be the subject of *The Triumph of Death* (FIG. 15-25)?

19.   Locate the following on the map on study guide page 172:

Siena   Padua
Pisa   Avignon

DISCUSSION QUESTIONS

1. Why do the authors refer to the thirteenth century in Italy as the "proto-Renaissance" rather than the Late Gothic period?

2. Compare the versions of the *Nativity* by Nicola and Giovanni Pisano (FIG. 15-2 and 15-3) with the Late Antique *Ludovisi Battle Sarcophagus* (FIG. 7-17). How are the Pisani works similar to this Roman example? How are they different from it and from each other?

3. Compare Giotto's *Death of St. Francis* (FIG. 15-15) with Duccio's *Betrayal of Jesus* (FIG. 15-8); note particularly the use of space, three-dimensional volume, and the sense of drama.

4. Compare Simone Martini's *Annunciation* (FIG. 15-19) with the figures on the west façade of Reims Cathedral (FIG. 10-33). Which of the French figures seem most closely related to those of Simone's version? Discuss the historical factors that account for the French influence in his work.

5. Discuss the effects of social and economic changes between the late thirteenth and late fourteenth centuries on Italian art of the period.

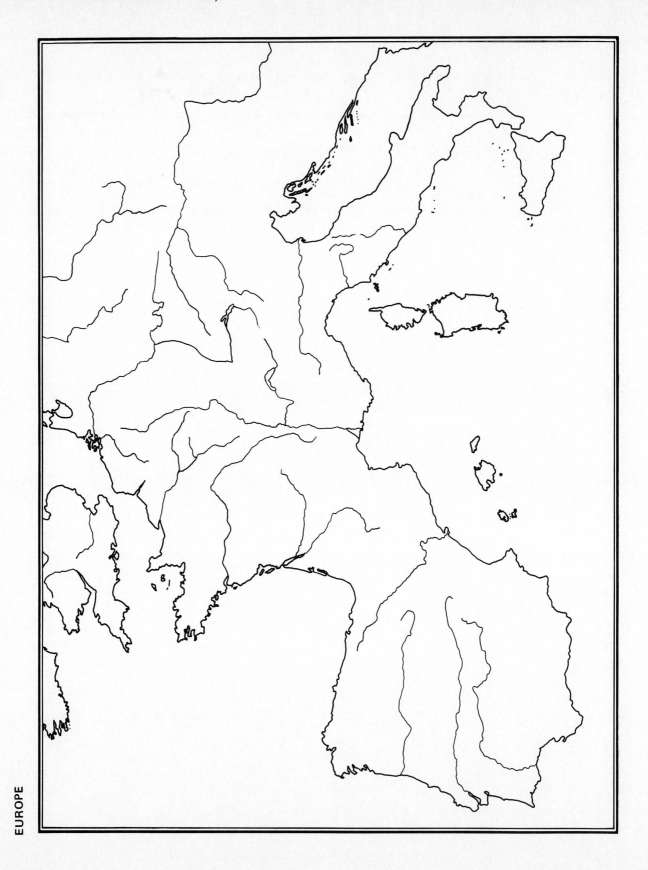

EUROPE

Chapter Sixteen

Fifteenth-Century Italian Art

THE FIRST HALF OF THE FIFTEENTH CENTURY   Text Pages 550–75

1. Define the following terms:

    predella

    aerial perspective

    linear perspective

    orthogonals

    vanishing point

    horizon

    rusticated stone

    dressed stone

    stringcourse

    cortile

    sacra conversazione

2. Identify the following individuals:

    Cosimo de' Medici

    Lorenzo de' Medici

    Marsilio Ficino

Leo X

"Gattamelata"

Giorgio Vasari

Jacobus de Varagine

3. Which Italian city played the most important role in the development of Renaissance ideas and art forms in the early fifteenth century?

4. Who were the chief competitors for the commission of the north doors of the baptistry of Florence?

   a.

   b.

   c.

   When was the competition held? _____ Who won it? _____

5. Who was the Sienese sculptor who competed unsuccessfully for the baptistry commission and whose powerfully muscled figures later influenced Michelangelo?

6. In what way do Nanni di Banco's *Quattro Santi Coronati* (FIG. 16-4) differ in relation to their architectural setting from the portal figures of French Gothic churches (FIG. 10-32)?

7. According to the text, what three elements constitute the art and personality of Donatello?

   a.

   b.

   c.

8. In what figure did Donatello first utilize the principle of weight shift (*ponderation*)?

   Describe contrapposto.

9. In what ways does Donatello's *St. George* (FIG. 16-6) differ from the Medieval figure *St. Theodore* (FIG. 16-7)?

    a.

    b.

10. Describe how Donatello's *Zuccone* (FIG. 16-8) differs strikingly from traditional representations of prophets.

    a.

    b.

    c.

11. The invention of linear perspective is generally attributed to _____.

12. What is the major significance of Donatello's bronze statue of *David* (FIG. 16-12)?

    Describe the Classical characteristics that are apparent in the figure.

    a.

    b.

    What new feature has Donatello added that embodies a dominant theme of the Renaissance?

13. Why did Brunelleschi design the dome of Florence Cathedral with an ogival rather than a semicircular section?

14. Name two possible sources for the round arches supported by slender columns and framed by pilasters that Brunelleschi used as the major element for his design of the Ospedale degli Innocenti.

    a.   b.

    What characteristics of the building create an impression of Classical rationality and logic?

    a.

    b.

    c.

    d.

15. Which of Brunelleschi's buildings most closely approximates the centralized plan?

    When was it begun?

16. The text names only one feature of the church of Santo Spirito (FIGS. 16-17 and 16-18) that uses proportions in a ratio of 1:2, namely:

    Can you find others in the plan?

17. Who designed the Palazzo Medici–Riccardi?

    The design of the courtyard shows the influence of _____.

18. Although an artistic descendant of _____, Masaccio used light to model his bulky figures in an entirely new way. How?

19. Three basic characteristics of Masaccio's style seen in *The Tribute Money* (FIG. 16-26) are:

    a.

    b.

    c.

20. What two Renaissance interests are summed up in Masaccio's *Holy Trinity* fresco (FIG. 16-28)?

    a.

    b.

21. List four fifteenth-century Italian painters who were deeply concerned with linear perspective.

    a.   c.

    b.   d.

22. Piero della Francesca's great fresco cycle in San Francesco at _____, represents episodes from _____. The scene of the *Annunciation* (FIG. 16-34), with its simplified, immobile figures, represents one solution to a problem that concerned him: namely, _____ _____.

23. What compositional device, which was very popular with Renaissance artists, is used effectively by Piero in the *Resurrection* (FIG. 16-36)?

24. List five features of Piero's work that sum up developments in Italian painting in the first half of the fifteenth century.

    a.

    b.

    c.

    d.

    e.

25. Fra Angelico combined elements from many styles in his work. Describe three elements he used in his fresco of the *Annunciation* (FIG. 16-37) and name their sources.

    a.

    b.

    c.

26. Under the influence of reliefs by Ghiberti and Donatello, Fra Filippo Lippi abandoned a style based on Masaccio's massive forms and developed his mature style, which is characterized by:

    a.

    b.

    c.

27. Locate the following on the map on study guide page 172:

    Urbino
    Florence

DISCUSSION QUESTIONS

1. Analyze the relative strength of the Classical and Gothic elements of Ghiberti's style by comparing the nude youth from his *Sacrifice of Isaac* (FIG. 16-2) with the Greek figure of Hermes (FIG. 5-65) and the Gothic figure of Christ from Reims (FIG. 10-34). Also compare Ghiberti's draped figure of Abraham from the same panel with the Greek figures from the Parthenon (FIG. 5-52) and the Gothic figures from Chartres (FIG. 10-31).

2. What degree of Classical influence is found in the work of Nanni di Banco (FIG. 16-4) in comparison with earlier works by Nicola Pisano (FIG. 15-2) and the figures from Reims Cathedral (FIG. 10-33)? Note particularly the mastery of the contrapposto pose. As your standard of comparison, use the Classical Aurelian relief of the second century (FIG. 6-66).

3. What major change had taken place in the representation of pictorial space between the time Ghiberti created the panel of *The Sacrifice Isaac* (FIG. 16-2) and his completion of the "Gates of Paradise" (FIG. 16-10)? How well did Ghiberti utilize the new ideas?

4. How does Donatello's *Gattamelata* (FIG. 16-13) differ from the equestrian portrait of the emperor Marcus Aurelius (FIG. 6-72) and the Medieval *Bamberg Rider* (FIG. 10-55)? What was the apparent purpose of the high pedestal used with the *Gattemelata*?

5. Both the Church of the Katholikon (FIGS. 7-45, 7-46, 7-48) and the Pazzi Chapel (FIGS. 16-19, 16-20, 16-21) are characterized by a centralized plan, yet one is typical of Medieval Byzantine structures while the other is often used as the prime example of a Renaissance building. In what ways are the Humanism and rationality of the Renaissance apparent in Brunelleschi's building?

6. Masaccio's style owes much to the work of Giotto, which is apparent when you compare Masaccio's fresco of *The Tribute Money* (FIG. 16-26) with Giotto's rendition of the *Lamentation* (FIG. 15-14). What has he learned from the older master? What innovations has he made?

7. What characteristics of style are shared by Simone Martini's *Guidoriccio da Fogliano* (FIG. 15-20) and Ucello's *Battle of San Romano* (FIG. 16-29)? To what style do these characteristics relate? What feature of the Uccello work indicates that it was painted in the fifteenth century?

8. What made perspective so important to Renaissance painters? Discuss Piero della Francesca's use of it in the *Resurrection* (FIG. 16-36).

9. Compare Piero della Francesca's *Annunciation* (FIG. 16-34) with Duccio's related composition (FIG. 15-9). What change has Piero made that lends his figures the air of momumental nobility? In what ways is Fra Angelico's *Annunciation* (FIG. 16-37) related to earlier versions? What has he learned from his contemporaries?

10. Discuss the use of space and line and the placement of the figures in Fra Filippo Lippi's *Madonna and Child with Angels* (FIG. 16-38) and Giotto's version of the same theme (FIG. 15-12). What is the religious impact of the different figure types and of the landscape background used by Fra Filippo?

THE SECOND HALF OF THE FIFTEENTH CENTURY   Text Pages 575-97

1. Name four cultural centers in Italy that became important in the second half of the fifteenth century, and note the leading family of each.

   a.

   b.

   c.

   d.

2. What literary and cultural developments mark the second half of the century?

   a.

   b.

   c.

   d.

3. Describe the effects that the conquest of Constantinople by the Turks in 1453 had on the cultural and economic life of Italy.

4. What fifteenth-century Renaissance scholar, known primarily for his achievements in architecture, comes closest to realizing the Renaissance ideal of *l'uomo universale*?

5. Three principles advocated by Alberti in his *De re aedificatoria* were:

   a.

   b.

   c.

6. Define the following terms:

   pilaster

   entablature

   bottega

   tondo

   engraving

   di sotto in sù

7. What feature does the Palazzo Rucellai (FIG. 16-39) share with the Roman Colosseum (FIGS. 6-45 and 6-46)?

In what way is it markedly different?

8. Which Romanesque church seems to have influenced Alberti when he designed the façade of Santa Maria Novella?

    How did he modify the Romanesque original to create a highly sophisticated Renaissance design?

9. Which building did Alberti renovate for Sigismondo Pandolfo Malatesta to serve as a neopagan temple?

    The design for the façade was based on that of a Roman _____.

10. The two Roman architectural motifs that Alberti locked together on the façade of Sant' Andrea in Mantua were:

    a.

    b.

    How does the plan of the church break with a centuries-old Christian building tradition?

11. Why was the central plan felt to be appropriate for religious architecture during the Renaissance period?

12. The Renaissance ideal of a central-plan church was most nearly realized in the fifteenth century by the church of _____, which was designed by _____.

13. The tomb of Leonardo Bruni in Santa Croce by _____ best expresses the Humanistic concern with _____.

    Name two elements of the tomb's design that are Humanistic and classicizing.

    a.

    b.

14. In what way does Antonio Rossellino's bust of Matteo Palmieri (FIG. 16-49) differ from its Roman proto-types?

15. The fifteenth-century sculptor _____ is best known for his production of glazed terra-cotta reliefs.

16. One of the most important Italian sculptors of the second half of the fifteenth century, who was also a painter, was _____.

    How does his *David* (FIG. 16-52) differ from Donatello's version (FIG. 16-12)?

    a.

    b.

    c.

17. What seems to have been Pollaiuolo's main artistic interest?

18. The secularization of sacred themes can be seen in the portraits of Florentine women as represented in the fresco *The Birth of the Virgin* (FIG. 16-57) by _____.

19. Botticelli's Classical compositions were influenced by the philosophical system known as _____ _____, which attempted to reconcile Classical philosophy with the beliefs of _____.

20. By what means did Marsilio Ficino believe that the soul could ascend toward union with God?

21. List three characteristics of Botticelli's style.

    a.

    b.

    c.

22. Who was Girolamo Savonarola?

23.   The Umbrian painter who exerted considerable influence on Michelangelo was _____ .

What interest did this artist share with Pollaiuolo?

Another Umbrian painter, Perugino, was more concerned with _____ .

24.   One of the most brilliant and influential northern Italian artists of the fifteenth century was _____ .

His style is characterized by:

a.

b.

c.

25.   Who introduced the Venetian painters to the technique of painting with oils?

26.   Locate the following on the map on study guide page 172:

Mantua
Venice

DISCUSSION QUESTIONS

1.   Who was Vitruvius? Why was his treatise important to Renaissance architects?

2.   Why were Renaissance architects so fascinated with the central-plan church design? What are its advantages and its disadvantages?

3.   Discuss the extent to which Alberti translated the principles of his theoretical writings on architecture into the specific buildings he designed.

4.   Compare and contrast the images of *condottieri*, or military leaders, created by Donatello (FIG. 16-13) and Verrocchio (FIG. 16-53).

5.   How did the members of Lorenzo de' Medici's Platonic Academy of Philosophy influence the art produced in Florence in the second half of the fifteenth century?

6.   Compare Renaissance portraits such as the bust of *Matteo Palmieri* (FIG. 16-49) and the equestrian portrait of *Bartolommeo Colleoni* (FIG. 16-53) with similar Classical works; for example, the *Head of a Roman* (FIG. 16-14), the heads of *Vespasian* (FIG. 6-69) and *Hadrian* (FIG. 6-71), and the equestrian portrait of Marcus Aurelius (FIG. 6-72). In what ways are the Renaissance examples similar to the Roman portraits? In what ways do they differ?

7.   How do the authors account for the popularity of the profile portrait in fifteenth-century Italy? What are its advantages and disadvantages?

Chapter Seventeen

Sixteenth-Century Italian Art

LEONARDO, BRAMANTE, AND RAPHAEL   Text Pages 600–613

1. What dates are generally accepted as the span of the High Renaissance?

2. Who were the major art patrons in Rome during the High Renaissance?

3. According to Leonardo, what was the major purpose of his scientific investigations?

4. When did Leonardo move from Florence to Milan?

    Who was his patron in that city?

    As what did Leonardo advertise himself to his new employer?

5. What two elements did Leonardo consider to be the heart of painting?

    a.

    b.

6. What compositional devices did Leonardo use in *The Virgin of the Rocks* (FIG. 17-1) to knit the figures together?

    a.

    b.

7. Define the following terms:

    atmospheric chiaroscuro

    cartoon (in fine arts usage)

8. What two fifteenth-century trends does Leonardo synthesize in *The Last Supper* (FIG. 17-3)?

    a.

    b.

9. Although Leonardo's significance as scientist may be disputed, what tradition, which is indispensible to modern science, did his investigations in anatomy originate?

10. Briefly describe four aspects of the sculptural appearance of Bramante's Tempietto.

    a.

    b.

    c.

    d.

11. Who was Julius II?

12. How much of the building of the new St. Peter's was completed during Bramante's lifetime?

    Name two architects other than Bramante who worked on St. Peter's during the sixteenth century.

    a.   b.

13. List six terms that typify High Renaissance Classical ideals of design.

    a.   d.

    b.   e.

    c.   f.

14. What is the basic, structural form of the church of Santa Maria della Consolazione?

15. The influential Palazzo Caprini was designed by _____.

    What feature of the building most clearly distinguishes its façade from those of fifteenth-century Italian palaces?

16. Who designed the Farnese Palace?

    Who was his patron?

    How does it differ from the Palazzo Medici–Riccardi?

17. Raphael was apprenticed to _____, who had been trained in Verrocchio's Shop with Leonardo.

    Based on a comparison of FIGS. 17-15 and 16-62, what do you think Raphael learned from his teacher?

    In what ways did Raphael improve on his master's work?

18. Raphael worked in Florence from _____ to _____.

19. List three characteristics of Raphael's style as seen in the *Madonna del Cardellino* (FIG. 17-16).

    a.

    b.

    c.

20. Name the four general themes Raphael used for his paintings in the Stanza della Segnatura.

    a.   c.

    b.   d.

21. Who are the two central figures represented in Raphael's *School of Athens* (FIG. 17-17), and what aspects of philosophy does each represent?

    a.

    b.

22. On the death of Julius II, a son of Lorenzo de' Medici was elected as Pope _____.

23. Who was Castiglioni?

24. Locate the following on the map on study guide page 172:

    Rome
    Milan

DISCUSSION QUESTIONS

1. How did the status of the visual artist change in the High Renaissance? What was the reason for this?

2. Compare the compositions of *The Last Supper* by Leonardo (FIG. 17-3) and Andrea del Castagno (FIG. 16-30) from the point of view of style, handling of space and form, and dramatic impact.

3. Compare Leonardo's *Mona Lisa* (FIG. 17-4) with Ghirlandaio's *Giovanna Tornabuoni* (FIG. 16-58); consider the placement of the figures, the definition of form, and the emotional effect achieved by each artist in creating a portrait.

4. Why is Bramante's Tempietto often referred to as the first High Renaissance building? What are the basic qualities that distinguish it from a typical Early Renaissance building?

5. How does the church of Santa Maria della Consolazione (FIGS. 17-9 and 17-10) "express the Classical ideals of the High Renaissance"? Do you feel that the building reflects a religious attitude that is different from the Medieval one? If so, what is the difference? How is it expressed?

6. How does the iconography of the Stanza della Segnatura relate to the ideals of the High Renaissance?

7. Compare Raphael's *Galatea* (FIG. 17-18) with Botticelli's *Birth of Venus* (FIG. 16-60); note the differences in the handling of the space and the representation of the bodies. What are the sources for the two subjects?

MICHELANGELO, ANDREA DEL SARTO, AND CORREGGIO AND MANNERISM   Text Pages 614–38

1. Michelangelo's belief that beauty is a reflection of the divine in the material world derives from what philosophical system?

2. To what extent did Michelangelo utilize the mathematical procedures used by other Renaissance sculptors to achieve harmonious proportion?

3. What is meant by the term *terribilità*?

4. In what two cities did Michelangelo do most of his work?

   a.   b.

5. List three figures that Michelangelo is believed to have created for the tomb of Julius II.

   a.

   b.

   c.

6. What are the two slaves thought to represent?

7. Briefly describe the iconography of the Sistine Chapel ceiling.

8. Characterize Michelangelo's style with four adjectives or phrases.

    a.

    b.

    c.

    d.

9. Describe briefly the iconography of the tombs of Lorenzo and Giuliano de' Medici.

    What are the tombs thought to symbolize?

10. Name some of the "anti-Classical" features in Michelangelo's design for the vestibule of the Laurentian Library.

    a.

    b.

    c.

    d.

11. With what urban project did Michelangelo enter the field of city planning?

What limitations did he have to cope with?

12. Describe the changes Michelangelo made in Bramante's original designs for St. Peter's.

    a. In the plan:

    b. In the elevation:

13. Who completed the dome of St. Peter's?

14. Which late work by Michelangelo best reflects the conditions brought on by the Protestant Reformation and the changed religious climate of Italy?

15. List three stylistic characteristics of Andrea del Sarto's *Madonna of the Harpies* (FIG. 17-37) that identify the painting as a High Renaissance work.

    a.

    b.

    c.

16. What was Corregio's most enduring contribution to the field of painting?

17. When was the Mannerist style most popular?

18. List some of the characteristics of Mannerist painting that can be called "anti-Classical" and that distinguish the Mannerist from the High Renaissance style.

    a.   d.

    b.   e.

    c.

19. Name three Mannerist painters.

    a.   b.   c.

20. Which Italian Mannerist sculptor most strongly influenced the development of French Renaissance art at Fontainebleau?

21. Which Mannerist sculptor developed the compositional device of the spiral?

22. Describe at least four features of the Palazzo del Tè that are "irregular" from the point of view of Renaissance architectural practice.

    a.

    b.

    c.

    d.

DISCUSSION QUESTIONS

1. Compare Michelangelo's *David* (FIG. 17-20) with Polykleitos' *Doryphoros* (FIG. 5-61) from the stylistic point of view. What similarities do you see? what differences? What distinguishes Michelangelo's *David* as a High Renaissance figure?

2. Choose a typical composition by Raphael, one by Leonardo, and one by Michelangelo, and decide in what ways they are stylistically related and in what ways they differ. Do you think the differences relate to the personalities of the artists? Are the similarities helpful in allowing us to make any generalizations about High Renaissance style?

3. Discuss the influence of Neo-Platonism on the art of Michelangelo; cite specific works and explain the Neo-Platonic ideals implicit in each.

4. Compare Michelangelo's Sistine Ceiling (FIG. 17-25) with his *Last Judgment* (FIG. 17-35). How does each represent Michelangelo's religious and philosophical beliefs at the time he painted it? Discuss the role of beauty in Michelangelo's art.

5. What Mannerist characteristics do you see in the art of Michelangelo? Would you call Michelangelo a Mannerist?

6. What did Michelangelo mean when he wrote: "The members of an architectural structure follow the laws exemplified in the human body?

7. Compare Domenico Veneziano's *St. Lucy Altarpiece* (FIG. 16-32), Andrea del Sarto's *Madonna of the Harpies* (FIG. 17-37), and Parmigianino's *Madonna with the Long Neck* (FIG. 17-43); consider the handling of space, the logic (or lack of it) of the compositions, and the treatment of the figures, including placement and proportions. What emotional effect does each artist create? Which painting do you like best? Why?

8. Compare the façade designs of Antonio da Sangallo's Farnese Palace (FIG. 17-12), Alberti's Palazzo Rucellai (FIG. 16-39), Michelangelo's Museo Capitolino (FIG. 17-31), and Giulio Romano's Palazzo del Tè (FIGS. 17-48 and 17-49). Which building seems to be the most monumental? Why?

VENICE   Text Pages 638-53

1. The State Library of San Marco in Venice was designed by _____.
    What feature of the building seems to have been modeled after the Roman Colosseum?

    What decorative scheme was used for the second story?

    How did the treatment of the roofline differ from traditional practice?

    In what ways does the library harmonize with the older Doge's Palace opposite it?

2. What was most significant about Palladio's writings?

3. What geometric forms did Palladio use to create the basic structure of the Villa Rotunda?

4. Describe the device Palladio used for the façade of San Giorgio Maggiore (FIG. 17-54) to integrate the high central nave and low aisles.

5. In what ways does Palladio's architectural style differ from:
    a. Mannerism?

    b. the style of Michelangelo?

6. What were the major formative influences on Bellini's style of painting?

    Where does the *Madonna of the Trees* (FIG. 17-56) fit into his stylistic development?

7. What major High Renaissance characteristics found in Bellini's *San Zaccaria Altarpiece* (FIG. 17-58) distinguish it from his earlier *San Giobbe Altarpiece* (FIG. 17-57)?
    a.

    b.

    c.

8. What concerns distinguish the art of Venice from that of Florence and Rome?

                  Venice   Florence and Rome

   a.   a.

   b.   b.

   c.   c.

9. Briefly characterize the Venetian approach to landscape painting.

10. Briefly describe three aspects of Giorgione's style.

   a.

   b.

   c.

11. What is the myth of Arcadia?

12. Why is Titian generally considered to be "the father of the modern mode of painting"?

13. Which painting of his teacher, Bellini, did Titian complete?

14. In the allegory *Sacred and Profane Love* (FIG. 17-61) the nude figure symbolizes _____,
   while the dressed figure symbolizes _____.

15. What characteristics of Titian's *Madonna of the Pesaro Family* (FIG. 17-62) are typical of High Renaissance painting?

   a.

   b.

   What features of the work are not typical of the High Renaissance?

   a.

   b.

16. Which of Titian's paintings established the compositional essentials for the representation of the female nude in much of later Western art?

17.   Emperor _____ and his son _____ were among Titian's greatest patrons.

18.   Titian's late style, as seen in *Christ Crowned with Thorns* (FIG. 17-65) is characterized by:

a.

b.

c.

19.   Tintoretto aspired to combine the color of _____ with the drawing of _____.

20.   What devices does Tintoretto use to identify Christ in his version of *The Last Supper* (FIG. 17-67)?

How did Leonardo identify him (FIG. 17-3)?

What style did Tintoretto anticipate?

21.   List three characteristics of Tintoretto's painting style that are *not* Manneristic.

a.

b.

c.

22.   Veronese's favorite subjects were:

a.

b.

His architectural settings often reflect the style of _____.

The Holy Office of the Inquisition objected to what aspects of his paintings?

23. What is the difference in the type of illusion created by Veronese in *The Triumph of Venice* (FIG. 17-69) and that created by Correggio in *The Assumption of the Virgin* for the dome of Parma Cathedral (FIG. 17-38)?

DISCUSSION QUESTIONS

1. What was Venice's political and economic situation during the sixteenth century? How do you account for the apparent fact that Venice reached the height of its artistic productivity during a period of political and economic decline? Can you think of more recent parallels to this phenomenon?

2. In what respects is the Villa Rotunda *not* typical of Palladio's general villa style? How does the building combine functional qualities with esthetic ideals that were important to Renaissance architects?

3. Compare Palladio's San Giorgio Maggiore (FIGS. 17-54 and 17-55) with Sant' Andrea by Alberti (FIGS. 16-42, 16-43, 16-44). What differences do you see in the articulation of the façades and the interiors? Note also the degree of plasticity of the surfaces.

4. Compare Titian's *Madonna of the Pesaro Family* (FIG. 17-62) with Bellini's *San Giobbe Altarpiece* (FIG. 17-57). Discuss the organization of space, the compositional devices used, and the treatment of the figures in each painting.

5. Compare Bronzino's *Venus, Cupid, Folly, and Time* (FIG. 17-44) with Giorgione's (and/or Titian's?) *Pastoral Symphony* (FIG. 17-60). Note the poses of the figures, the settings, and the compositions. What do you think were the major concerns of each artist?

6. Discuss the different styles preferred by artists of Venice and those of Florence. What factors do you think might have influenced these preferences?

7. In what ways are the styles of the Early Renaissance in Florence, the High Renaissance in Rome, Mannerism in Florence, and the Late Renaissance in Venice typified in the portraits by Botticelli (FIG. 16-59), Raphael (FIG. 17-19), Bronzino (FIG. 17-45), and Titian (FIG. 17-64)?

SUMMARY: THE ITALIAN RENAISSANCE   Text Pages 528–653

Fill in the following charts as much as possible from memory; then check your answers against the text in Chapters 15–17 and complete the charts.

HISTORICAL BACKGROUND

	Political Leaders and Events	Cultural and Scientific Developments
"Proto-Renaissance"		
15th-Century Florence		
15th Century Outside Florence		
High Renaissance		
Mannerism		

SUMMARY OF "PROTO-RENAISSANCE" ART IN ITALY

	Typical Examples	Stylistic Characteristics
Nicola Pisano		
Giovanni Pisano		
Andrea Pisano		
Maniera Greca		
Duccio		
Giotto		
Simone Martini		
The Lorenzetti		

SUMMARY OF FIFTEENTH-CENTURY ITALIAN RENAISSANCE PAINTING

	Typical Examples	Stylistic Characteristics
Masaccio		
Uccello		
Andrea del Castagno		
Piero della Francesca		
Fra Angelico		
Pollaiuolo		
Ghirlandaio		
Botticelli		
Signorelli		
Perugino		
Mantegna		

SUMMARY OF SIXTEENTH-CENTURY ITALIAN PAINTING OUTSIDE VENICE

	Typical Examples	Stylistic Characteristics
Leonardo		
Raphael		
Michelangelo		
Andrea del Sarto		
Correggio		
Pontormo		
Rosso Fiorentino		
Parmigianino		
Bronzino		

SUMMARY OF SIXTEENTH-CENTURY VENETIAN PAINTING

	Typical Examples	Stylistic Characteristics
Bellini		
Giorgione		
Titian		
Tintoretto		
Veronese		

SUMMARY OF RENAISSANCE AND MANNERIST SCULPTURE IN ITALY

	Typical Examples	Stylistic Characteristics
Ghiberti		
Donatello		
Antonio Rossellino		
Verrocchio		
Michelangelo		
Cellini		
Giovanni da Bologna		

SUMMARY OF RENAISSANCE AND MANNERIST ARCHITECTURE IN ITALY

	Typical Examples	Stylistic Characteristics
Brunelleschi		
Michelozzo di Bartolommeo		
Alberti		
Bramante		
Antonio da Sangallo		
Michelangelo		
Giulio Romano		
Sansovino		
Palladio		

Chapter Eighteen

The Renaissance Outside of Italy

Text Pages 654–707

THE FIFTEENTH CENTURY Text Pages 656–82

1. Describe the role played by the Guild of St. Luke in the life of the northern painter in the fifteenth century and how a young man attained membership in the guild.

2. What painting technique was perfected by the fifteenth-century Flemish painters?

Briefly describe the technique.

In what respects did it prove to be superior to the tempera technique?

3. Define the following terms:

genre scenes

triptych

polyptych

alla prima

impasto

retable

hatching

4. What seem to have been the major artistic concerns of northern painters in the fifteenth century?

   a.

   b.

   c.

5. Name the two main sources of wealth in fifteenth-century Bruges.

   a.

   b.

6. Who were the most powerful rulers in northern Europe during the first three-quarters of the fifteenth century?

   Whom did they generally support during the Hundred Years' War? Why?

7. Name the two northern dukes who are generally considered to have been the greatest patrons of the arts in northern Europe in the late fourteenth and early fifteenth centuries.

   a.   b.

8. List four adjectives or phrases that characterize Sluter's sculptural style.

   a.

   b.

   c.

   d.

   In comparison with the figures of Donatello, what seems to be missing from Sluter's conception of the figure?

9. What four subjects did Broederlam depict on the wings of the altarpiece he painted for the Chartreuse de Champmol?

   a.   c.

   b.   d.

10. What characteristics of the International style are found in Broederlam's work?

    a.

    b.

    c.

    d.

11. In what ways did the earlier techniques of stained glass and illuminated-manuscript painting influence fifteenth-century panel painting in the north?

    a.

    b.

12. Who was Jean Pucelle?

13. What is a "Book of Hours"?

14. Describe the stylistic characteristics that link the illuminations done by the Limbourg brothers with fourteenth-century Sienese painting.

    a.

    b.

    c.

15. Who was the Master of Flémalle?

    List three characteristics of his style.

    a.

    b.

    c.

16. What did the book, candle, sink, and towels symbolize in *The Mérode Altarpiece* (FIG. 18-6)?

17. Who was Hubert van Eyck? What part of the original *Ghent Altarpiece* has recently been attributed to him?

18. To what event do the scenes depicted on the outside of *The Ghent Altarpiece* (FIG. 18-7) symbolically refer?

What is the general theme of the interior of the altarpiece?

Write the subjects of the various panels in the corresponding spaces below.

What is symbolized by the following groups on the lower wings?

Hermits: Knights:

Pilgrims: Judges:

19. How does Jan van Eyck use perspective in his *Virgin with the Canon van der Paele* (FIG. 18-10)?

What does this indicate about Van Eyck's conception of pictorial space?

20. What is new and significant about the pose of the *Man in a Red Turban* (FIG. 18-11)?

21. How did Nicholas of Cusa's writings provide a justification for the intense realism of fifteenth-century Flemish artists?

22. The probable purpose of the painting of *Giovanni Arnolfini and His Bride* (FIG. 18-12) was:

    List four symbols contained in the painting and give their meanings.

    a.

    b.

    c.

    d.

23. Which Flemish artist had the greatest influence on later fifteenth-century northern art?

24. In contrast to the complex symbolism and optimism of Jan van Eyck, what did Rogier van der Weyden stress in his paintings?

25. List the Flemish characteristics of Rogier's *Portrait of a Lady* (FIG. 18-15) that distinguish it from the work of Italian artists such as Ghirlandio (FIG. 16-58).

26. Name the two fifteenth-century Flemish painters who demonstrated the greatest interest in the depiction of space and cubic form.

    a.   b.

27. Recent studies indicate that _____ was the first northern artist to utilize a single vanishing point for construction of an architectural interior.

28. Describe the distinctive qualities of style that set Hugo van der Goes' paintings apart from those of his contemporaries.

29.　Who was Tommaso Portinari?

30.　What is the symbolic meaning of the following items in the central panel of *The Portinari Altarpiece* (FIG. 18-18)?

Iris and columbine:

Sheaf of wheat:

Harp of David:

Where was *The Portinari Altarpiece* displayed?

31.　In what sort of subject matter did Memling specialize?

Briefly describe his style.

32.　What are the primary subjects of the panels of Bosch's *Garden of Earthly Delights*?

Left:

Center:

Right:

Exterior:

List some of the sources that have been suggested for Bosch's iconography.

a.

b.

c.

d.

33. What is alchemy?

34. How was the style of Fouquet modified by his Italian experiences?

35. *The Avignon Pietà* seems to be most closely related to the work of which Flemish artist?

   What Italian elements are apparent in the painting?

36. What is meant by the "soft" style in German painting?

37. List three characteristics of the style of Witz.
   a.

   b.

   c.

38. What subject did Stoss depict in the center of the Kraków altarpiece (FIG. 18-28)?

   List some typical Late Gothic characteristics of his style.
   a.

   b.

   c.

39. What mood is most typically expressed in the figures carved by Riemenschneider?

40. What Italian artist seems to have influenced the style of Pacher?

What features of his style do Pacher's work reflect?

a.

b.

c.

41. Briefly describe the technique of the woodcut.

42. Locate the following on the map on study guide page 172:

Burgundy	Flanders	Bruges
Dijon	Paris	Ghent
Tournai	Cologne	

DISCUSSION QUESTIONS

1. Compare Sluter's figure of Moses (FIG. 18-1) with Donatello's *St. Mark* (FIG. 16-5). In what way do these figures typify the concerns of northern and Italian artists?

2. Compare the treatment of the landscape in the works by the Limbourg Brothers (FIGS. 18-4 and 18-5) with that in Ambrogio Lorenzetti's *Peaceful Country* (FIG. 15-24). In what ways are they similar? In what ways do they differ?

3. Masaccio's *Holy Trinity* fresco (FIG. 16-28) and Campin's *Mérode Altarpiece* (FIG. 18-6) were done at about the same time. Compare them from the point of view of scale, medium, and treatment of space. Does Campin use linear perspective? Identify the orthogonals in each and locate the vanishing point, if one exists. How do the two works reflect the different concerns of Italian and northern artists?

4. How does Jan van Eyck's approach to portraiture as shown in the head of Canon van der Paele (FIG. 18-10) differ from the approach of Italian portraitists?

5. According to Lotte Brand Philip's reconstruction, how was *The Ghent Altarpiece* displayed that differs from its present state? Does her reconstruction seem reasonable? If not, why?

6. Discuss *The Portinari Altarpiece* (FIG. 18-18) by Hugo van der Goes; note especially iconography and the meaning of the disguised symbols. What stylistic influence do you see from Jan van Eyck? How does this altarpiece differ from his work?

7. How does Bosch's conception of the Creation and man's fate (FIGS. 18-21, 18-22, 18-23) compare with Michelangelo's as expressed in the latter's Sistine Ceiling (FIG. 17-25) and *Last Judgment* frescoes (FIG. 17-35)? Compare both the iconography and the style of the two artists.

8. Compare Bosch's *Carrying of the Cross* (FIG. 18-21) with Titian's *Christ Crowned with Thorns* (FIG. 17-65) from the points of view of technique, meaning, and emotional impact.

THE SIXTEENTH CENTURY   Text Pages 682–707

1. Identify the following individuals:

    Martin Luther

    Erasmus of Rotterdam

    Thomas More

    Henry VIII

    Francis I

    Charles V

    Phillip II

    Rudolf II

    St. Ignatius of Loyola

2. By what means did sixteenth-century German artists become aware of the developments in Italian art?

    a.   c.

    b.

3. To what period of Italian art does the most brilliant period of German sixteenth-century art correspond?

4. What was the Danube style?

    Who was its primary representative?

5. Who is generally credited with having painted the first landscape without human figures in Western art?

6. Who painted *The Isenheim Altarpiece*?

    How is the altarpiece constructed?

List three characteristics of the artist's style.

a.

b.

c.

7. Name an important Italian work that was done about the same time as *The Isenheim Altarpiece*.

    Point out at least two differences between the works.

    a.

    b.

8. What is the subject of the predella of *The Isenheim Altarpiece*?

9. Which northern artist is generally considered to have been the first to fully understand the basic aims of the Italian Renaissance?

    Name two Renaissance masters whose works he copied.

    a.   b.

    His interest in scientific illustration and artistic theory was similar to that of _____.

10. In what year did Dürer create the Apocalypse series?

    The woodcut series is based upon the vision of _____ as related in the book of _____.

    List three stylistic characteristics of the woodcut series.

    a.

    b.

    c.

11. The poses of Dürer's Adam and Eve are similar to the figures of:

12. Describe the major difference that you see between Dürer's portrait of *Hieronymus Holzschuher* (FIG. 18-39) and Raphael's portrait of *Baldassare Castiglione* (FIG. 17-19).

13. Give a brief description of the possible meaning of Dürer's *Melencolia I* (FIG. 18-40).

14. Point out those characteristics of Dürer's *Four Apostles* (FIG. 18-41) that it shares with Italian High Renaissance works.

    Which features of the work are essentially "Germanic" and thus set it apart from Italian art?

15. In what type of painting did Holbein specialize?

16. Why is Holbein believed to have left Basel for England?

17. List five characteristics of Holbein's style that are seen in his double portrait of *The French Ambassadors* (FIG. 18-42).

    a.

    b.

    c.

    d.

    e.

18. What does *anamorphic* mean?

19. Name two early-sixteenth-century artists who tried, with varying degrees of success, to integrate Italian Renaissance characteristics into their native Netherlandish style.

    a.   b.

20. List four new types of painting that became popular in sixteenth-century Flemish art.

    a.   c.

    b.   d.

21. The leading artist of the School of Antwerp during the early decades of the sixteenth century was

    _____.

22. What was a Flemish "Romanist"?

23. What name did Jan Gossaert adopt?

    Which features of his *Neptune and Amphitrite* (FIG. 18-45) are Classical?

    Which are not?

24. Joachim Patinir specialized in:

    In what two ways did he achieve effects of recession?

    a.

    b.

25. Describe three ways in which Bruegel's landscape paintings differ from those of Patinir.

    a.

    b.

    c.

26. What is thought to have been the meaning of Bruegel's *Peasant Dance* (FIG. 18-49)?

27.   What contemporary political events do some of Bruegel's paintings seem to reflect?

28.   Who painted a famous portrait of Francis I?

29.   Name two Italian Mannerists who were instrumental in the formation of the School of Fontainebleau.

a.   b.

30.   What Manneristic characteristics are seen in the decoration of the Gallery of Francis I at Fontainebleau?

a.

b.

c.

31.   Analyze the plan and elevation of the Château de Chambord. What are its Italian Renaissance features?

a.

b.

c.

What are its French and Gothic features?

a.

b.

32.   Identify those features of the façade of the Louvre courtyard (FIG. 18-53) that are derived from the Italian Renaissance and those that are essentially French.

Italian:

a.

b.

c.

French:

a.

b.

c.

33. The architect who designed the Square Court of the Louvre was _____

    and the sculptor who ornamented the façade was _____.

34. What characteristics of Pilon's style are derived from the Fontainebleau style?

    a.

    b.

    In what ways does his style differ from that of the School of Fontainebleau?

    a.

    b.

35. Define "Plateresque."

36. What features of Bramante's Tempietto (FIG. 17-6) did Machuca use in the palace he designed for Charles V in Granada (FIG. 18-57)?

37. The Escorial was constructed for King _____ of Spain.

    Describe the style of the building.

38. Two seemingly opposing spiritual trends appear to have been expressed in Spanish art of the Counter-Reformation period. What are they?

    a.

    b.

39. Describe the elements of El Greco's style that seem to be related to Italian Mannerism.

    a.

    b.

    Describe those elements that point toward the Baroque.

    a.

    b.

Describe two purely personal stylistic traits that are found in El Greco's work.

a.

b.

40. Locate the following on the map on study guide page 172:

Nuremberg	Basel	Antwerp
Granada	Toledo	Madrid

DISCUSSION QUESTIONS

1. What different conceptions of the nude and of Classical mythology are apparent in Correggio's *Jupiter and Io* (FIG. 17-40) and Cranach's *Judgment of Paris* (FIG. 18-33)?

2. Make a stylistic comparison of Grünewald's *Resurrection* (FIG. 18-35) with that of Piero della Francesca (FIG. 16-36). Discuss color, form, composition, structure, and dramatic impact. Which do you like better? Why?

3. Compare Grünewald's *Isenheim Altarpiece* (FIGS. 18-34 and 18-35) with Jan van Eyck's *Ghent Altarpiece* (FIGS. 18-7 and 18-8). Discuss the iconography, the handling of light, color, and space, as well as the emotional impact. What kind of landscape setting does each use? How does each treat the human figure?

4. Compare the pose and proportions of the Van Eycks' (FIG. 18-8) and Dürer's (FIG. 18-37) representations of Adam and Eve. How do these figures relate to Classical proportions and the contrapposto pose?

5. In what ways do you think Dürer and Leonardo were alike? In what ways do you think they were different?

6. List what you believe to be the six most important works of art done between 1500 and 1520. Include at least one from the Netherlands and one from Germany. Why do you believe they are the most important? What differences do you see between the ones you have selected from the north and those from Italy? What do you think these differences reveal about the different conceptions of man held by the two regions? Which set of beliefs do you think is the closest to the one we hold today?

7. Discuss the implications of Dürer's statement: "We regard a form and figure out of nature with more pleasure than any other, though the thing itself is not necessarily altogether better or worse."

8. Compare the Classicism of the Escorial (FIG. 18-58) with that of the Château de Chambord (FIG. 18-52). What does each building tell about the life and interests of the kings who commissioned them?

9. Compare Pilon's *Descent from the Cross* (FIG. 18-55) with similar subjects by Rogier van der Weyden (FIG. 18-14), the Master of *The Avignon Pieta* (FIG. 18-25), and Giotto (FIG. 15-14). Which moves you the most? Why?

10. What stylistic features does El Greco (FIG. 18-61) share with the following artists: Parmigianino (FIG. 17-43), Bronzino (FIG. 17-44), Rosso and Primaticcio (FIG. 18-51), Spranger (FIG. 18-46), Cellini (FIG. 17-46), and Goujon (FIG. 18-54)? How does his work differ from theirs?

SUMMARY: THE RENAISSANCE OUTSIDE OF ITALY   Text Pages 654–707

Fill in the following charts as much as you can from memory; then check your asnwers against the text and complete the charts.

HISTORICAL BACKGROUND

	Political Leaders and Events	Religious, Cultural, and Scientific Developments
15th-Century Flanders		
16th-Century Flanders		
15th-Century France		
16th-Century France		
15th-Century Germany		
16th-Century Germany		

SUMMARY OF RENAISSANCE PAINTING IN FIFTEENTH-CENTURY FLANDERS

	Typical Examples	Stylistic Characteristics
Broederlam		
Limbourg Brothers		
Campin		
Jan van Eyck		
Rogier van der Weyden		
Christus		
Bouts		
Hugo van der Goes		
Memling		
Bosch		

SUMMARY OF RENAISSANCE PAINTING IN SIXTEENTH-CENTURY NETHERLANDS

	Typical Examples	Stylistic Characteristics
Metsys		
Gossaert		
Spranger		
Patinir		
Bruegel		

SUMMARY OF FRENCH RENAISSANCE ART

	Typical Examples	Stylistic Characteristics
Fouquet		
Clouet		
Rosso at Fontainebleau		
Goujon		
Pilon		
Lescot		

SUMMARY OF GERMAN RENAISSANCE ART

	Typical Examples	Stylistic Characteristics
Lochner		
Witz		
Riemen-schneider		
Pacher		
Schongauer		
Altdorfer		
Cranach		
Grünewald		
Dürer		
Holbein		

Chapter Nineteen
Baroque Art

INTRODUCTION   Text Pages 710–12

1. Give the approximate dates that embrace the Baroque period.

2. List as many adjectives or phrases that describe the Baroque style as you can think of.

    a.   f.

    b.   g.

    c.   h.

    d.   i.

    e.   j.

3. What discoveries in the physical sciences fascinated Baroque artists and may be held responsible, at least in part, for the change in style from the Renaissance to the Baroque?

    a.

    b.

    c.

4. Poussin and Rubens were considered as the two poles in the Baroque debate between the forces of passion and reason. Which pole did each artist represent? What characteristics in the work of each artist reflect their attitudes?

    Rubens:

    Poussin:

THE SEVENTEENTH CENTURY IN ITALY AND SPAIN   Text Pages 712–36

1. The city that is generally thought to have been the birthplace of Baroque art is _____.

2. With what religious movement is much of the Baroque art in Catholic countries associated?

3. Why is the church of Il Gesù important?

    Who were its architects?

    a.   b.

    What were the two most influential features of the building?

    a.   b.

4. Name four architects who worked on St. Peter's and note the primary contribution of each.

    a.

    b.

    c.

    d.

5. Describe the illusionistic devices that Bernini used to make the Scala Regia appear longer.

    a.

    b.

6. What is a *baldacchino*?

7. List some major characteristics of Bernini's sculpture that are typical of Baroque art in general.

    a.

    b.

    c.

    d.

8. Why did the design of fountains fascinate Baroque artists?

9. Who developed the sculptural architectural style to its extreme?

   Name two buildings designed by him.

   a.   b.

   Both are located in the city of _____.

10. While the circle had been the ideal geometric figure to the Renaissance architects, Baroque planners pre-
    ferred the _____.

    Why?

11. What is the purpose of the lateral, three-part division of Baroque palace façades?

    Upon what human psychological tendency does it seem to be based?

12. In what countries were the architectural styles of Borromini and Guarini particularly influential?

    a.

    b.

    c.

13. What Venetian church may have inspired the centralized plan used by Longhena for the church of Santa
    Maria della Salute?

    Describe the features of Santa Maria della Salute that look back to the Renaissance.

    Describe the features that can be considered more typically Baroque.

14. The "naturalistic" strain in Baroque art was most pronounced in the countries of _____
    and _____.

15. List the three assumptions that were basic to the teaching of art at the Bolognese academy.

    a.

    b.

    c.

Who was the founder of that academy?

16. What earlier work strongly influenced Annibale Carracci's ceiling frescoes in the gallery of the Farnese Palace in Rome?

How did Carracci modify the original to achieve heightened illusionism?

17. Define the following terms:

quadro-riportato

tenebrism

18. The common purpose of Caravaggio's *Conversion of St. Paul* (FIG. 19-26) and Bernini's *St. Theresa* (text page 520) was:

19. List three characteristics of Caravaggio's style.

a.

b.

c.

20. Why were some of Caravaggio's works refused by the people who had commissioned them?

21. What was Caravaggio attempting to present in his religious pictures?

What pictorial devices did he use to achieve his goal?

22. Describe the features of Domenichino's *Last Communion of St. Jerome* (FIG. 19-28) that were adapted from Caravaggio.

a.

b.

Describe the features that reflect the mood of the High Renaissance.

a.

b.

c.

23. List three of the social factors that tended to exclude women from training and practice in the arts.

a.

b.

c.

24. Which artist most influenced the style of Artemisia Gentileschi?

25. Who were Judith and Holofernes?

26. Who is credited with developing the "classical" or "ideal" landscape?

What were its roots?

27. Briefly describe Rosa's landscape style.

28. Name an Italian Baroque artist who specialized in illusionistic ceiling painting.

29. Ribera's style was influenced by the "dark manner" of _____.

30. What type of lighting did Zurbarán prefer?

31. Velázquez was court painter to King _____.

32. In contrast to the idealized Italian treatment of Classical themes, Velázquez depicted Bacchus and his followers in a style that could be described as:

33. Who suggested to Velázquez that he visit Italy?

How did this visit affect Velázquez's style?

34. What is the subject of *Las Meninas*?

How many levels of reality can you find in the picture?

Briefly describe them.

What painting technique did Velázquez use in *Las Meninas*?

DISCUSSION QUESTIONS

1. Compare Bernini's *David* (FIG. 19-10) with Michelangelo's version (FIG. 17-20). Discuss the pose of the figures, the closed or open quality of the composition, and the mood that is created by these technical devices.

2. Study the elevations and plans of Giuliano da Sangallo's Church of Santa Maria delle Carceri at Prato (FIGS. 16-45, 16-46, 16-47) and Borromini's San Carlo alle Quattro Fontane (FIGS. 19-13 and 19-14). Contrast the basic shapes used in the plans, and describe how these forms relate to the elevations of the buildings.

3. Discuss the different views of the interrelation of realism and of Classical antiquity as illustrated in Titian's *Venus of Urbino* (FIG. 17-63) and Velázquez's *Los Borrachos* (FIG. 19-35).

4. Compare Ribera's *Martyrdom of St. Bartholomew* (FIG. 19-33) with Antonello da Messina's *Martyrdom of St. Sebastian* (FIG. 16-67). Discuss composition, painting technique, and emotional impact. What major concerns of the Italian Renaissance and the Counter-Reformation in Spain are demonstrated by these works?

5. Some critics feel that Baroque style is not opposed to Renaissance style, but rather that it is a logical development and continuation of it. What evidence do you find for this statement?

6. Bernini's art has been described as "theatrical." If you agree, give examples of its theatricality.

7. Discuss the role played by art in the revitalization of the Catholic church and Catholic beliefs during the seventeenth century.

THE SEVENTEENTH CENTURY IN FLANDERS AND HOLLAND   Text Pages 736-53

1. Why did the northern provinces of the Low Countries break away from Spain?

The northern provinces constitute the modern country of _____,
while those in the south constitute the country of _____.
During the seventeenth century, this southern region was known as _____.

2.   The painting style of Rubens synthesizes those of the Renaissance masters _____
and _____ with the styles of the Baroque masters
_____ and _____.

3.   Rubens' favorite theme was:

What sort of a mood do his paintings most often reflect?

4.   What member of the famous Florentine House of Medici commissioned Rubens to paint a cycle memorializing and glorifying her career and that of her late husband?

5.   In what type of paintings did Van Dyck specialize?
How could his style best be characterized?

Who was Van Dyck's principal patron?

6.   List a few of the political, social, and religious distinctions between seventeenth-century Flanders and seventeenth-century Holland that influenced the art of the two regions.

a.

b.

c.

7.   How did the religious and economic conditions in seventeenth-century Holland affect artistic production?

a.

b.

c.

8. Who were the "Caravaggisti"?

    Name one.

9. Frans Hals was the leading painter of the _____ School, who specialized in

    _____.

    What are the main elements of his style that distinguish his works from those of his contemporaries?

10. Briefly describe Rembrandt's use of light and shade.

11. Whose influence is apparent in the lighting effects in Rembrandt's early works such as the *Supper at Emmaus* (FIG. 19-47)?

    How did his interpretation of the same theme (FIG. 19-48) change in his later years?

12. Using the adjectives you listed on page 220 to describe the Baroque style, to what degree would you classify Rembrandt's *Return of the Prodigal Son* as Baroque?

    How does this painting relate to the mood of Rembrandt's late portraits?

13. Briefly describe the technique of etching.

    What are its advantages over engraving?

14. What major change did Rembrandt make in the fourth state of *The Three Crosses* (FIG. 19-53) in comparison with the earlier states?

15. Why was Rembrandt's late work not acceptable to his contemporaries?

16. What aspect of Jan van Eyck's art was carried on in seventeenth-century Holland?

17. Vermeer's favorite type of subject matter was:

18. In what way does Vermeer's use of light differ from Rembrandt's?

19. On what principle does a *camera obscura* work?

20. Describe the mood created by Vermeer's compositions.

21. Write down three important facts about the optics of color that are illustrated in Vermeer's paintings (note FIG. 19-55).

    a.

    b.

    c.

22. Name one seventeenth-century Dutch painter who specialized in landscape painting.

    In what way can his landscape paintings be considered "Protestant"?

23.   Locate the following on the map on study guide page 172:

Haarlem
Utrecht
Amsterdam

DISCUSSION QUESTIONS

1.   Compare Rubens' *Rape of the Daughters of Leucippus* (FIG. 19-39) with Giorgione's (and/or Titian's) *Pastoral Symphony* (FIG. 17-60). Compare composition, color, and mood. What is Baroque about the Rubens?

2.   In what ways do the works and lives of Rubens and Rembrandt reflect the different social and religious orientations of seventeenth-century Flanders and Holland?

3.   Compare Rembrandt's *Self Portrait* (FIG. 19-51) with Raphael's portrait of *Baldassare Castiglione* (FIG. 17-19). How have the artists depicted the different psychological states of the subjects? How do these two works illustrate major differences in the philosophies of the times in which they were painted?

4.   Compare Vermeer's *Young Woman with a Water Jug* (FIG. 19-54) with Van Eyck's *Giovanni Arnolfini and His Bride* (FIG. 18-12) and Hals's *Malle Babbe* (FIG. 19-45). Discuss painting surface, composition, and mood. Do you think Vermeer's work is closer to that of Van Eyck or to that of his contemporary Hals? Why?

5.   Discuss the effect of the economic and religious climate of seventeenth-century Holland on its artists.

THE SEVENTEENTH CENTURY IN FRANCE AND ENGLAND   Text Pages 753–67

1.   The period from 1660 to 1715 in Europe is referred to as the "age of _____."

2.   What formal traits of style give unity to the arts in France during the second half of the seventeenth century?

How can that style best be characterized?

3.   Which French artist was most influenced by the northern "Caravaggisti"?

In what ways does his style differ from theirs?

4.   The French artist Callot is best known for his works done in the medium of _____.

His *Miseries* series realistically depicts scenes of _____.

5.   What French artist is credited with having established seventeenth-century Classical painting?

Where did he spend most of his life?

The two Italian artists he most admired were:

a.   b.

6. What four characteristics of the 1640 version of *Et in Arcadia Ego* are typical of Poussin's fully developed Classical style?

a.

b.

c.

d.

7. What type of subjects did Poussin consider to be appropriate for paintings done in the "grand manner"?

What did he think should be avoided?

8. In what major way does the landscape in Poussin's *Burial of Phocion* (FIG. 19-62) differ from Van Ruisdael's *View of Haarlem* (FIG. 19-57)?

9. What was Claude Lorraine's primary interest in landscape painting?

In what country did he do most of his painting?

10. Describe the features that create the impression of dignity and sobriety apparent in Mansart's work at Blois (FIG. 19-64).

a.

b.

What feature of the building is typically Baroque?

11. The French Royal Academy of Painting and Sculpture was established in the year _____.

   What was its primary purpose?

12. Three architects collaborated to design the east façade of the Louvre. They were:

   a.   b.   c.

   What form is used for the central pavilion of the Louvre?

13. Who was the principal director for the building and decoration of the palace of Versailles?

   Name the two architects who were responsible for the design of the garden façade.

   a.   b.

   What Baroque device was used to subdivide the façade?

14. Who designed the park of Versailles?

15. What is symbolized by the vast complex of Versailles?

16. Which feature of Jules Hardouin-Mansart's Church of the Invalides is most Baroque?

   Which is most classical?

17. Why was the work of the French sculptor Puget not accepted at the French court?

   Which sculptor was a court favorite?

18. Which of the visual or plastic arts was most important in seventeenth-century England?

19. Name the Italian architect who had the strongest influence on the buildings of Inigo Jones?

20. Who designed St. Paul's Cathedral in London?

   What feature of the building shows the influence of Borromini?

   What feature is taken over from the east façade of the Louvre?

DISCUSSION QUESTIONS

1. To what extent can the term "Classical Baroque" appropriately be applied to the art of seventeenth-century France? Cite specific examples from painting, architecture, and sculpture to support your argument.

2. Discuss the relative balance between Baroque and Renaissance features in the following buildings: the east façade of the Louvre (FIG. 19-65), the Church of the Invalides in Paris (FIGS. 19-71 and 19-72), the Banqueting House at Whitehall (FIG. 19-75), and St. Paul's in London (FIG. 19-76).

3. In what ways did Louis XIV influence French art of the seventeenth century? How did his utilization of art differ from that of Philip IV in Spain?

4. Could Rubens' *Lion Hunt* (FIG. 19-40) and Van Honthorst's *Supper Party* (FIG. 19-43) serve as illustrations of Poussin's "grand manner"? If not, why?

5. Who was chiefly responsible for the development of "classical" landscape painting in Italy? How did his approach differ from those of Poussin (FIG. 19-62), Rosa (FIG. 19-31), and Van Ruisdael (FIG. 19-57)?

Chapter Twenty

The Eighteenth Century: Rococo and the Rise of Romanticism Text Pages 768–801

LATE BAROQUE AND ROCOCO   Text Pages 770–85

1. The authors of the text divide the eighteenth century into two stages. What do they consider to be the major characteristic of the first stage?

   Of all the changes that took place in the second half of the eighteenth century, which do the authors consider to have been of greatest importance for the development of the modern world?

2. List three of the social effects caused by the discovery and utilization of the steam engine.

   a.

   b.

   c.

3. What was the "third estate"?

   Why did it become more important in the second half of the eighteenth century?

4. What was the primary purpose of art for the eighteenth-century nobility?

5. Briefly characterize the differences between Baroque and Rococo as seen in Rigaud's portrait of *Louis XIV* (FIG. 20-1) and Watteau's *L'Indifferent* (FIG. 20-2).

Baroque	Rococo
a.	a.
b.	b.
c.	c.

6. In what ways does Juvara's Superga near Turin (FIG. 20-3) differ from the Baroque palaces of his predecessor Guarini (FIG. 19-18)?

    a.

    b.

7. Blenheim Palace in England was designed by _____ for _____ _____, but even before it was completed it was criticized being _____ _____.

8. In reaction to Baroque buildings like Blenheim, the restraint of _____ was restated in buildings like Chiswick House, which was designed by _____ and _____. List four of its characteristic features.

    a.   c.

    b.   d.

9. What was the major objective of artists who worked for the eighteenth-century French aristocracy?

    Write down a few adjectives that describe the type of art they created.

    a.   c.

    b.   d.

10. Compare the photographs of the Salon de la Princesse of the Hôtel de Soubise (FIG. 20-6) and the Galerie des Glaces of Versailles (FIG. 19-69). List three adjectives or phrases that describe each.

Salon de la Princesse	Galerie des Glaces
a.	a.
b.	b.
c.	c.

11. One of the best examples of French Rococo architecture, known as the _____, was built in Munich. It was designed by _____.

In sharp contrast to the restraint of Chiswick House, the Rococo features of this small building can be described as:

a.

b.

c.

12. Name the two Baroque architects who most influenced the Rococo architecture of southern Germany and Austria.

   a.   b.

13. The church of Vierzehnheiligen was designed by _____.

   What features of the building are reminiscent of the work of Borromini?

   a.

   b.

   In what way does it differ from his work?

   How does the effect of the interior differ from that of typical Baroque interiors?

14. Name the eighteenth-century Italian painter who is best known for his elegant, illusionistic ceiling paintings.

15. Theatrical illusionism is an important characteristic of the work of the German Baroque sculptor

   _____.

16. What two seventeenth-century artists inspired the debate in eighteenth-century France between the advocates of color and those of form as the most important element in painting?

   Color: Form:

   Which element did Watteau consider to be the most important?

17. List the characteristics of Watteau's *Return from Cythera* (FIG. 20-14) that are typical of Rococo art in general.

   a.

   b.

   c.

   d.

18. List three Baroque devices used by Boucher in *Cupid a Captive* (FIG. 20-15).

   a.

   b.

   c.

   In what ways does the painting differ from a Baroque composition such as Rubens' *Elevation of the Cross* (FIG. 19-38)?

19. In what type of subject matter did Rosalba Carriera and Quentin de la Tour specialize?

   What was their favorite medium?

20. From what social class did the majority of Chardin's patrons come?

   Why did his work appeal to them?

21. What stylistic feature did Hogarth borrow from continental Rococo artists?

   What type of subject matter did he portray?

DISCUSSION QUESTIONS

1. How did the patronage of the nobility and of the bourgeoisie affect eighteenth-century art? Which artists did each social class patronize? What type of subject matter did each prefer?

2. Discuss the influence of Palladian Classicism on eighteenth-century architecture.

3. How are social attitudes reflected by Versailles (FIGS. 19-66 to 19-70), the Amalienburg (FIGS. 20-7 and 20-8), Blenheim (FIG. 20-4), and Chiswick House (FIG. 20-5)?

4. Discuss the development of Italian ceiling painting by comparing the works of Mantegna (FIG. 16-65), Michelangelo (FIG. 17-25), Veronese (FIG. 17-69), Annibale Carracci (FIG. 19-23), Reni (FIG. 19-24), Guercino (FIG. 19-25), Pozzo (FIG. 19-32), and Tiepolo (FIG. 20-12).

5. Compare Fragonard's *The Swing* (FIG. 20-16) with Bronzino's *Venus, Cupid, Folly, and Time* (FIG. 17-44). Although both works have strong erotic overtones, they are very different in their emotional effects. What makes one Rococo and the other Mannerist?

6. What are the stylistic similarities between Asam's *Assumption of the Virgin* (FIG. 20-13) and Riemenschneider's version of the same subject (FIG. 18-29)? What are the differences? What makes Asam's version Baroque?

THE RISE OF ROMANTICISM   Text Pages 785–801

1. What values were stressed during the so-called "age of sensibility"?

   a.

   b.

   c.

2. What virtues were stressed during the revolutionary age?

   a.

   b.

3. What feeling was evoked by the "sublime" in art and nature for those possessing "Romantic sensibility"?

4. What is meant by the term "gothick"?

5. The shift from reason to feeling, from objective nature to subjective emotion, is characteristic of the attitude of mind known as _____.

6. In what sense can Neoclassicism be considered one of the aspects of the Romantic movement?

7. What is an important source of the informality of so-called "English gardens"?

8. What style did Walpole revive at Strawberry Hill (FIG. 20-21)?

9. Who was Johann Winckelmann? Why was he important to the development of art?

10. Neoclassicism was stimulated by the excavation of the Roman cities of _____ and _____ in the mid- _____ century.

11. List three eighteenth-century architects who worked in the Neoclassical style.

    a.   b.   c.

12. Name two buildings that apparently influenced Jefferson's designs for Monticello.

    a.   b.

13. List three characteristics of Clodion's late eighteenth-century sculptures.

    a.

    b.

    c.

14. How do Houdon's portraits differ from typical Rococo and Neoclassical works?

15. Although Gainsborough preferred to paint landscapes, he is best know for his _____.

16. The French painter Vigée-Lebrun specialized in _____ .

    In contrast to Rococo artificiality, the style of her self-portrait can be described as:

17. Although he espoused the Italian Baroque theory that "general" nature is always superior to "particular" nature, Reynolds' own portraits were often characterized by:

18. Name an American painter who was a pioneer in the Anglo-American school of history painting.

19. Sentimentality is an obvious trait of the work of the French painter _____ .

20. Angelica Kauffmann worked in the style called:

21. Which painter stressed his desire "to work in a pure Greek style," saying "I feed my eyes on ancient statues; I even have the intention of imitating some of them."?

22. What is the importance of the subject matter in the *Oath of the Horatii* (FIG. 20-38)?

    List at least two Neoclassical stylistic features that are found in this work.

    b.

23.   Whose *Pietà* seems to have influenced David's painting of *The Death of Marat*?

24.   Briefly describe the style of Flaxman.

25.   What type of subject matter was preferred by Flaxman's contemporary Fuseli?

26.   Who was William Blake?

27.   Piranesi worked primarily in the medium of _____.

His work combined _____ and _____.

DISCUSSION QUESTIONS

1.   Compare Greuze's *Return of the Prodigal Son* (FIG. 20-36) with Rembrandt's version of the same subject (FIG. 19-49). What emotional states does each composition depict? What devices has each artist used to create his effects? Which painting do you like better? Why?

2.   Discuss the changing tastes of eighteenth-century France by comparing Clodion's *Nymph and Satyr* (FIG. 20-28), Houdon's *Diana* (FIG. 20-29), David's *Oath of the Horatii* (FIG. 20-38), and Fuseli's *Nightmare* (FIG. 20-41).

3.   To what extent do you consider David's art to be propaganda? Do you believe that creating "propaganda" art is an appropriate activity for an artist? Why or why not?

4.   Compare West's *Death of General Wolfe* (FIG. 20-35) with El Greco's *Burial of Count Orgaz* (FIG. 18-61). What similarities and what differences do you see, both thematically and stylistically?

5.   Discuss the development of eighteenth-century architecture through a comparison of Juvara's Superga (FIG. 20-3), Vanbrugh's Blenheim Palace (FIG. 20-4), Neumann's Vierzehnheiligen (FIGS. 20-9, 20-10, 20-11), and Soufflot's Panthéon (FIG. 20-25).

6.   Among the other works you have studied, which do you feel are closest in spirit to Neumann's pilgrimage church of Vierzehnheiligen (FIGS. 20-9, 20-10, 20-11) and Asam's *Assumption of the Virgin* (FIG. 20-13)? Why?

SUMMARY: SEVENTEENTH- AND EIGHTEENTH-CENTURY ART   Text Pages 708–801

Fill in the following charts as much as possible from memory; then check your answers against the text in Chapters 19 and 20 and complete the charts.

HISTORICAL BACKGROUND

	Political Leaders and Events	Religious Orientation	Cultural and Scientific Developments
Italy			
Spain			
Flanders			
Holland			
France			
England			
Germany			

SUMMARY OF SEVENTEENTH-CENTURY PAINTING IN FLANDERS, HOLLAND, AND FRANCE

	Major Works	Country and Stylistic Characteristics
Rubens		
Van Dyck		
Van Honthorst		
Hals		
Rembrandt		
Vermeer		
Van Ruisdael		
Georges De la Tour		
Le Nain		
Poussin		
Claude Lorraine		

SUMMARY OF SEVENTEENTH-CENTURY PAINTING IN ITALY AND SPAIN

	Major Works	Country and Stylistic Characteristics
Annibale Carracci		
Reni		
Guercino		
Caravaggio		
Domenichino		
Gentileschi		
Pozzo		
Ribera		
Zurbarán		
Velázquez		

SUMMARY OF EIGHTEENTH-CENTURY PAINTING

	Major Works	Country and Stylistic Characteristics
Rigaud		
Tiepolo		
Watteau		
Boucher		
Fragonard		
Carriera		
Quentin De la Tour		
Chardin		
Hogarth		
Gainsborough		

SUMMARY OF EIGHTEENTH-CENTURY PAINTING (continued)

	Major Works	Country and Stylistic Characteristics
Vigée-Lebrun		
Reynolds		
West		
Kauffmann		
Greuze		
David		
Fuseli		
Flaxman		
Blake		
Piranesi		

SUMMARY OF SEVENTEENTH- AND EIGHTEENTH-CENTURY ARCHITECTURE

	Major Works (Give dates of buildings)	Country and Stylistic Characteristics
Maderno		
Bernini		
Borromini		
Guarini		
	Louvre:	
	Versailles:	
Jones		
Wren		
Juvara		
Vanbrugh		
Boyle and Kent		

SUMMARY OF SEVENTEENTH- AND EIGHTEENTH-CENTURY ARCHITECTURE (continued)

	Major Works (Give dates of buildings)	Country and Stylistic Characteristics
Boffrand		
Cuvilliés		
Neumann		
Walpole		
Soufflot		
Jefferson		

SUMMARY OF SEVENTEENTH- AND EIGHTEENTH-CENTURY SCULPTURE

	Major Works	Stylistic Characteristics	Country and Century
Bernini			
Puget			
Giradon			
Clodion			
Houdon			

SUMMARY: THE RENAISSANCE AND THE BAROQUE AND ROCOCO   Text Pages 520–801

ICONOGRAPHIC STUDY

While stylistic analysis tells us how a thing is represented, iconographic analysis helps us understand what is represented. Images of saints are usually identified by certain attributes that are associated with their particular story. Look at the representations of the following saints in Chapters 15 through 19 and briefly describe the way you would identify them in terms of their iconography.

St. Anthony

St. Catherine

David

St. Francis

St. George

Judith and Holofernes

Mary Magdalene

Moses

St. John the Baptist

St. Peter

St. Paul

St. Sebastian

St. Stephen

St. Theresa

Self-Quiz

PART FOUR: THE RENAISSANCE AND THE BAROQUE AND ROCOCO

I. **Matching.** Choose the identification in the right column that best corresponds to the term or name in the left column and enter the appropriate letter in the space provided.

_____ 1. Franciscans		a. soft, smoky modeling
_____ 2. tondo		b. "weight-shift" pose
_____ 3. baldacchino		c. monastic preaching order
_____ 4. Lorenzo de' Medici		d. extreme contrasts of light and dark
_____ 5. Giulio Romano		e. Florentine political leader and Humanist
_____ 6. chiaroscuro		f. High Renaissance pope
_____ 7. Girolamo Savonarola		g. a canopy with columns, often over an altar
_____ 8. Julius II		h. gradations of light and dark to produce the effect of modeling
_____ 9. St. Ignatius of Loyola		i. Mannerist architect
_____ 10. Ludovico Sforza		j. multi-paneled altarpiece
_____ 11. sfumato		k. Florentine monastic reformer
_____ 12. tenebrism		l. painting technique using no underpainting
_____ 13. triptych		m. German religious reformer
_____ 14. Martin Luther		n. a circular painting or relief sculpture
_____ 15. predella		o. three-paneled altarpiece
_____ 16. genre		p. founder of Jesuit order
_____ 17. Louis XIV		q. eighteenth-century style using Chinese motifs
_____ 18. Francis I		r. sixteenth-century French king
_____ 19. chinoiserie		s. a narrow panel at the bottom of an altarpiece
_____ 20. polyptych		t. northern painters using extreme light–dark contrasts of Caravaggio
_____ 21. alla prima		u. Duke of Milan
_____ 22. Baldassare Castiglione		v. scenes of everyday life
_____ 23. orthogonal		w. seventeenth-century French king
		x. a perspective line perpendicular to the picture plane
		y. Italian author of High Renaissance period

II. Matching. Choose the architect in the right column that corresponds to the building in the left column and enter the appropriate letter in the space provided.

_____ 24.	Villa Rotunda near Venice	a. Michelangelo
_____ 25.	Campidoglio, Rome	b. Jones
_____ 26.	Sant' Andrea, Mantua	c. Alberti
_____ 27.	Palazzo Rucellai, Florence	d. Brunelleschi
_____ 28.	Dome of Florence Cathedral	e. Neumann
_____ 29.	Palazzo del Tè, Mantua	f. Wren
_____ 30.	Tempietto, Rome	g. Perrault, Le Vau, and Le Brun
_____ 31.	Square Court of the Louvre, Paris	h. Le Vau and Mansart
_____ 32.	Scala Regia, Vatican	i. Palladio
_____ 33.	East façade of the Louvre, Paris	j. Giulio Romano
_____ 34.	San Carlo alle Quattro Fontane, Rome	k. Bernini
_____ 35.	Church of Vierzehnheiligen, near Bamberg	l. Lescot
_____ 36.	Pazzi Chapel, Florence	m. Borromini
_____ 37.	Palazzo Carignano, Turin	n. Guarini
_____ 38.	St. Ivo, Rome	o. Vanbrugh
_____ 39.	Banqueting House, Whitehall	p. Michelozzo

q. Giuliano da Sangallo
r. Giacomo della Porta and Vignola
s. Bramante
t. Maderno

III. Matching. Choose the artist in the right column that corresponds to the art work in the left column and enter the appropriate letter in the space provided.

_____ 40.	*Lamentation* (Arena Chapel)	a. Bernini
_____ 41.	*The Isenheim Altarpiece*	b. Michelangelo
_____ 42.	*The School of Athens*	c. Leonardo
_____ 43.	*The Ghent Altarpiece*	d. Rogier van der Weyden
_____ 44.	*The Garden of Earthly Delights*	e. Raphael
_____ 45.	Sistine Ceiling	f. Dürer
_____ 46.	*Las Meninas*	g. Ghiberti
_____ 47.	*The Ecstasy of St. Theresa*	h. Masaccio
_____ 48.	"Gates of Paradise"	i. Grünewald

j. Velázquez
k. Ribera
l. Bosch
m. Bruegel
n. Giotto
o. Donatello
p. Jan van Eyck
q. Rubens

IV. Multiple Choice. Circle the most appropriate answer.

49. Which of the following architects best exemplifies the principles of High Renaissance style? a. Guarini
b. Bramante   c. Brunelleschi   d. Borromini   e. Michelozzo

50. Which one of the following Dutch artists specialized in landscape? a. Hals   b. Van Honthorst   c. Van Ruisdael   d. Steen   e. Vermeer

51. "Bourgeois moralism" is most often found in the work of   a. Watteau   b. Greuze   c. Boucher   d. Velázquez   e. Bernini

52. The combination of Germanic and Italian characteristics is most apparent in the work of   a. Leonardo   b. Cranach   c. Bosch   d. Dürer   e. Grünewald

53. The counter-positioning of a figure about its central axis, with the weight of the body on one leg and with the other leg relaxed is called   a. chiaroscuro   b. contrapposto   c. condottiere   d. orthogonal   e. sfumato

54. Rococo artists most valued   a. disproportion and disturbed balance   b. magnificence and order   c. pyramidal composition and chiaroscuro   d. pleasure and delicacy   e. symmetry and balance

55. A painting using much gold, flat patterns, a high horizon line, elegant figure style, many details from nature, and curvilinear line would most likely be   a. High Renaissance   b. Early Renaissance   c. "proto-Renaissance"   d. International Gothic   e. Baroque

56. The paintings of Vermeer most often convey a feeling of   a. agitation   b. ostentation   c. serenity   d. pomposity   e. fury

57. Which of the following artists best exemplifies French Classical Baroque style?   a. Boucher   b. Poussin   c. Rigaud   d. Rubens   e. Watteau

58. In which of the following cities did Borromini build the majority of his buildings?   a. Rome   b. Florence   c. Paris   d. Venice   e. Milan

59. Rembrandt found the models for many of his religious paintings   a. among the Dutch militia   b. in the Jewish ghettoes   c. in older religious art   d. in local brothels   e. in extant Roman sculpture.

60. Most characteristic of seventeenth-century Dutch painting was that they were   a. commissioned by the aristocracy   b. commissioned by the church   c. painted to glorify military leaders   d. sold on the open market   e. scarce and hard to find

61. Which of the following is *least* characteristic of Baroque art?   a. dramatic use of light   b. emphasis on diagonal lines   c. calm, Classical figures   d. a reflection of the ideals of the Counter-Reformation   e. energy and complexity of design

62. Which is *least* characteristic of Baroque architecture?   a. three-part division of the façade   b. compact, centralized plan   c. emphasis on a grand central entrance   d. greater variation in the depth of wall surface   e. preference for rectangular and circular motifs

63. Developed as a reaction against the formality of Louis XIV, this court style is characterized by a light and delicate treatment of sensual subjects   a. Mannerism   b. Rococo   c. Classical Baroque   d. High Baroque   e. High Renaissance

64. Which building is located in Paris?   a. Palazzo Vecchio   b. Campidoglio   c. Louvre   d. Farnese Palace   e. St. Ivo

65. Oil painting was first used by the   a. fifteenth-century Flemish   b. fifteenth-century Florentines   c. sixteenth-century Venetians   d. fifteenth-century Germans   e. sixteenth-century Germans

66. Two versions of *The Virgin of the Rocks* were painted by   a. Botticelli   b. Leonardo   c. Raphael   d. Andrea del Sarto   e. Bellini

67. The frescoes in the Arena chapel were painted by   a. Masaccio   b. Michelangelo   c. Giotto   d. Duccio   e. Raphael

68. Which artist was commissioned to design a tomb for Julius II?   a. Donatello   b. Verrocchio   c. Michelangelo   d. Giovanni da Bologna   e. Bernini

69. A concern for realism, psychological portraiture, and emotional expression best describes the style of the   a. Italian "proto-Renaissance"   b. International Gothic   c. Italian High Renaissance   d. German Renaissance   e. Mannerism

70. Which of the following *least* characterizes the International Gothic style?   a. intricate ornamentation   b. rational perspective   c. splendid processions   d. uptilted ground plane   e. brilliant color and costuming

71. An important characteristic of much fifteenth-century Flemish art was the use of   a. linear perspective   b. disguised symbolism   c. contrapposto   d. sfumato   e. painterly brush strokes

72. The use of sfumato, full figures, psychological interpretation, and anatomical accuracy most correctly describes the work of   a. the Lorenzetti   b. El Greco   c. Leonardo   d. Duccio   e. Botticelli

73. Which of the following is *not* characteristic of High Renaissance figure painting?   a. slow, rhythmic movement   b. rational control   c. restrained gravity   d. balance and order   e. elongation and distortion

74. Which artist created paintings protesting the brutality of an occupying force in his country?   a. Jan van Eyck   b. Holbein   c. Cranach   d. Bruegel   e. Campin

75. The Limbourg brothers are known for their   a. frescoes   b. engravings   c. panel paintings   d. manuscript illuminations   e. woodcuts

76. Giotto's work is best classified as   a. Italian High Renaissance   b. fifteenth-century Flemish   c. International Gothic   d. Italian proto-Renaissance   e. Mannerist

77. An important Mannerist painter was   a. Botticelli   b. Ghirlandaio   c. Andrea del Sarto   d. Parmigianino   e. Correggio

78. Which of the following Baroque painters did *not* do frescoed ceilings?   a. Pozzo   b. Guercino   c. Caravaggio   d. Reni   e. Annibale Carracci

79. The major part of El Greco's work was done in: a. Greece   b. Italy   c. Netherlands   d. France   e. Spain

80. Which of the following architects did *not* take part in the building of St. Peter's or its piazza?   a. Bramante   b. Michelangelo   c. Maderno   d. Bernini   e. Borromini

V.   Chronological Chart. Fill in the names of the major architects, painters, and sculptors in the following charts by country of origin and the century in which they did the major part of their work.

13th–14th Centuries	15th Century	16th Century
_____	_____	_____
_____	_____	_____
_____	_____	_____
_____	_____	_____
_____	_____	_____
_____	_____	_____
_____	_____	_____
	_____	_____
	_____	_____
	_____	_____
	_____	_____
	_____	_____

Italy

	13th–14th Centuries	15th Century	16th Century
Flanders (Netherlands)	_____	_____ _____ _____ _____ _____	_____ _____ _____ _____
Germany		_____ _____ _____ _____	_____ _____ _____ _____
France		_____	_____ _____ _____ _____

	17th Century	18th Century
Italy	_____ _____ _____ _____ _____ _____ _____	_____ _____ _____ _____

	17th Century	**18th Century**
France	_____ _____ _____ _____ _____ _____	_____ _____ _____ _____ _____ _____
Holland	_____ _____ _____ _____ _____ _____	
Flanders (Belgium)	_____ _____	
Spain	_____ _____ _____ _____	_____
England	_____ _____	_____ _____
Germany		_____ _____

VI.   Identification.

81.   Compare the two pictures of the Virgin Madonna below, attributing each to an artist, country, century, and
style. Give the reasons for your attributions.

Artist: _____

Country: _____

Century: _____

Style: _____

Artist: _____   Country: _____

Century: _____   Style: _____

Reasons:

82. Compare the plan and photograph of a building below, attributing it to an artist, country, century, and style. Give the reasons for your attributions.

Artist: _____

Century: _____

Country: _____

Style: _____

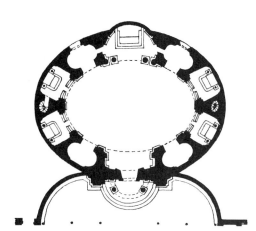

Reasons:

83.   These two very different interpretations of the sky were painted in the same century but in different countries. Attribute these paintings to a century and assign a country to each. Describe the artistic concerns that link these paintings to the same period as well as the differences between them. How might these differences have been affected by the patrons for whom the artists worked?

Century: _____

A. Country: _____

B. Country: _____

Describe the similarities and differences of these paintings below.

84.   Compare the two paintings below, attributing each to an artist, country, and century. How do these paintings illustrate the different approaches to the use of light that characterize the works of these two artists?

A. Artist: _____

    Country: _____

    Century: _____

B. Artist: _____

    Country: _____

    Century: _____

Describe below the different approaches to the use of light in these paintings.

85. Compare the two sculptures below, attributing each to an artist, country, century, and style. Give the reasons for your attributions.

A. Artist: _____

    Country: _____

    Century: _____

    Style: _____

B. Artist: _____

    Country: _____

    Century: _____

    Style: _____

Reasons:

PART FIVE: THE MODERN WORLD

Chapter Twenty-one

The Nineteenth Century:
Pluralism of Style

Text Pages 806–85

THE FIRST HALF OF THE NINETEENTH CENTURY   Text Pages 808–35

1. What was the "doctrine of Progress"?

    What values did many fear might be lost to such a doctrine?

2. Who were the major patrons of artists in the nineteenth century?

3. What two general directions can be identified within the welter of nineteenth-century styles?

    a.

    b.

4. List three nineteenth-century innovations that drastically affected the artist as producer of unique pictures.

    a.   c.

    b.

5. List four of the social attitudes inherent to the Romantic view of life.

    a.

    b.

    c.

    d.

6. What can be considered to be the most central conviction of the Romantics?

7. List four sources of subject matter that were favored by Romantic artists.

    a.   c.

    b.   d.

8. What was the original purpose of La Madeleine?

    What are its primary stylistic features?

9. What style did Barry and Pugin use for the rebuilding of the Houses of Parliament in London?

10. What style did Nash use for the Royal Pavilion in Brighton?

11. List three features that the Paris Opéra (FIG. 21-4) shares with the east façade of the Louvre (FIG. 19-65).

    a.

    b.

    c.

12. Which aspect of Canova's portrait of *Pauline Borghese as Venus* (FIG. 21-5) comes from earlier Rococo style?

    Which aspect is realistic?

    Which features are Neoclassical?

13. List three Baroque stylistic features reflected in Rude's *"La Marseillaise."*

    a.

    b.

    c.

14. Goya's work cannot be confined to a single stylistic classification. Briefly summarize his varied concerns as expressed in the following works:

    "The Dream of Reason" (FIG. 20-44):

    The Family of Charles IV (FIG. 21-9):

    The Third of May, 1808 (FIG. 21-10):

    Saturn Devouring His Children (FIG. 21-12):

15. In what respects does Gros' *Pest House at Jaffa* (FIG. 21-14) differ stylistically from David's *Oath of the Horatii* (FIG. 20-38)?

    a.

    b.

    c.

16. Name three artists whose influence can be seen in Géricault's *Raft of the Medusa* (FIG. 21-15).

    a.   b.   c.

17. For Géricault, suffering and death, frenzy, and madness are characteristic of _____.

18. What qualities of mind did Delacroix most admire?

    a.   b.   c.

    List three adjectives that describe his technique.

    a.   b.   c.

19. Write down one of Delacroix's observations on the way to apply color to the canvas.

20. In breaking with David, Ingres adopted a manner that he felt was based on true and pure Greek style. Two characteristics of this style are:

a.

b.

21. Who said "Drawing is the probity of art"?

22. Name two Renaissance artists whose influence is apparent in Ingres's *Grande Odalisque* (FIG. 21-22).

a.   b.

23. Define *epigones*.

24. Which characteristic of Ingres' style did Chassériau utilize in *Esther Adorning Herself* (FIG. 21-26)?

Which feature did he adopt from Delacroix?

25. What is the allegorical reference of Couture's *Romans of the Decadence* (FIG. 21-27)?

26. Briefly describe the new type of "history painting" that developed in the nineteenth century.

Name two nineteenth-century artists who specialized in it.

a.   b.

27. What did Daguerre invent?

How did artists generally react to his invention?

28. What other art form is most closely linked to the approach of English artists to landscape painting?

29. Who was John Ruskin?

30. What features of Turner's work were most influential in liberating painting from the so-called "Tradition"?

a.

b.

31. Constable felt that painters should be _____ as well as poetic. How did he create the sparkling shimmer of light seen in so many of his landscape paintings?

32.   To what group did Cole belong?

How did his own work differ from that of his fellow members?

33.   What was the significance of landscape painting for Runge?

34.   What did Friedrich believe that the artist should paint?

DISCUSSION QUESTIONS

1.   How does each of the following artists appear to view the Classical past: David in the *Oath of the Horatii* (FIG. 20-38); Poussin in *Et in Arcadia Ego* (FIG. 19-61); Couture in *Romans of the Decadence* (FIG. 21-27); Gérôme in *Thumbs Down!* (FIG. 21-28); and Cole's *The Course of Empire*: *Desolation* (FIG. 21-31)?

2.   Compare Ingres' *Grande Odalisque* (FIG. 21-22) with Titian's *Venus of Urbino* (FIG. 17-63); note composition, body type and distortion, and degrees of idealization.

3.   How do Ingres' and Delacroix's portraits of *Paganini* (FIGS. 21-24 and 21-25) typify each artist's approach to his subject?

4.   Why is *The Burial of Atala* (FIG. 21-13) considered to be quintessentially Romantic? How did Girodet's concerns differ from those of David and Delacroix?

5.   Do you think there are remnants of Romanticism alive today in our society? If so, can you identify them? How are they reflected in the arts? What film that you have seen recently best embodies the ideas of Romanticism? What artist working today would you consider to be Romantic?

6.   Is there such a thing as a "contemporary Classicism" in the arts? If so, what artist would you put in that category and why?

7.   Look for examples of "revival" architecture in your community and try to find at least one example each of Gothic and Classical revival buildings to share with your class. Be prepared to explain the architectural features that identify each as a Neo-Gothic or Neoclassical building.

8.   Discuss the difference in approach to landscape painting of Van Ruisdael (FIG. 19-57), Claude Lorraine (FIG. 19-63), Turner (FIG. 21-29), Constable (FIG. 21-30), Cole (FIG. 21-31), Runge (FIG. 21-32), and Friedrich (FIG. 21-33). How was Schelling's definition of the transcendent role of the artist (see text page 834) expressed by each?

THE SECOND HALF OF THE NINETEENTH CENTURY   Text Pages 836-85

1.   What was the primary focus of the mid-nineteenth-century debate between the proponents of "Realism" and those of "Romanticism"?

2.   The Realists believed that the only suitable subjects for artists to depict were:

3. What is the "paradox of Realism" found in the work of Manet and the Impressionists?

4. Which aspect of Corot's work points toward Impressionism?

5. Identify the Barbizon School.

6. Although Daumier did many fine paintings, he is primarily known for his work in the medium of _____ _____.

7. Name two artists who were concerned principally with the realistic portrayal of the working classes.

   a.   b.

8. Give Courbet's definition of the art of painting.

   What aspect of Courbet's painting is essentially traditional?

   What aspects are "new"?

9. *Le Déjeuner sur l'herbe* (FIG. 21-39), the painting that caused such a scandal at the Salon des Refusés of 1863, was painted by _____.

   Which aspects of the picture shocked the public?

   What was the artist's major concern when he painted the work?

10. What was Manet's major concern in the *Bar at the Folies-Bergère* (FIG. 21-41)?

In what ways does his handling of the picture surface differ radically from past practice?

11. How did the American public receive Eakins' *Gross Clinic* (FIG. 21-42)?

How would Eakins' approach to his art best be characterized?

12. List artists from each of the following countries who adhered to the Realists' credo of depicting modern scenes in a realistic manner;

United States:

France:

England:

Germany:

Russia:

13. Name an English artist who tried to apply the Realistic style to fictional and historical subjects.

14. List three of the concerns that were shared by the men who formed the Pre-Raphaelite Brotherhood.

a.

b.

c.

15. List three adjectives that best describe the style of Burne-Jones.

a.   b.   c.

16. The German painter Feuerbach found his inspiration in the art of the _____ and

_____.

17. Why was Pierre Puvis de Chavannes accepted by the art establishment?

Why was he admired by the avant-garde?

18. In what way do the Classical figures painted by Bouguereau differ from those painted by Puvis?

19. What earlier style seems to have influenced Bonheur's monumental *Horse Fair* (FIG. 21-53)?

20. Which styles converge in Bastien-Lepage's *Joan of Arc* (FIG. 21-54)?

21. In the nineteenth century, the art style concerned almost exclusively with purely visual sensations is known as _____.

22. Name five Impressionist painters.

    a.

    b.

    c.

    d.

    e.

23. During what two decades did the Impressionists hold cooperative exhibitions?

24. List four characteristics of Impressionism.

    a.

    b.

    c.

    d.

25. How did Degas' concerns differ from those of the other Impressionists?

26. What features of Japanese prints did the Impressionists admire?

    a.

    b.

    c.

In what ways does Degas' work show the influence of Japanese prints?

a.

b.

c.

27. What were Cassat's favorite subjects?

With which group did she regularly exhibit?

28. In what way did the Impressionists continue the Romantic preoccupation with the self of the artist?

29. Name four major Post-Impressionist painters.

a.

b.

c.

d.

What aspects of Impressionism did they criticize?

How are these criticisms reflected in the oeuvre of each of the artists you named?

a.

b.

c.

d.

30. Define the following terms:

    divisionism

    pointillism

31. What features did Seurat adapt from Renaissance formalists like Ucello and Piero della Francesca?
    a.

    b.

32. Who said, "I want to make of Impressionism something solid and lasting like the art in the museums"?

33. What two roles does color play in Cézanne's paintings?
    a.

    b.

34. For Van Gogh, the primary purpose of color in his paintings was:

    How did Van Gogh apply paint to his canvas? What type of effect does his application of paint produce?

35. How did Gauguin's use of color differ from Van Gogh's?

36. Where did Gauguin spend the last ten years of his life?

37. Briefly describe Toulouse-Lautrec's approach in his subjects.

    How does his style emphasize this approach?

38. In what year did the manifesto of literary Symbolism appear? in what city?

39. What did the Symbolist artists consider to be their primary task?

40. Who were the Nabis?

41. List three stylistic characteristics of the work of Moreau.

    a.

    b.

    c.

42. According to Redon, his originality consisted in:

43. Name three painters whose harsh colors and distorted forms express the *fin-de-siècle* malaise.

    a.   b.   c.

44. By the end of the nineteenth century, what three major changes had occurred in the artist's vision of reality?

    a.

    b.

    c.

45. As painters around the turn of the century moved away from the portrayal of the optical world of common experience, which two media preserved that concern?

    a.   b.

46. What style did Saint-Gaudens utilize for his monument to Mrs. Henry Adams?

47. Which stylistic influences are most evident in the sculpture of Carpeaux?

48. Name two earlier sculptors whose work influenced Rodin's style.

    a.   b.

In what major ways did his work differ from theirs?

Which aspects of Rodin's work can be described as Impressionistic?

Which can be described as Expressionistic?

49. Describe the effect of the use of iron on nineteenth-century architectural structure.

50. Which characteristics of Sullivan's buildings earned for him the title of "the first truly modern architect"?

51. Who designed the Peacock Room?

What styles influenced its design?

DISCUSSION QUESTIONS

1. Compare Daumier's *Rue Transnonain* (FIG. 21-36) with Goya's *Third of May, 1808* (FIG. 21-10). David's *Oath of the Horatii* (FIG. 20-38), and Delacroix's *Liberty Leading the People* (FIG. 21-19). What is the style and the social message of each? Which do you feel is the most effective? Why?

2. Compare Manet's *Le Déjeuner sur l'herbe* (FIG. 21-39) with Giorgione's (and/or Titian's) *Pastoral Symphony* (FIG. 17-60). In what ways are they similar? In what ways are they different?

3. What characteristics does Courbet share with the Impressionists? In what ways does he differ significantly from them? Should the Impressionists be considered Realists?

4. Realism in art raises some deep questions about the nature of art. Why can we say one photograph looks more like a person than another one does? Is it because one photo captures what we see as the real essence of the person? Does it focus our attention on some essential quality and eliminate others we consider accidental? Can we say a photographer or an artist who does a good portrait has only *underlined* something *in* nature? Or has the photographer or artist *added* something *to* nature? Take these general questions at a more concrete level. Is the man who exhibits himself as a work of art really creating a work of art? Con-

versely, is the dummy in the wax museum really a work of art? Finally what are the essential differences between life and art, art and life?

5. Compare Cézanne's still life (FIG. 21-65) with Kalf's (FIG. 19-56); note differences in composition, the treatment of color, painting technique, and distortion of form.

6. Compare Seurat's *Sunday Afternoon on the Island of La Grande Jatte* (FIG. 21-64) with Renoir's *Le Moulin de la Galette* (FIG. 21-57) and Piero della Francesca's *The Proving of the True Cross* (FIG. 16-35). What characteristics does Seurat's painting share with each?

7. Discuss briefly the development of art theory from the Renaissance through the end of the nineteenth century. Consider how Alberti, Poussin, Delacroix, Ingres, Courbet, and Cézanne might have reacted to Picasso's statement: "Nature and art, being two different things, cannot be the same thing. Through art we express our conception of what nature is not."

8. Discuss the significant contribution made by each of the major Post-Impressionists. In what ways are their works a continuation of historical artistic traditions?

9. In what sense is the slogan "form follows function" accurate or inaccurate as a summary description of most of today's architecture? For examples in probing this question consider buildings in your own community. As esthetic ideals, are functionality and beauty in basic agreement or in basic opposition? Why?

SUMMARY: THE NINETEENTH CENTURY   Text Pages 806–85

Fill in the following charts as much as possible from memory; then check your answers against the text and complete the charts.

STYLISTIC SUMMARY OF NINETEENTH-CENTURY ART

	Painters	Sculptors	Characteristics of the Style	Influential Historical and Cultural Factors
Romanticism				
Neoclassicism				
Academicism				
Realism				
Impressionism				
Post-Impressionism				
Fin-de-Siècle Period				

SUMMARY OF NINETEENTH-CENTURY PAINTING

	Major Works	Country and Stylistic Characteristics
Goya		
Gros		
Géricault		
Delacroix		
Ingres		
Turner		
Constable		
Cole		
Friedrich		
Corot		

SUMMARY OF NINETEENTH-CENTURY PAINTING (continued)

	Major Works	Country and Stylistic Characteristics
Daumier		
Courbet		
Manet		
Eakins		
Repin		
Homer		
Millais		
Pierre Puvis de Chavannes		
Bouguereau		
Bonheur		
Monet		
Pissarro		

SUMMARY OF NINETEENTH-CENTURY PAINTING (continued)

	Major Works	Country and Stylistic Characteristics
Renoir		
Degas		
Cassatt		
Seurat		
Cézanne		
Van Gogh		
Gauguin		
Toulouse-Lautrec		
Ensor		
Munch		
Rousseau		

SUMMARY OF NINETEENTH-CENTURY ARCHITECTURE

Building	Architect(s)	Country and Date	Style	Description
La Madeleine, Paris:				
Houses of Parliament, London:				
Royal Pavilion, Brighton:				
The Opéra, Paris				
Reading Room, Bibliothèque Ste.-Geneviève, Paris:				
Crystal Palace, London:				
Galerie Des Machines, Paris:				
Marshall Field Warehouse, Chicago:				
Guaranty Building, Buffalo:				

SUMMARY OF NINETEENTH-CENTURY SCULPTURE

	Major Works	Country and Stylistic Characteristics
Canova		
Greenough		
Rude		
Barye		
Saint-Gaudens		
Préault		
Carpeaux		
Rodin		

Chapter Twenty-two

The Twentieth Century

PAINTING BEFORE WORLD WAR II   Text Pages 888–917

1. Did Freud's discoveries underscore the Romantic or the Classical humanistic view of man's nature? How?

2. What did Paul Klee feel was the task of the artist?

3. Explain the phrase *épater le bourgeois.*

4. From what sources did the Symbolists draw their themes?

5. What stylistic characteristics did Klimt share with other Symbolist painters?
    a.

    b.

    c.

6. In their reaction to industrialization and mass production, artists working in the Art Nouveau style drew inspiration from:
    a.

    b.

7. In what year was the exhibition held in which the name "Fauve" was coined?

8. Describe the characteristics that Fauve paintings have in common.

   a.

   b.

9. Name two Fauve painters.

   a.   b.

10. What were *Die Brücke* and *Der Blaue Reiter*?

11. List four characteristics that German Expressionism shared with earlier German art.

    a.

    b.

    c.

    d.

12. Name three German Expressionists whose work expresses terror and indignation.

    a.   b.   c.

    Name one who expresses a mood of pity and concern for the poor.

13. By what year had Kandinsky developed abstract art?

14. What qualities and values did Kandinsky attribute to color in his treatise, *Concerning the Spiritual in Art*?

15. The Post-Impressionist painter who most strongly influenced the movements known as Cubism and Constructivism was:

    What aspect of his theory and practice became the chief concern of the Cubists?

16. Name two probable sources of the dislocation of form seen in Picasso's *Les Demoiselles d'Avignon* (FIG. 22-12).

    a.

    b.

17. What is the basis of Cubist pictorial space? How does it differ from Renaissance perspective?

18. Define *collage*.

19. How does "synthetic" Cubism differ from "analytic" Cubism?

    a.

    b.

20. What characteristic best distinguishes Braque's Cubist works from those of Picasso?

21. Which of the Cubists was most interested in the depiction of modern urban life?

22. The Cubist shattering of Renaissance space was influential in the development of a number of twentieth-century styles. Name two of them.

    a.   b.

23. What were the Futurists trying to express in their art?

24. What other art form influenced Duchamp's *Nude Descending a Staircase #Z* (FIG. 22-19)?

25. What basic colors and forms characterize Mondrian's mature work?

26. In contrast to Mondrian's geometric severity, O'Keeffe's approach to abstraction can be characterized as:

27. What did Malevich name his nonobjective style?

28. What was the original purpose of the Dada movement?

Although short-lived, Dada had important consequences for later art. What were they?

29.   Name two artists connected with the Dada movement.

a.   b.

30.   Who was the major practitioner of the style known as *pittura metafisica*?

31.   According to André Breton, what was the purpose of the Surrealist movement?

32.   According to the authors, the distinction between abstract and nonobjective art is:

33.   Name three painters connected with the Surrealist movement.

a.   b.   c.

34.   Name two major artists of the twentieth century who dealt primarily with fantasy but were not members of the Surrealist group.

a.   b.

35.   How are Carl Jung's theories related to the art of Klee?

36.   The theme of the murals that Orozco executed at Dartmouth College is:

37.   What is the dominant mood of Hopper's *Eleven A.M.* (FIG. 22-34)?

Which features of the painting create that mood?

DISCUSSION QUESTIONS

1. It has been said that the Renaissance died in the holocaust of World War I. Explain why you agree or disagree with that statement. What are some of the factors other than the war that have contributed to the changed conception of the world presented by many twentieth-century artists?

2. Can you relate the works of art studied in this chapter to the proposition that "meaning," "truth," and "reality" are now considered to be only relative, not absolute concepts?

3. Relate Maurice Denis' statement that "a picture before being a war horse, a nude woman, or some anecdote, is essentially a plane surface covered with colors assembled in a certain order" to the paintings you have studied in this chapter. Does his view differ from the traditional one regarding the meaning and purpose of a painting? How? Do you think Social Realists would agree with Maurice Denis? Surrealists? Who then would agree with him?

4. Compare Klimt's *Death and Life* (FIG. 22-1) with El Greco's *Burial of Count Orgaz* (FIG. 18-61); note the differences in composition, handling of surface, space, color, and the distortion of form. What world view is represented by each composition?

5. Discuss the different conceptions of Renaissance and Cubist space.

6. If you equate "Classical" with rational/objective and "Romantic" with emotional/subjective, which twentieth-century approaches to art (e.g., Expressionism, Cubism, Surrealism, etc.) would you consider to be essentially "Classical" and which "Romantic?" Why?

7. Discuss the role of chance in both the Dada and Surrealist movements. What connection do you see between the Dada movement and art movements today?

8. What did Mondrian mean when he wrote: "Cubism did not accept the logical consequences of its own discoveries . . ."?

SCULPTURE AND ARCHITECTURE BEFORE WORLD WAR II   Text Pages 918–36

1. How did Maillol's sculptural style differ from that of Rodin?

   a.

   b.

   c.

2. Name one sculptor who was strongly influenced by the Expressionist aspect of Rodin's work.

   What became characteristic of his style?

3. What twentieth-century German sculptor was influenced by the forms of Medieval art?

4. Name two Cubist sculptors.

   a.   b.

5. Name one Futurist sculptor.

6. What basic shape did Brancuşi believe was "the most natural?

7. Define *biomorphic abstraction*.

8. Gonzalez's primary contribution to the development of modern sculpture was:

9. In what country did Constructivism develop?

    An outstanding representative of that movement was _____ , who was influenced by

    _____.

10. List three new materials used by Gabo.

    a.   b.   c.

11. Who invented mobiles?

12. Name the artist who first selected common objects, which he called "ready-mades," and exhibited them as art.

13. Who worked with Duchamp to introduce Dada to America in 1921?

14. What attitudes did Dada bequeath to contemporary artists?

15. List three characteristics of the sculpture of Moore.

    a.

    b.

    c.

16. How does Giacometti's sculpture differ from that of Moore?

17. What two factors helped revolutionize architecture in the twentieth century?

    a.

    b.

18. Name two architects who were influenced by the forms of Art Nouveau.

    a.   b.

19. How was Wright's concern for "organic" form reflected in his buildings?

    a.

    b.

    c.

20. What are "curtain" walls?

    What makes their construction possible?

21. Define the following terms:
    reinforced concrete

    prestressed concrete

    cantilever

    functionalism (in architecture)

22. List three major principles of International style architecture.

    a.

    b.

    c.

23. Who defined a "functional" house as a "machine for living"?

24. How does Le Corbusier's Villa Savoye (FIG. 22-61) differ from the houses designed by Frank Lloyd Wright (FIGS. 22-57 and 22-62)?

a.

b.

c.

25. Identify The Bauhaus.

Who founded it?

Who was its post-World War I director?

What did its curriculum emphasize?

26. What feature does Gropius' Bauhaus building share with earlier Classical architecture?

27. List three characteristics of Mies van der Rohe's architectural style.

a.

b.

c.

28. What effect did the mechanical control of the interior environment have on the style of twentieth-century buildings?

DISCUSSION QUESTIONS

1. Compare Brancuși's *Bird in Space* (FIG. 22-45) with Oldenburg's *Clothespin* (FIG. 22-100). In what ways are the forms similar, and in what ways are they different? How does each artist explain the techniques and goals of his art?

2. If you compare Boccioni's *Unique Forms of Continuity in Space* (FIG. 22-44) with the *Nike of Samothrace* (FIG. 5-76), as the authors suggest, what really are the basic differences of the two sculptures?

3. Compare the use of mass, space, and decorative detail in the Villa Rotunda (FIG. 17-52), the Chiswick House (FIG. 20-5), the Villa Savoye (FIG. 22-61), and the Kaufmann House (FIG. 22-62). Which do you like best? Why?

4. Why was Constructivism banned in Russia? Do you think the ban was good or bad for the development of Russian art? Why?

5. One reason for the stylistic similarity of International-style buildings, whether erected in Brasilia, Tokyo, Paris, or New York, is the architects' dependence on intricate machinery to control the interior climates of their buildings. Do you feel that increasing reliance on complex technology is still justified in view of dwindling energy sources and the threat of accompanying economic and social upheavals throughout the world? What practical alternatives, if any, do you see?

6. What attitudes toward the relationship between the human being and society are expressed in the figural groupings by Giacometti (FIG. 22-54) and Rodin (FIG. 21-82)? Could you consider either or both to reflect Romantic attitudes? Why?

PAINTING, SCULPTURE, AND ARCHITECTURE AFTER WORLD WAR II   Text Pages 936–75

1. As twentieth-century artists rejected most of the values that underlay traditional art expressions, they retained the value of the artistic expression itself. What impact has this had on twentieth-century art?

2. According to what two fundamental principles have the authors attempted to order and classify the numerous currents in twentieth-century art?

3. Fear and an almost insane terror are visible in the portrait of Pope Innocent X by:

    Although the work is figural, the painting techniques are derived from:

4. Which European artist who taught in America most influenced the development of American Abstract Expressionism?

    Against what artistic trends did Abstract Expressionism rebel?

5. The emphasis on process rather than structure is most important in a type of painting known as _____

    _____.

    Who was an outstanding practitioner of this art form?

6. Name three New York Abstract Expressionists and briefly characterize the style of each.

    a.

    b.

    c.

    How does Andrew Wyeth's style differ from theirs?

    What does he share with them?

7. What style is favored in the Soviet Union and the People's Republic of China?

    What, for them, is the purpose of art?

8. When was the Armory show held and what was its importance?

9. Name one American painter who was strongly influenced by Cubism.

10. What is Post-Painterly Abstraction?

    Some of its "allied manifestations" are:

11. What features of Newman's work were important for artists of the 1960s?

12. Name one artist who worked in what is known as Color-Field painting.

13. Name a painter who worked in the style called Op Art.

14. Name two sculptors who worked primarily with welded metals in the post-World War II period.

    a.   b.

15. What sort of meaning did Smith want his sculptures to convey?

16. For many years Nevelson worked primarily in the medium of _____,

    using a technique of _____.

17. In works like the cubes illustrated in FIG. 22-82, Judd asserts his doctrine of:

18. Like Judd, Bladen and other artists of the "Minimal" School sought to create an art that:

19. Name one sculptor who is a major representative of the movement known as Earth Art.

20. What is Kinetic Art?

    Describe the difference between Calder's and Bury's approach to Kinetic Art.

21. What was Tinguely's *Homage to New York* (FIG. 22-86) intended to do?

22. What did Lawrence Alloway mean by the name "Pop Art"?

23. What subject matter was characteristic of Pop Art of the 1960s?

24. What are "combine paintings"?

    Who developed them?

What distinguishes Rauschenberg's works from those of the Dadaists of the 1920s?

25. John's *Painted Bronze* (FIG. 22-89) is similar in many ways to the "ready mades" first exhibited by:

26. How does New Realism differ from traditional Realism?

27. What is the basic claim of Process Art?

of Conceptual Art?

28. What is Christo's primary medium?

29. "Modernism" is now being defined as a style. List three of its axioms.
     a.

     b.

     c.

30. Briefly characterize the aims of Post-Modernist art.

31. What medium does Schnabel use?

     How does his use of it differ from that of earlier artists?

32. List two artists of the 1980s who use news photographs as prime sources for their works, and briefly characterize the style of each.

    a.   b.

33. Describe the effect produced by Oldenburg's Clothespin.

34. List two contemporary works that were designed to be exhibited briefly, then dismantled.

    a.

    b.

    What do you think is the purpose of such work?

35. In the appropriate columns below, list the twentieth-century artists and/or movements that you feel best epitomize the poles of Romantic/subjective and Classical/formalist art that we have been studying.

    Romantic/subjective   Classical/formalist

    a.   a.

    b.   b.

    c.   c.

    d.   d.

    e.   e.

    f.   f.

36. List one building by each of the following architects that seems to fuse the principles of sculpture with those of architecture.

    Le Courbusier:

    Wright:

    Saarinen:

37. Name the three twentieth-century architects whom the authors consider to be "pioneers of an architecture free of reference to earlier architectural styles.

    a.   b.   c.

38. What revolutionary structural system is exploited by Otto in the roof of the Olympic Stadium in Munich (FIG. 22-112)?

How does it differ from traditional structural principles?

What are its advantages?

39. What structural system did Birkerts use in his tower in Minneapolis (FIG. 22-113)?

What effect did it have on the space below and around the building?

40. What modern industrial concept found experimental application in Habitat (FIG. 22-114) at Montreal's Expo '67?

Who was its architect?

41. Who designed the new East Building of the National Gallery in Washington, D.C. (FIG. 22-115)?

How did he deal with the irregular site?

42. What earlier building does the Paris "Beaubourg" (FIG. 22-117) recall?

How are the functional aspects of the "Beaubourg" handled?

43. List three sources for Venturi's eclectic Brant-Johnson House (FIG. 22-119) in Vail Colorado.
    a.

    b.

    c.

44. What value is shared by so-called Post-Modernist architects?

45. Why are International-style buildings not energy-efficient?

46. Describe the energy-conserving system used in Duke's design of a state office building in Sacramento, California.

47. What were the primary purposes of Moore's Piazza d' Italia (FIG. 22-121)?

48. List four of the historical references found in the piazza.

    a.

    b.

    c.

    d.

    In what way will the architecture of the future resemble that of the Gothic period?

DISCUSSION QUESTIONS

1. Can you relate Bladen's *X* (FIG. 22-83) and Tinguely's *Homage to New York* (FIG. 22-86) to the earlier traditions of Classical and Romantic art? How?

2. Compare Hamilton's *Just What Is It That Makes Today's Homes So Different, So Appealing?* (FIG. 22-87) with Campin's *Mérode Altarpiece* (FIG. 18-6). Discuss the compositional structure and the symbolism of both works, along with their cultural meanings.

3. Compare Estes' *Nedick's* (FIG. 22-93) with Léger's *City* (FIG. 22-18) and Monet's *Rouen Cathedral* (FIG. 21-55). What similarities and what differences do you see?

4. What observations on the life and society of their time do you think Kienholz and Ghirlandaio were making in *Birthday* (FIG. 22-92) and *The Birth of the Virgin* (FIG. 16-57)?

5. Discuss the effects of mass production and financial speculation on the role of the artist in the twentieth-century world.

6. Discuss the use of modular measurement in the architecture of Le Corbusier and Alberti. Is one the revival of the other? What relationships do you see between the Palazzo Rucellai (FIG. 16-39) and the Unité de'Habitation (FIG. 22-104)? or between the designs for Sant' Andrea in Mantua (FIGS. 16-42, 16-43, 16-44) and Notre Dame du Haut at Ronchamp (FIGS. 22-105 and 22-106)?

7. If it is true that resources and talent are invested in those undertakings that a society values most, what do the types of buildings we have studied from different periods say about the social values of the people who commissioned and built them? You might wish to select one building from each of the architectural survey charts you did at the end of the various chapters.

8. Recently, the International style, which has dominated the architecture of the past fifty years, seems to have fallen into disfavor. What criticisms have been leveled against it? Are they justified? What are some possible alternatives?

9. Compare the structural techniques used by the Roman architects of the Baths of Caracalla (FIG. 6-55) and Beauvais Cathedral (FIG. 10-30) with those used by contemporary architects like Nervi (FIG. 22-109), Otto (FIG. 22-112), and Birkerts (FIG. 22-113). Which creates the greatest effect of mass? Which creates the greatest effect of lightness?

10. Compare the urban dwellings constructed by the ancient Romans (FIGS. 6-24 and 6-25) with those constructed by Le Corbusier (FIG. 22-104), Mies van der Rohe (FIG. 22-103), and Safdie (FIG. 22-114). Where would you rather live? Why?

11. Some recent trends in contemporary architecture have been called "Baroque." Who are the main representatives of these trends? What are their stylistic features?

SUMMARY: THE TWENTIETH CENTURY   Text Pages 886–975

Fill in the following charts as much as possible from memory; then check your answers against the text and complete the charts.

SUMMARY OF TWENTIETH-CENTURY ART MOVEMENTS

	Painters	Sculptors	Characteristics of the Style	Influential Historical and Cultural Factors
Symbolism				
Art Nouveau				
The Fauves				
Expressionism				
Cubism				
Futurism				
De Stijl				

SUMMARY OF TWENTIETH-CENTURY ART MOVEMENTS (continued)

	Painters	Sculptors	Characteristics of the Style	Influential Historical and Cultural Factors
Suprematism				
Dada				
Surrealism				
Constructivism				
Pittura Metafisica				
Social Realism				
Abstract Expressionism				

SUMMARY OF TWENTIETH-CENTURY ART MOVEMENTS (continued)

	Painters	Sculptors	Stylistic Characteristics	Influential Historical and Cultural Factors
New Realism				
Abstract Formalism (Minimal Art, Earth Art, etc.)				
Op Art				
Kinetic Art				
Pop Art				
Post-Modernism				

TWENTIETH-CENTURY ARCHITECTURE

	Style and Country	Major Buildings and Dates	Characteristics
Horta			
Gaudí			
Wright			
Le Corbusier			
Rietveldt			
Gropius			
Mies van der Rohe			
Nervi			
Saarinen			
Otto			
Birkerts			
Safdie			
Pei			
Johnson			
Venturi			

Self-Quiz

PART FIVE: THE MODERN WORLD

I. Matching. Choose the architect in the right column that corresponds to the building in the left column and enter the appropriate letter in the space provided.

_____ 1. Notre Dame du Haut, Ronchamp

_____ 2. Guggenheim Museum, New York

_____ 3. Casa Milá, Barcelona

_____ 4. Chiswick House, near London

_____ 5. Panthéon, Paris

_____ 6. State Capitol, Richmond

_____ 7. Piazza d' Italia, New Orleans

_____ 8. Schroeder House, Utrecht

_____ 9. Kaufmann House, Bear Run, Pennsylvania

_____ 10. Bauhaus, Dessau

_____ 11. Crystal Palace, London

_____ 12. Marshall Field Warehouse, Chicago

_____ 13. Houses of Parliament, London

_____ 14. The Opéra, Paris

_____ 15. National Gallery addition, Washington, D.C.

a. Adam
b. Labrouste
c. Sullivan
d. Wright
e. Walpole
f. Mies van der Rohe
g. Garnier
h. Gaudí
i. Paxton
j. Gropius
k. Le Corbusier
l. Otto
m. Nervi
n. Soufflot
o. Boyle and Kent
p. Rietveldt
q. Barry and Pugin
r. Pei
s. Jefferson
t. Birkerts
u. Moore

II. **Matching.** Choose the art style/movement in the right column that corresponds to the artist in the left column and enter the appropriate letter in the space provided.

_____ 16.	Mondrian	a. Romanticism
_____ 17.	Ingres	b. Neoclassicism
_____ 18.	Malevich	c. Realism
_____ 19.	Cézanne	d. Impressionism
_____ 20.	Oldenburg	e. Post-Impressionism
_____ 21.	Picasso	f. Symbolism
_____ 22.	Delacroix	g. Art Nouveau
_____ 23.	Duchamp	h. The Fauves
_____ 24.	Matisse	i. Expressionism
_____ 25.	Monet	j. Cubism
_____ 26.	Boccioni	k. Futurism
_____ 27.	Pissarro	l. De Stijl
_____ 28.	Gros	m. Surrealism
_____ 29.	David	n. Dada
_____ 30.	Klimt	o. Suprematism
_____ 31.	Tansey	p. Constructivism
_____ 32.	Lichtenstein	q. Pittura metafisica
_____ 33.	Seurat	r. Abstract Expressionism
_____ 34.	Nolde	s. Abstract Formalism
_____ 35.	De Chirico	t. Op Art
_____ 36.	Dali	u. Pop Art
_____ 37.	Braque	v. Post-Modernism
_____ 38.	Derain	
_____ 39.	Daumier	
_____ 40.	Géricault	
_____ 41.	Gabo	
_____ 42.	Van Gogh	
_____ 43.	Riley	
_____ 44.	Rothko	
_____ 45.	Kline	

III. **Multiple Choice.** Circle the most appropriate answer.

46. The most important Realist painter of the mid-nineteenth century was   a. Degas   b. Ingres   c. Courbet   d. Delacroix   e. Géricault

47. The first Impressionist exhibition was held in the year   a. 1855   b. 1863   c. 1874   d. 1886   e. 1895

48. The most important painter of the French Revolutionary period was   a. Delacroix   b. Courbet   c. David   d. Ingres   e. Monet

49. A group portrait of the family of Charles IV was painted by   a. Ingres   b. Goya   c. Courbet   d. Géricault   e. David

50. An important French academic painter of the mid-nineteenth century was   a. Daumier   b. Courbet   c. Delacroix   d. Gérôme   e. Manet

51. The famous Armory show, which introduced modern art to the American public, was held in New York in the year   a. 1874   b. 1886   c. 1913   d. 1927   e. 1935

52. The artist who developed "combine paintings" was   a. Oldenburg   b. Rauschenberg   c. Kelly   d. Estes   e. Paolozzi

53. Movement is an important element in much of the art of   a. Calder   b. Smith   c. Kline   d. Bladen   e. Maillol

54. An important Social Realist of the 1930s was   a. Chagall   b. Klee   c. Duchamp   d. Tansey   e. Schwitters

55. An architect who worked primarily in the Neoclassical style was   a. Garnier   b. Walpole   c. Soufflot   d. Sullivan   e. Wright

56. The famous *Oath of the Horatii* was painted by   a. Ingres   b. David   c. Gros   d. Delacroix   e. Goya

57. An important sculptor who worked primarily in the Neoclassical style was   a. Rodin   b. Saint-Gaudens   c. Canova   d. Barye   e. Lehmbruck

58. A sculptor whose work was most closely associated with Cubism was   a. Lipchitz   b. Rodin   c. Tinguely   d. Giacometti   e. Moore

59. The architect who was associated with the Art Nouveau movement was   a. Wright   b. Gaudí   c. Nervi   d. Mies van der Rohe   e. Gropius

60. Strong Expressionist tendencies are seen in the work of   a. Mondrian   b. Munch   c. Seurat   d. Cézanne   e. Matisse

61. The artist who believed that "the art of painting can consist only in the representation of objects visible and tangible to the painter" was   a. Ingres   b. Delacroix   c. Goya   d. Courbet   e. Dali

62. The concern with images deriving directly from the subconscious is most apparent in the work of the   a. Expressionists   b. Impressionists   c. Cubists   d. Surrealists   e. Post-Painterly Abstractionists

63. The mural entitled *Guernica* was painted by   a. Léger   b. Picasso   c. Kollwitz   d. Grosz   e. Beckmann

64. The first exhibition of the Fauves took place in   a. 1874   b. 1890   c. 1905   d. 1915   e. 1925

65. A Monument to the Third International was designed by   a. Gabo   b. Malevich   c. Tatlin   d. Archipenko   e. Arp

66. Line is stressed over color in the works of   a. Ingres   b. Delacroix   c. Turner   d. Monet   e. Pissarro

67. Which artist uses a formal approach to painting that is closest to that of Mondrian?   a. Rubens b. Vermeer   c. Delacroix   d. Fragonard   e. Turner

68. Which of the following artists has the least Romantic or Expressionist approach to landscape painting? a. Friedrich   b. Van Ruisdael   c. Turner   d. Cézanne   e. Van Gogh

69. An important Abstract Expressionist was   a. Pollock   b. Dali   c. Malevich   d. Johns   e. Brancuşi

70. The artist most representative of the Impressionist style was   a. Van Gogh   b. Renoir   c. Manet d. Toulouse-Lautrec   e. Munch

71. The Spanish painter who most effectively combined realism and fantasy was   a. Velázquez b. Zurburán   c. Goya   d. Miró   e. Ribera

72. The sculptor who effectively combined aspects of Impressionism, Romanticism, and Expressionism in his work was   a. Canova   b. Taylor   c. Rodin   d. Maillol   e. Lehmbruck

73. The Post-Impressionist who based his work on the color theories of Delacroix and the scientists Helmholtz and Chevreul was   a. Van Gogh   b. Gaugin   c. Cézanne   d. Seurat   e. Toulouse-Latrec

74. The death of the revolutionary hero Marat was painted by   a. Goya   b. David   c. Gros d. Géricault   e. Ingres

75. The harsh, flat lighting and the juxtaposition of a nude woman with two men dressed in contemporary clothes shocked the public when Manet first exhibited his famous work entitled   a. *Le Déjeuner sur l'herbe*   b. *Le Moulin de la Galette*   c. *Sunday Afternoon on the Island of La Grande Jatte*   d. *The Spirit of the Dead Watching*   e. *The Night Café*

76. The *fin-de-siècle* artist who was considered a "primitive" was   a. Ensor   b. Rousseau   c. Munch d. Gaudí   e. Toulouse-Lautrec

77. An important member of the Barbizon School was   a. Millet   b. Friedrich   c. Turner   d. Constable   e. Delacroix

78. The landscape painter who influenced Delacroix and anticipated both the attitude and technique of Impressionism was   a. Turner   b. Constable   c. Friedrich   d. Van Ruisdael   e. Courbet

79. The *Raft of the Medusa* was painted by   a. Delacroix   b. Goya   c. Gérôme   d. Géricault e. Gros

80. A large construction of Earth Art, called *Spiral Jetty*, was designed by   a. Smith   b. Bladen c. Paolozzi   d. Smithson   e. Bury

IV. Identification.

81.   Compare the two sculptures below, attributing each to an artist, country, and decade. Give the reasons for your attributions.

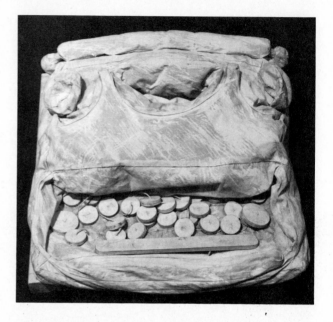

A.   Artist:_____

Country:_____

Decade:_____

B.   Artist:_____

Country:_____

Decade:_____

Reasons:

82. Compare the two sculptural groups below, attributing each to an artist, country, approximate date, and
style. Give the reasons for your attributions.

A.   Artist:_____

Country:_____

Date:_____

Style:_____

B.   Artist:_____

Country:_____

Date:_____

Style:_____

Reasons:

83. Compare the two abstractions below, attributing each to an artist and approximate date. Give the reasons for your attributions.

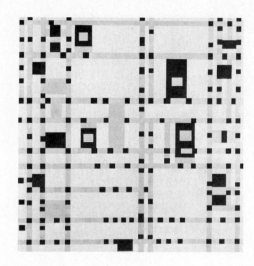

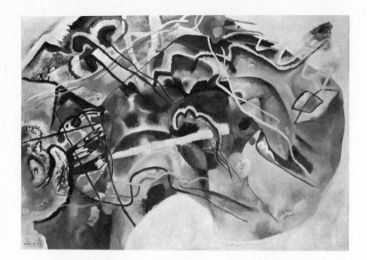

A. Artist:_____

    Date:_____

B. Artist:_____

    Date:_____

Reasons:

84. Compare the two landscape below, attributing each to an artist and approximate date. Give the reasons for your attributions.

A.   Artist:_____

      Date:_____

B.   Artist:_____

      Date:_____

Reasons:

85. Explain in the space provided below when you think these two buildings were built and how they relate to architectural styles of the twentieth century?

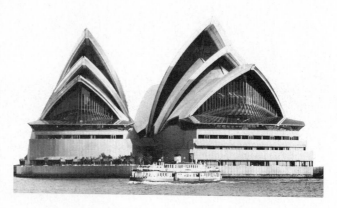

A.

B.

Answer:

86. The two paintings reproduced here reflect very different ways of depicting a still life. Attribute each to an artist, a style or stylistic grouping, and a decade. Give the reasons for your attributions. What do you think were the major concerns of each artist?

A. Artist:_____

    Style: _____

    Decade:_____

B. Artist: _____

    Style: _____

    Decade: _____

Reasons:

Answers for Self-Quizzes

PART ONE: THE ANCIENT WORLD

I. 1. h 2. r 3. s 4. a 5. i 6. k 7. 1 8. o 9. u 10. n 11. b 12. e 13. r 14. e 15. f 16. c 17. q 18. t 19. f 20. t 21. 1 22. u 23. d 24. r 25. p 26. p 27. h 28. m 29. j 30. k **II.** 31. n 32. h 33. a 34. 1 35. f 36. i 37. m 38. o 39. k 40. q 41. e 42. g 43. j 44. b 45. v 46. w 47. x 48. t 49. s 50. c 51. p 52. d 53. u 54. y 55. r **III.** 56. e 57. b 58. c 59. e 60. b 61. a 62. b 63. b 64. e 65. d 66. a 67. e 68. b 69. d 70. c 71. c 72. b 73. c 74. a 75. c 76. d 77. a 78. c 79. b 80. a

IV. 81. A. Greek, fifth century B.C.* (Detail from the Parthenon frieze, *c.* 440–423 B.C. British Museum, London.)

B. Assyrian, ninth to seventh century B.C. (*Banquet Relief of King Ashurbanipal,* Nineveh, 668–627 B.C. British Museum, London.)

As you compare these two reliefs, which illustrate the differences between the Assyrian and Classical Greek handling of relief sculptures, you might have made the following observations. The Greek relief shows the same characteristics that were noted in the other reliefs from the Parthenon: the balance between the "ideal" and the "real," between the tactile and optical approaches to form. The texture of the drapery folds contrasts with the smooth, monumental forms of the bodies. The human figures are the dominant element in the relief; a plain background and few props give only a summary indication of the setting. The greater three-dimensionality of the Greek relief contrasts with the lower bas-relief technique used by the Assyrians. In contrast to the relaxed and idealized Greek figures, which seem to be engaging in easy and familiar conversation, the conventionalized Assyrian figures seem stiff and tense. While the Classical Greek figures are fully understood anatomically and move freely and naturally in space, the Assyrian figures are rendered in an age-old combination of front and side views. The short, stocky, heavily muscled figures are characteristic of the reliefs of both Ashurnasirpal II and Ashurbanipal, as are the tight curls of hair and beard. The stylized details of the plant forms and the furniture are combined to reinforce a rather stiff formality similar to that of the Assyrian relief illustrated in the text (FIG. 2-29).

82. Roman, Republican period, second century B.C. to first century A.D. (Maison Carrée, Nimes, France, beginning of first century B.C.)

Although this temple bears a close resemblance to a Greek peripteral temple, it is obviously Roman for several reasons: like the Temple of "Fortuna Virilis" in Rome (FIG. 6-16), it is set on a high podium and is approached by stairs only from the front. Greek temples, by contrast, which were ordinarily set on the tiered stylobate and stereobate, were much more easily approached from all sides. The cella of this temple, like that of the Roman Temple of "Fortuna Virilis," extends the full width of the podium, with the result that the columns around the cella are attached to its walls as engaged columns, and only those of the porch are free-standing. This type of construction is known as "pseudoperipteral" and was very popular with Roman architects. Another typically Roman feature is the use of the Corinthian order, which was used by Roman architects more often than were the Greek Doric and Ionic orders.

83. A. Roman, second century B.C. to first century A.D. (*Roman Head,* Republican period, first century B.C. Glyptothek, Munich.)

B. Greek, fifth to fourth century B.C. (Praxiteles, *Head of Hermes*, detail of *Hermes and Dionysos, c.* 340 B.C. Museum, Olympia.)

These two heads illustrate the contrast between Greek idealism and Roman realism. As you identified them, you probably noted the difference between the youthful beauty of the Greek head and the mature dignity of the Roman head. The Greek head has the rounded face, the slightly pouting lips, small eyes, and straight nose and brow line that are characteristic of heads from the Classical period. The locks of the hair are loosely rendered, and shadows that slightly soften the formal perfection of the features are apparent around the eyes, a softening that is seen in the style of Praxiteles. In contrast to the smooth perfection and generalization of the features of

*In each of the answers to the identification questions, the first date given is the range within which you should have dated the work, and the second, in parentheses, is the actual date accepted by scholars.

the Greek face, the Roman face is deeply lined and strongly particularized. The wrinkles seem to be his and his alone, etched by profound experiences of life. With painstaking care the artist has indicated every change in the contour of the face, an approach to portraiture that was particularly popular during the years of the Roman Republic and that has been called "veristic."

84. Egyptian, New Kingdom, Amarna period, fourteenth century B.C. (*Relief of Akhenaton and his family*, Tel el-Amarna, Eighteenth Dynasty, *c.* 1360 B.C. Ägyptisches Museum, Berlin)

The hieroglyphics and the unique shape of the tall crowns identify the work as Egyptian. The relief can be precisely placed in the Amarna period, for it clearly demonstrates the new sense of life and movement introduced by the artists who worked for Akhenaton. Although the Egyptian figural conventions of head and legs shown in profile with shoulders seen from the front is still observed, the bodies seem to be much more relaxed and lively than those found in traditional figural representations. In this relief one also sees the predilection for fluid curved lines and attenuated bodies that was typical of the Amarna style, as well as the strange combination of naturalism and stylization favored by artists of the period. All the members of the family, even the tiny children, show the wide hips, sinuous bodies, long graceful necks, and elongated heads that were seen in representations of Akhenaton himself. The intimacy and the informality of the family grouping, in which the children gesticulate freely and fondle their royal parents, is similar to the informality seen in the Amarna relief of King Smenkhkare and his wife Meritaten (FIG. 3-38).

85. A. Byzantine, sixth century A.D. (Detail of *Procession of Female Saints*, mosaic from Sant' Apollinare Nuovo, Ravenna, Italy, *c.* A.D. 561.)
B. Roman, second century B.C. to second century A.D. (*Judgment of Paris*, fresco from Pompeii, first century B.C. National Museum, Naples.)

These two works illustrate the change from Roman illusionism (as seen at Pompeii) to the more abstract and symbolic style of Early Byzantine art. Even from black-and-white reproductions, you should have been able to distinguish between the media of the two works: the fresco technique, which was so commonly used by the Romans for wall decorations, and the glistening mosaic preferred by Byzantine artists. Although the media contributed to a certain degree to the style seen in the two works—the quick, painterly brush strokes adding to the illusionism of the Roman example and the glass chips of the mosaic emphasizing the flat, otherworldly quality of the Byzantine frieze—the artists manipulated the media to produce the effects favored by their respective cultures. To achieve the illusion of the world in which we live is of obvious interest to the Roman artist; his figures are placed to emphasize their existence in three-dimensional space and modeled in the round with rapid, painterly strokes to heighten a sense of their reality. The Byzantine artist, on the other hand, uses formal means to minimize real space and to set his figures in a transcendental world. Instead of overlapping his figures as the Roman artist has done, he places them in a line, separates them from each other by date palms, and thus creates a rhythmically repeated pattern. The heads and feet all extend to the same level, and the ground on which they stand seems to be tilted upward. As in other sixth-century mosaics, the artist tells his story in terms of an array of symbols, lined up side by side. The details of costume and trees create a rich tapestry design. The flat background and the relative lack of modeling in the figures themselves keep us from confusing our world with theirs; they abide solely on another plane of reality.

PART TWO: THE MIDDLE AGES

I. 1. l 2. j 3. a 4. b 5. d 6. e 7. i 8. c 9. a 10. b 11. c 12. i 13. j 14. i 15. b 16. j 17. l 18. l 19. l 20. j 21. g 22. f 23. i 24. f 25. b 26. a 27. h 28. l 29. k 30. k **II.** 31. f 32. p 33. b 34. d 35. j 36. k 37. n 38. u 39. i 40. g 41. a 42. m 43. o 44. q 45. e 46. c 47. h 48. r 49. t 50. x **III.** 51. b 52. c 53. a 54. b 55. a 56. c 57. e 58. b 59. d 60. b 61. e 62. c 63. c 64. e 65. d 66. c 67. b 68. c 69. a 70. e 71. b 72. b 73. a 74. c 75. c 76. c 77. e 78. e 79. d 80. c

IV. 81. A. Hiberno-Saxon, sixth to ninth century A.D. (*Matthew the Evangelist*, from *Book of Darrow*, seventh century A.D. Trinity College, Dublin.)
B. Carolingian, eighth to ninth century A.D. (*John the Evangelist,* from the *Gospel Book of Archbishop Ebbo of Reims, c.* 816–835 Bibliothèque Nationale, Paris.)

These two evangelist pages illustrate two very different approaches to form that were used by artists working the Early Middle Ages. Illustration A is typical of the fusion of Germanic and Celtic styles found in Hiberno-Saxon manuscripts. The artist was not in the least concerned with illusionism, but instead created a style that was abstract, decorative, and (except for the figure's feet) bilaterally symmetrical. The flat form of the body with its complex inlay patterns is closely related to the jewelry forms created by Germanic craftsmen, while the spirals around the frame reflect the complicated interlace so popular with Celtic artists. The entire page decoration is flat and linear, and there is no interest whatsoever in three-dimensional form. The artist who created the Evangelist from the *Ebbo Gospels,* however, was very much interested in creating the illusion of three-dimensional form and undoubtedly based the drawing on prototypes that were derived from the illusionistic, Late Antique style, a practice encouraged by the emperor Charlemagne. The strange perspective of the writing desk and stool indicate that the Carolingian artist did not fully understand the spatial illusionism of the model. Yet the overall linear technique of this northern artist has given a new vitality to the old models. The nervous, spontaneous line and the tense energetic figure is closely related to the other illuminations produced by artists of the Reims School in the first half of the ninth century.

82. A. Romanesque, twelfth century (*Prophet Isaiah*, from the portal of the church of Souillac, Lot, France, *c.* 1130–1140.)
  B. Gothic, thirteenth to fourteenth century (*Virgin*, from the north transept, Notre Dame, Paris, second half of the thirteenth century.)

These two figures demonstrate some of the changes that took place in French monumental sculpture between the Romanesque and Gothic periods. The elegant prophet with his elongated body and decorative drapery resembles many Romanesque figures from southern France. The incised linear detail, the swinging drapery folds, and the cross-legged, almost dancing pose shows a close relationship to the Jeremiah carved on the trumeau of St. Pierre at Moissac (FIG. 9-28). In both cases, the artist seems to be using the forms of the body and drapery to express the mystic inner state of his figures rather than to describe their physical presence. The low relief of the Romanesque figures has given way in the Gothic statue to a body carved much more fully in the round, and the trancelike ecstacy of the Romanesque prophet has been transformed into the fully ripened corporality of the Gothic style. Like the figures from the Reims portal (FIG. 10-33), the drapery of the Virgin is heavy, falling in massive folds quite different from the delicate arabesques of the Romanesque drapery. The Virgin demonstrates the Gothic concern for natural appearances, as is apparent in the more naturalistic rendering of the drapery and the more natural proportions of the body; however, this naturalism is blended with a kind of Classical calm and monumentality that is seen in many High Gothic figures. The graceful swing of the drapery shows hints of the mannered elegance that began with the angel from Reims and continued in fourteenth-century Gothic figures like *The Virgin of Paris* (FIG. 10-38), as does the upward tilt of the hips, which gives the figure a typical Gothic S-curve.

83. Romanesque, Cluniac-Burgundian, principally twelfth century (Santiago de Compostela, Spain, 1077–1211.)

Both the plan and elevation of this Romanesque church bear a strong resemblance to the church of St. Sernin at Toulouse (FIGS. 9-4, 9-5, 9-6), and it is one of those that were built along the pilgrimage road in southern France and northwestern Spain. This particular church marked the site that was the goal of the pilgrimage. Many of the churches along this road were built in the Cluniac-Burgundian style, a style characterized by semicircular stone vaults, a square crossing, extreme regularity and precision, and an ambulatory with radiating chapels. As in the church of St. Sernin, the square crossing of this church is used as a module for the rest of the building, with each nave bay measuring exactly one-half and each aisle square measuring exactly one-fourth of the crossing square. The floor plan is carried up the walls by the attached columns that mark the edges of each bay and then over the vault by the transverse arches. The wall elevation, like that of St. Sernin, is marked by aisle arcades surmounted by tribunes. The heavy masonry vaults in both cases preclude the creation of a clerestory, thus creating dark interiors. The aisles are covered by groin vaults, but while St. Sernin has a double row of aisles, this church has only one. It does, however, have the same type of ambulatory with radiating chapels, a feature that was particularly popular in the pilgrimage churches, since it permitted the pilgrims to view the relics without disrupting the monastic services.

While this building shares the clear articulation and segmentation of space that characterize Gothic churches, the round arches, the lack of rib vaulting as well as the lack of a clerestory, and the use of a gallery rather than a triforium mark it as Romanesque.

84. Notre Dame, Paris, late twelfth to mid-thirteenth century (1163–1250), Early and High Gothic styles. Check the accuracy of your identification of the various parts of the building from the diagrams below.

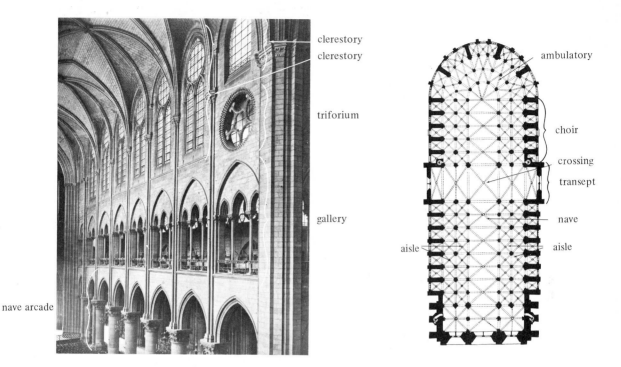

The illustration shows clearly the transition from Early to High Gothic architecture, as described in the text. Most significant is the change in the nave-wall elevation from a quadripartite elevation to a tripartite elevation. The four parts of an Early Gothic elevation—nave arcade, gallery, triforium, and clerestory—seen in the right bay were changed in the other bays of the nave to a tripartite elevation by merging the two upper windows to allow more light to penetrate the nave. The retention of the gallery in the tripartite elevation shows this to be a modification of Early Gothic rather than a true High Gothic elevation, which typically consists of a nave arcade, triforium, and clerestory. The six-part vault system used in the nave is typical of Early Gothic buildings, but the alternate-support system used in Early Gothic churches has been abandoned.

PART THREE: THE NON-EUROPEAN WORLD

I. 1. b 2. g 3. c 4. a 5. h 6. e 7. d 8. l 9. i 10. k 11. u 12. m 13. q 14. j 15. t 16. n 17. r 18. p 19. o 20. s **II.** 21. b 22. a 23. f 24. h 25. f 26. a 27. b 28. e 29. c 30. a 31. d 32. f 33. f 34. h 35. c 36. b 37. h 38. f 39. e 40. c 41. b 42. c 43. e 44. a 45. g **III.** 46. c 47. d 48. b 49. c 50. a 51. b 52. b 53. d 54. d 55. c 56. a 57. c 58. c 59. a 60. b 61. b 62. c 63. d 64. a 65. d 66. a 67. c 68. e 69. a 70. b 71. b 72. b 73. b 74. c 75. b 76. c 77. b 78. d 79. c 80. c

IV. 81. A. Japan, Jomon, first to sixth century (*Haniwa* figure of a warrior, Tumulus period, fifth century.)
    B. China, Ch'in dynasty, third century B.C. (*Charioteer,* Lintong, Shensi Province, China, 221–206 B.C.)

Figure A is an example of the haniwa figures that were produced in Japan during the Jomon period. It is molded in tubular form, with the legs and torso echoing the cylindrical shape of the base. The slit eyes, the necklace, and the swelling legs are very similar to those of the haniwa figure illustrated in the text (FIG. 13-1), although this one is more complete and is represented wearing his helmet and padded armor. The forward motion of the arms seems to indicate that he is in the act of drawing his sword. As in other haniwa figures, the simple, direct forms of this warrior seem to express a type of energy and creativity that is specifically Japanese.

The Chinese warrior—stiff and formal, rigidly frontal, done with simple volumes and sharp, realistic detail—shows all the stylistic characteristics of the warriors discovered in the tomb mount in Shensi, China. With his detailed armor, he represents one member of the vast army who made up the imperial bodyguard (see FIGS. 12-4 and 12-5). Since his hands are stretched out in front, he was probably a charioteer. The realistic style seems to be much more sophisticated than that of the energetic Japanese haniwa figure.

82. A. Japan, Ashikaga period, fifteenth to sixteenth century (Attributed to Soami, detail of a six-fold screen, 1525. Metropolitan Museum of Art, New York.)
     B. Japan, Tokugawa or Edo period, nineteenth century (Hokusai, *Fuji Above the Storm,* c. 1823. Woodblock print.)

If you guessed Chinese for the misty landscape, don't feel bad, because although it is Japanese, it comes from a period when Japanese art was strongly influenced by that of China, particularly the delicate misty land-scapes of the Sung period. Here the Japanese artist has used the Sung device of dividing the landscape into fore-ground, middle ground, and far distance, with a cliff in the middle distance and pale mountain peaks suggested in the far distance. The three areas are similarly held together by a field of mist. The painting also used some of the bolder brushwork that was introduced by Zen Buddhist masters of the Yüan period. You should have no trouble, however, in identifying the specifically Japanese qualities of the representation of Mt. Fuji, for the boldness and strength of this woodblock print is unlike anything produced in China. The bold lines and patterns of this wood-block resemble closely those of the Hokusai woodblock print reproduced in the text (FIG. 13-30), and one finds the same assymetrical composition. Both reflect Hokusai's grand and monumental view of nature.

83. Benin, fifteenth to eighteenth century (*The King with Two Chiefs,* sixteenth to seventeenth century. Bronze. The British Museum, London.)

The bronze panel showing the king flanked by two chiefs is very closely related to the Benin altar illustrated in the text (FIG. 14-44). The figures are depicted with the same simplified, somewhat rigid naturalism; the hel-meted heads, the decorated necks, and the bodies are all part of the same cylindrical form to which small arms and legs are attached. The patterns of armor, helmets, and necklaces further emphasize the rigidity of the forms and the hieratic dignity of the king. As in the Benin altar, the background is covered with engraved decoration; no surfaces except faces, hands, and feet are free from it. Like many Benin bronzes, this one glorifies the power of the devine king.

84. China, Shang, sixteenth to eleventh century B.C. (Wine vessel in the shape of a bird. Bronze. The Art Institute of Chicago, Lucy Maud Buckingham Collection.)

This bronze vessel is a typical example of the most outstanding type of art produced during the Shang period in China. It possesses the dynamic sculptural shape and rich surface decoration that is typical of such pieces. Although of a different shape and design, it bears strong stylistic resemblance to the twelfth-century B.C. bronze *Kuang* illustrated in the text (FIG. 12-1). Both pieces are a masterly blend of naturalistic and abstract forms; the strange zoomorphic creatures both sport horns that would belong neither to the feline creature repre-sented in the text nor to the bird that forms the basis of this vessel. The silhouettes of both vessels are dynamic and broken, and in both cases the decoration seems to be an integral part of the sculptural whole rather than mere surface embellishment. The decoration of both vessels, and undoubtedly the shapes themselves, carried a symbolic meaning that was important to the ritual purpose of Shang bronzes.

85. A. India, Andhra period, first century B.C. to fourth century A.D. (*Aspara,* from the Kandarya Mahadeva Temple, Khajuraho, India.)
     B. China, T'ang, seventh to tenth century (Terra-cotta funerary statuette, 618–906. Museum Rietberg, Zurich.)

These two very different representations of women are typical of those found respectively in traditional Indian and traditional Chinese art. The sensuous and undulating curves of the Indian figure are reminiscent of those of the woman carved on the façade of the chaitya hall at Karli (FIG. 11-9) and of the voluptuous yakshis, or nature spirits, carved at Sanchi. The exaggeration of the sexual characteristics, the rich jewelry, and flimsy veil all emphasize the eroticism that played a much greater role in Indian art than it did in the Chinese tradition. The dainty Chinese lady represents an entirely different spirit. This delicate little figure, which was created by T'ang potters, was placed in a tomb and was intended to provide entertainment for the deceased in the world beyond. Its charm and delicacy indicates its relationship to the graceful dancing woman illustrated in the text (FIG. 12-17). The figure shown here is a sleeve dancer, as is the one in the text. Her body is completely covered by a long flowing garment, very different from the revealing garments of the Indian figure, which were intended to emphasize rather than conceal bodily charms.

PART FOUR: THE RENAISSANCE AND THE BAROQUE AND ROCOCO

I. 1. c 2. n 3. g 4. e 5. i 6. h 7. k 8. f 9. p 10. u 11. a 12. d 13. o 14. m 15. s 16. v 17. w 18. r 19. q 20. j 21. l 22. y 23. x **II.** 24. i 25. a 26. c 27. c 28. d 29. j 30. s 31. l 32. k 33. g 34. m 35. e 36. d 37. n 38. m 39. b **III.** 40. n 41. i 42. e 43. p 44. l 45. b 46. j 47. a 48. g **IV.** 49. b 50. c 51. b 52. d 53. b 54. d 55. d 56. c 57. b ·58. a 59. b 60. d 61. c 62. e 63. b 64. c 65. a 66. b 67. c 68. c 69. d 70. b 71. b 72. c 73. e 74. d 75. d 76. d 77. d 78. c 79. e 80. e

V. Answers for Chronological Chart: (More artists could be listed than the number of spaces provided.)
Italy: 13th-14th centuries: Nicola Pisano, Giovanni Pisano, Andrea Pisano, Berlinghieri, Duccio, Cimabue, Cavallini, Giotto, Simone Martini, Gaddi, Pietro Lorenzetti, Ambrogio Lorenzetti, Traini
Italy: 15th century: Ghiberti, Jacopo della Quercia, Nanni di Banco, Donatello, Brunelleschi, Michelozzo di Bartolommeo, Masaccio, Uccello, Andrea del Castagno, Piero della Francesca, Fra Angelico, Fra Filippo Lippi, Alberti, Giuliano da Sangallo, Rossellino, Desiderio da Settignano, Andrea del Verrocchio, Pollaiuolo, Ghirlandaio, Botticelli, Signorelli, Perugino, Mantegna
Italy: 16th century: Leonardo, Bramante, Antonio da Sangallo, Raphael, Michelangelo, Andrea del Sarto, Correggio, Jacopo Pontormo, Rosso Fiorentino, Parmigianino, Cellini, Giovanni da Bologna, Giulio Romano, Palladio, Bellini, Giorgione, Titian, Tintoretto, Veronese
Netherlands: 13th-14th centuries: Sluter, Broederlam
Netherlands: 15th century: Limbourg Brothers, Campin, Jan van Eyck, Rogier van der Weyden, Christus, Bouts, Hugo van der Goes, Memling, Bosch
Netherlands: 16th Century: Gossaert, Patinir, Bruegel, Metsys, Spranger
Germany: 15th century: Riemenschneider, Pacher, Lochner, Witz, Schongauer, Stoss
Germany: 16th century: Altdorfer, Cranach, Grünewald, Dürer, Holbein
France: 15th century: Fouquet
France: 16th century: Clouet, Goujon, Lescot, Pilon
Italy: 17th century: Giacomo da Vignola, Giacomo della Porta, Maderno, Bernini, Borromini, Guarini, Annibale Carracci, Reni, Guercino, Caravaggio, Domenichino, Pozzo, Gentileschi
Italy: 18th century: Tiepolo, Juvara, Piranesi, Carriera
France: 17th century: Georges de la Tour, Le Nain, Poussin, Claude, Mansart, Perrault, Le Vau, Le Brun, Puget, Girardon
France: 18th century: Watteau, Boucher, Fragonard, Chardin, Quentin de la Tour, Greuze, Houdon, Vigée Lebrun
Holland: 17th century: Van Honthorst, Hals, Rembrandt, Vermeer, Kalf, Van Ruisdael
Belgium: 17 century: Rubens, Van Dyck
Spain: 17th century: El Greco, Ribera, Zurbarán, Velázquez
Spain: 18th century: Goya
England: 17th century: Jones, Wren
England: 18th century: Vanbrugh, Hogarth, Gainsborough, Reynolds, Kauffmann, West, Fuseli, Blake

VI. 81.   A.   Jan van Eyck, Flanders, fifteenth century, Northern Renaissance (*The Annunciation, c.* 1435. National Gallery, Washington, D.C.)

   B.   Raphael, Italy, sixteenth century, High Renaissance (*La Belle Jardinière,* 1507–1508. Louvre, Paris.)

The precision and absolute clarity of the rendition of every form in this annunciation scene indicate its fifteenth-century northern origin. The emphasis is on the specific, as shown in the rich brocaded robe, and the sparkling jewels point to Van Eyck as the artist. Similar details are seen in his painting of *The Virgin with the Canon van der Paele* (FIG. 18-10). The slightly awkward position of the Virgin of this panel is very similar to that of the Virgin on the exterior of his *Ghent Altarpiece* (FIG. 18-8). The slight upward tilt of the floor indicates that single-point linear perspective was not used to construct the architectural setting, as most likely would have been done by an Italian painter of the same period. Rich surface, precise detail, and symbolism are more important than unified space. As in other fifteenth-century Netherlandish works, disguised symbolism plays an important role in this painting, with such things as the scenes depicted on the capitals of the columns and the tiles of the floor adding to the devotional meaning of the altarpiece.

The Madonna with the Christ child and St. John is an excellent example of Raphael's High Renaissance style, for it demonstrates the tightly organized pyramidal composition that was favored by High Renaissance artists as well as the subtle chiaroscuro Raphael used to model the idealized faces. Like the *Madonna with the Goldfinch* (FIG. 17-16), this work demonstrates Raphael's striving to combine grace, dignity, and idealism with simplicity and logic. The beauty and calm dignity of these figures and their monumental form well illustrate Raphael's great achievement of merging Christian devotion with pagan beauty.

82.   Bernini, seventeenth century, Italy, Baroque (Sant' Andrea al Quirinale, Rome, 1658–1670).

The building illustrated here very clearly demonstrates the approach to form favored by Baroque architects. Variations on the oval were much more popular with Baroque architects than variations on the square and circle, which were the ideal forms for Renaissance architects. That preference is apparent in the plan of the Baroque church shown here. The façade also demonstrates the distinctive approach of Baroque architects. While the typical Renaissance façade is composed of discrete geometric units, carefully proportioned and coordinated, the façade of Sant' Andrea is composed of forms molded deeply in space, with curve playing against curve, creating a rich plastic surface. Many of the stylistic characteristics of this church, which was designed by Bernini, are apparent in other Baroque buildings as well, for example Borromini's church of San Carlo alle Quattro Fontane (FIGS. 19-13 and 19-14), Guarini's Palazzo Carignano (FIG. 19-18), and the piazza of St. Peter's (FIG. 19-3), which was also designed by Bernini. All share with this building the Baroque delight in dynamic forms that reach out and embrace space, plastic handling of surfaces, contrast of concave and convex forms, and preference for oval plans rather than the more static forms of circle and square preferred by Renaissance architects.

83.   A.   Holland, seventeenth century (Philips Koninck, *Landscape with a Hawking Party.* National Gallery, London.)

   B.   Italy, seventeenth century (Pietro da Cortona, Triumph of Barberini. 1633–39. Ceiling fresco. Gran Salone, Palazzo Barberini, Rome.)

These Baroque paintings share the seventeenth-century expansiveness and dynamism. Like Baroque scientists, the artists of these works see physical nature as matter in motion through space and time. However, while the Dutch artist paints the motion of clouds through a realistic landscape, dappled with a constantly changing light, the Italian artist gives an intense physical reality to his personifications of abstract ideas and then sets his massive figures into dynamic motion.

The differences between the paintings can be attributed in part to the desires and expectations of the patrons. The Italian artist was commissioned to paint an allegorical painting in praise of his powerful ecclesiastical patron and used a form similar to that used by Pozzo in his *Glorification of St. Ignatius* (FIG. 19-32), painted on the ceiling of one of the huge new Roman churches. The Dutch artist, on the other hand, was working for the open market, attempting to paint something that would be appreciated and purchased by a prosperous Dutch burgher to decorate his residence. These patrons were not interested in allegory, but rather in something real, such as portrayals of the changing moods of their beloved skies. The Dutch Protestant preferred to worship God reflected in his works, rather than under the majestic painted ceilings so popular in Catholic Rome.

84. A. Rembrandt, Holland, seventeenth century (*Aristotle with the Bust of Homer*, 1653. Metropolitan Museum of Art, New York.)
    B. Vermeer, Holland, seventeenth century (*Girl Reading a Letter*, c. 1655-1660. Staatliche Kunst-sammlungen, Dresden.)

Rembrandt and Vermeer shared with other seventeenth-century Dutch artists an intense interest in the optics of light. However, their handling of it was quite different. Vermeer was primarily concerned with the creation of pictorial illusion and with extremely subtle optical effects. His attention to the effects of a warm and sunny light entering a quiet room, its reflections on the glass, and the varying textures it illuminates is very clearly seen in this painting.

Rembrandt, on the other hand, used subtle modulations of light and dark to indicate spiritual or psychic states, to explore nuances of character and mood. The man represented here shares with many of the others portrayed by Rembrandt a sense of inwardness, of quiet contemplation. Only a portion of his face emerges out of the darkness, while the bust, on which he rests his hand, seems to glow with light. Rembrandt makes us wonder about the relationship between the man and the bust, even if we do not know that they represent Aristotle, the famous philosopher, contemplating a bust of the blind poet Homer. Is he recognizing the superiority of Homer's intuitive wisdom over his own, more worldly knowledge and success, symbolized by the golden chain? (Even if you didn't write anything about the subject Rembrandt was representing, I hope that you wrote something about the mysterious effects he created.)

85. A. Michelangelo, Italy, seventeenth century, High Renaissance (*The Bearded Giant*, 1530-1533. Galleria dell' Accademia, Florence.)
    B. Bernini, Italy, seventeenth century, Baroque (*Rape of Proserpine*, 1621-1622. Borghese Gallery, Rome.)

These two works are typical of the sculptural styles of Michelangelo and Bernini. While some of Michelangelo's works shared the qualities found in the work of other High Renaissance artists, this work demonstrates the quality of "terribilità" so characteristic of his personal style. Pent-up passion and power are represented here rather than calm and ideal beauty. This figure has an even more massive physique than the two slaves illustrated in the text (FIGS. 17-22 and 17-23) but like them, it seems to represent the human soul struggling to free itself from matter. The same straining of the huge limbs in contrary directions is seen in the unfinished figure of Day from the tomb of Guiliano de' Medici (FIG. 17-27). While the action of Michelangelo's figure can be understood from a single view—as is typical of most Renaissance sculpture—one must walk around the Bernini group in order to fully appreciate the complex composition, a characteristic of much Baroque sculpture. As he did in his rendition of *David* (FIG. 19-10), Bernini captures the split-second action of the most dramatic moment. The two struggling bodies pull against each other with great energy, and Bernini contrasts the strong musculature of the male figure with the softer quality of female flesh. Virtuoso treatment of surface textures, combined with great energy and movement, is typical of Bernini, as is the work's expansive quality as it reaches out into space and refuses to be confined to the block from which it is carved.

PART FIVE: THE MODERN WORLD

I. 1.k 2.d 3.h 4.o 5.n 6.s 7.u 8.p 9.d 10.j 11.i 12.c 13.q 14.g 15.r **II.** 16.1 17.b 18.p 19.e 20.u 21.j 22.a 23.n 24.h 25.d 26.k 27.d 28.a 29.b 30.f 31.v 32.u 33.e 34.i 35.q 36.m 37.j 38.h 39.c 40.a 41.p 42.e 43.t 44.r 45.r **III.** 46.c 47.c 48.c 49.b 50.d 51.c 52.b 53.a 54.d 55.c 56.b 57.c 58.a 59.b 60.b 61.d 62.d 63.b 64.c 65.c 66.a 67.b 68.d 69.a 70.b 71.c 72.c 73.d 74.b 75.a 76.b 77.a 78.b 79.d 80.d

IV. 81. A. David Smith, United States, 1960s (*Cubi XXVII*, 1965. Guggenheim Museum, New York.)
       B. Claes Oldenburg, United States, 1960s (*Model Ghost Typewriter*, 1963. Sidney Janis Gallery, New York.)

Both of these pieces of sculpture were created by American artists in the 1960s, and they represent two very different approaches to the art. Smith is representative of the Formalist/Structuralist approach, which aims to eliminate the human element in art in favor of formal machine-like perfection. Like the stainless-steel sculpture by Smith illustrated in the text (FIG. 22-80), this one shows his interest in arranging "solid-geometrical masses in a remarkable equilibrium of strength and buoyancy." Notice particularly the precarious balance of the columnar form on the upper right part of the sculpture. The beautifully machined surfaces of the forms demonstrate Smith's interest in contemporary machines, and his professed desire to turn his studio into a factory. Oldenburg's approach is almost diametrically opposed, for one of his goals was to humanize the machine, which he does with a kind of sly humor by means of his "soft" sculptures. Like the forms of the *Soft Toilet* (FIG. 22-91), the various mechanisms of the soft typewriter sag and assume a strangely grotesque organic quality, which completely denies its function as a machine. Oldenburg's fantasy seems to be a combination of Dada mockery of society and the interest of American Pop artists in the forms of the commercial world around them.

82. A. Rodin, France, late nineteenth to early twentieth century (Three Fates from *The Gate of Hell*, 1880–1917. Musée Rodin, Paris.)
    B. Canova, Italy or France, early nineteenth century, Neoclassicism (*Three Graces*, 1814. Nye Carlsburg Glyptych, Copenhagen.)

These two sculptured groups demonstrate the difference between Canova's cool and formal Neoclassicism and Rodin's much more emotional style, which combines elements from Romanticism, Impressionism, and an expressive Realism (FIGS. 21-82, 21-83, 21-84). Rodin's figures are cast in bronze from clay models, and his use of soft clay enabled him to create subtle variations and shifts of the planes under the play of light and thus to achieve effects that were impossible to an artist like Canova, who carved directly into marble. Rodin's fluid modeling is analogous to the deft Impressionist brush stroke, but the exaggerations of the forms and the striking gestures of the three figures as they point downward echo the dramatic intensity of Romantic and Expressionist works. The impression of work-in-progress created by the figures seems to derive from the unfinished works of Michelangelo, which influenced Rodin deeply. Rodin's concern with dramatic statement and with expressive bodily pose and gesture shows clearly the influence of Michelangelo. Canova's graceful female figures derive from very different sources. There is a lingering Rococo charm, but the precise technique used to create the idealized figures, which combine careful detailing and generalized forms, is clearly in the Classical tradition. These three figures are closely related to Canova's representation of *Pauline Borghese as Venus* (FIG. 21-5), for they demonstrate the same type of femininity: ideal and seemingly distant, yet human and accessible at the same time.

83. A. Mondrian, second-quarter twentieth century (*Broadway Boogie Woogie,* 1942–1943. Museum of Modern Art, New York.)
    B. Kandinsky, first-quarter twentieth century (*Picture with a White Edge*, 1913. Guggenheim Museum, New York.)

These two compositions illustrate the range of experimentation that was found in the development of abstract art in the early twentieth century. They could be said to represent the Romantic or Baroque approach as opposed to the Classical approach. Mondrian's composition, like the one illustrated in the text (FIG. 22-20), is composed exclusively of straight lines that form squares and rectangles of various sizes, arranged very carefully on a two-dimensional surface to create a subtle asymmetrical balance. He was interested in the idea of an absolute artistic order, but he did not want mechanical uniformity. This composition illustrates his belief that "true reality is attained through dynamic movement in equilibrium," for while there is a sense of balance in the composition, there is no symmetry, and the shapes of the rectangles are infinitely varied. Yet, he is not unlike the Neoclassical artists, since his approach, like theirs, can best be described as "deliberate and studious." Although the words used to describe the Romantic artist as "impetuous, improvisational, and instinctive" are out of place in describing Mondrian's work, they do seem to describe exactly the approach used by Kandinsky in the work illustrated here and in the text (FIG. 22-9). The painting demonstrates the point at which Kandinsky's exploration of the emotional and psychological properties of color, line, and shape have dispensed with the depiction of subject matter and have moved into the realm of pure abstraction. The title, which he used for many of the pictures of this time, including *Improvisation 28* in the text, aptly describes his approach and is very different from the deliberate, intellectual one of Mondrian. Where Mondrian's lines are vertical or horizontal, lines and masses of color move across Kandinsky's canvas in all directions, movements and arrangements that seem to burst directly from his subconscious. Kandinsky's own writing stresses the importance of allowing the instinctual world of the subconscious to emerge and to control directly the artistic expression of the artist. In this work we see the results of that technique.

84. A. Van Gogh, late nineteenth century (*Stairway at Auvers*, 1890. City Art Museum, St. Louis.)
    B. Cézanne, late nineteenth century (*The Gulf of Marseilles Seen from L'Estaque,* 1884–1886. Metropolitan Museum of Art, New York.)

These two paintings, done in late nineteenth-century France by two Post-Impressionists, show the same contrast in approach that we saw in the twentieth century between Mondrian and Kandinsky. Van Gogh's approach to the painting is instinctive and emotional, while Cézanne's is deliberate and intellectual. The Van Gogh landscape shows the same type of swirling, impulsive brush strokes that he used in *Starry Night* (FIG. 21-69). There are no stable forms; rather everything seems to be in motion. Unfortunately, the black-and-white reproduction does not show the intense color that Van Gogh loved and made such an important part of his painterly expression. Color was important to Cézanne too, but he used it to build up form and pictorial structure and not to express emotional states as did Van Gogh. The carefully interlocked planes he developed in his painting of *La Montagne Sainte-Victoire* (FIG. 21-66) are also used here, for the shape and size of the bay and the foreground land mass are almost the same and interlock forcibly on the two-dimensional surface of the canvas. As in his other landscapes, he has immobilized the shifting colors of Impressionism and has created a series of clearly defined planes. How much more stable this landscape looks than the one created by Van Gogh. Like Mondrian, Cézanne has achieved this stability by emphasizing vertical and horizontal lines in his composition, while Van Gogh, like Delacroix and Kandinsky, has created an emotional and constantly changing effect in his by using diagonal lines that undulate.

85. A. (Johnson and Burgee, AT&T Headquarters, New York, 1978–1983.)
    B. (Opera House, Sydney, Australia, 1970s.)

These two buildings, built in two different parts of the world—New York and Sydney, Australia—in the 1970s and early 1980s, demonstrate the great variety found in so-called Post-Modernist styles. The AT&T building pays its respects to the International style, and particularly to Mies van der Rohe, with its elegantly simple rectilinear shape, its ribbon windows, and vertical banding. However, the top of the building with its cutout that looks as though it were taken from a piece of Federal-style furniture, marks a sharp break with the stylistic orthodoxy of the International style and distinguishes the building as Post-Modernist.

The soaring wings of the Sydney Opera House demonstrate another strong tendency in modern architecture, a kind of "Romanticism" first seen in Le Corbusier's Notre Dame du Haut (FIG. 22-105) with its molded organic forms, a tendency carried even further by Saarinen in the Trans World Airline Terminal in New York (FIGS. 22-110 and 22-111). The malleability of poured concrete strengthened by structural steel enabled the architects of the Sydney Opera House to create huge overlapping shells that aid not only in the acoustics of the concert hall, but also in creating the dynamic organic tensions of the building. The Opera House is related to the structural explorations of such architects as Nervi, Otto, and Pei.

86. A. Picasso or Braque, Analytic Cubism, 1910s (Picasso, *Violin and Grapes*, 1912. Museum of Modern Art, New York.)
    B. Mark Tansey, Post-Modernist, 1980s (*Still Life*, 1982. Metropolitan Museum of Art, New York.)

The subject of painting A, which seems to be some sort of stringed instrument and a fruit resembling grapes, is not depicted according to our usual view, but rather is dissected, spread out across the picture plane, and compressed into a very shallow space. Shortly before 1910 Picasso and Braque began experimenting with ways to present the total reality of three-dimensional objects on a two-dimensional plane. They utilized multiple angles of vision and simultaneous presentations of discontinuous planes to represent various aspects of their subjects. Color was kept to a minimum in these works, and the surface was broken up as forms were subjected to careful analysis. All of these characteristics are seen in the painting reproduced here, although the color range is impossible to detect in this black-and-white reproduction.

Painting B shows us a traditional still life, but it is a painting within a painting. The style is a kind of careful realism like that used by a number of artists during the 1930s, but the pun is in the spirit of the work done by Mark Tansey in the 1980s. It is a kind of modern *memento mori*, not only for the flowers, which die while their painted representation lives on, but also for the painting style of so many artists of an earlier era. Although Tansey painted many of his images in the tones of grey of a news photograph in order to create an additional level of reality, this black-and-white reproduction does not allow us to detect the colors used in this still-life painting.

Both Picasso and Tansey set problems for the viewer to solve: Picasso's is the analysis of pictorial space, while Tansey's concern is with a wry dissection and analysis of the conventions of art and of the art world itself.

Geographical Index

Following is an alphabetical listing by country and by city of the locations of works illustrated in Gardner's *Art through the Ages,* eighth edition. Figures are identified by name of artist, title of work, date, culture or country of origin, art-historical period when appropriate, and art form. (Excluded are works no longer in existence, works whose present locations are unknown, and works in private collections.) Items located in the same museum or at the same site are grouped together and, within these groups, are arranged in the order in which they appear in the text.

ALGERIA   *fig. no.*

Timgad   Plan of Ruins of Roman city founded *c.* A.D. 100, Roman architecture in Africa   6-44

AUSTRALIA

Melbourne   Painting of hunter and kangaroo from Oenpelli, Arnhem Land (National   14-72
                                       Museum of Victoria), Australian bark painting
New South Wales   Mungarawai, The Djanggawul Sisters, from Yirrkala, Arnhem Land, Australian   14-71
                                       bark painting

AUSTRIA

Salzburg   Klimt, *Death and Life,* 1908 and 1911 (collection of Marietta Preleuthner),   22-1
                                       Austrian painting
Vienna   *Venus of Willendorf, c.* 20,000 B.C. (Naturhistorisches Museum), prehistoric   1-13
                                       sculpture
                                    Vienna Genesis, detail *Rebecca and Eliezer at the Well,* early 6th century   7-15
                                       Österreischeische Nationalbibliothek), book illumination
                                    Dürer, *The Great Piece of Turf,* 1503 (Graphische Sammlung Albertina),   18-38
                                       German painting

                                    Kunsthistorisches Museum

                                    St. Matthew, from the *Gospel Book of Charlemagne, c.* 800, Carolingian   8-9
                                       manuscript
                                    Mounted Warrior with Captive, detail of gold vessel, probably 9th century, from   8-14
                                       Nagy-szent-Miklos Hoard, Migration metalwork
                                    Corregio, *Jupiter and Io, c.* 1532, Italian painting   17-40
                                    Spranger, *Hercules and Omphale, c.* 1598, Austrian painting   18-46
                                    Bruegel, *Hunters in the Snow,* 1565, Flemish painting   18-48
                                    Bruegel, *The Peasant Dance, c.* 1567, Flemish painting   18-49
                                    Rembrandt, *Self-Portrait,* 1652, Dutch painting   19-50

BELGIUM

Antwerp   Rubens, *The Elevation of the Cross,* 1610 (Antwerp Cathedral), Flemish painting   19-38
                                    Ensor, *Christ's Entry into Brussels,* 1888 (Koninklijk Museum voor   21-75
                                       Schone Kunsten), Belgian painting
Bruges (West Flanders)   Jan van Eyck, *The Virgin with the Canon van der Paele,* 1436   18-10
                                       (Musée Communaux), Flemish painting
                                    Memling, *St. John Altarpiece,* 1479 (Hospitaal Sint Jan), Flemish painting   18-20
Brussels   Horta, Hotel van Eetvelde, 1895 (Palmerston Square), Belgian architecture   22-55

                                    Musée Royaux des Beaux-Arts de Belgique

                                    Metsys, *st. Anne Altarpiece,* 1507–1509, Netherlandish painting   18-44
                                    David, *The Death of Marat,* 1793, French painting   20-39

Ghent (East Flanders)   Hubert and Jan van Eyck, *The Ghent Altarpiece,* 1432 (church of St. Bavo),   18-7 to 18-9
                                       Flemish painting
                                    Bosch, *The Carrying of the Cross, c.* 1510(?), (Musée des Beaux-Arts),   18-21
                                       Flemish painting
Louvain   Bouts, *The Last Supper,* 1464–1468, (St. Peter's), Flemish painting   18-17
Tervuren   Ancestral figure, Kongo, Zaire, 19th to 20th century (Musée Royal de   14-50
                                       l'Afrique Centrale), sculpture
                                    Power figure, Songye, Zaire, 19th to 20th century (Musée Royal de   14-51
                                       l'Afrique Centrale), sculpture
                                    Mboom helmet mask, Kuba, Zaire, 19th to 20th century (Musée Royal de   14-54
                                       l'Afrique Centrale), carving

BOLIVIA

Tiahuanaco	Monolithic gateway, 9th century (?), Tiahuanaean style architecture	14-15

CANADA

Montreal	Safdie, Habitat, 1967 Israeli architecture in Canada	22-114
Ottawa	West, *The Death of General Wolfe*, 1771 (National Gallery of Canada), English painting	20-35
Toronto	Acropolis of Athens, Model of Parthenon, Erectheon, Propylaea, and Temple of Athena Nike, Greek architecture	5-44

CHINA

Kansu (province)	*Paradise of Amitabha*, Cave 139A, Tunhwang, T'ang dynasty, 9th century, Chinese cave painting	12-14
Kwangtung (province)	Pagoda of the Temple of the Six Banyan Trees, 537, Chinese architecture	12-30
Shansi (province)	*Colossal Buddha*, Cave XX, Yunkang, c. 460, Chinese sculpture	12-10
Shantung (province)	Wu family shrine, Later Han dynasty, A.D., 147–168, Chinese stone rubbing	12-6
Shensi (province)	*Soldiers of the Imperial Bodyguard*, tomb of Emperor Shih Huang Ti 221–206 B.C., Chinese sculpture	12-4
	Soldier Poised for Hand-to-Hand Combat, tomb of Emperor Shih Huang Ti, 221–206 B.C., Chinese sculpture	12-5
	Palace Ladies, from the tomb of Princess Yung-t'ai, near Sian, T'ang dynasty, 706, Chinese painting	12-15

TAIWAN

Taipei	**National Palace Museum**	
	Fan K'uan, *Travelers Among Mountains and Streams,* Northern Sung dynasty, early 11th century, Chinese scroll painting	12-18
	Huang Kung-Wang, *Dwelling in the Fu-ch'un Mountains,* Yüan dynasty, 1347–1350, Chinese scroll painting	12-22
	Wu Chen, *Bamboo*, Yüan dynasty, 1350, Chinese painting	12-23

EGYPT

Abu Simbel	Temple of Ramses II, 1257 B.C., Egyptian architecture	3-24, 3-25
Beni Hasan	Rock-cut tombs, c. 1900 B.C., Egyptian architecture	3-18, 3-19
	Tomb of Amenemhet, c. 1930 B.C., Egyptian architecture	3-20
	Feeding of Oryxes, from the tomb of Khnumhotep, c. 1900 B.C. Egyptian painting	3-21
Cairo	Mausoleum of Sultan Hasan, 1356–1363, Islamic architecture	7-80, 7-81
	Egyptian Museum	
	Palette of Narmer, Hierakonpolis, c. 3000 B.C., Egyptian sculpture	3-2
	Panel of Hesire, Saqqara, c. 2750 B.C., Egyptian sculpture	3-3
	Khafre, diorite statue from Gizeh, c. 2600 B.C., Egyptian sculpture	3-13
	Reserve head of a prince, from Gizeh, c. 2500 B.C., Egyptian sculpture	3-14
	Sheikh el Beled, from his tomb at Saqqara, c. 2400 B.C., Egyptian sculpture	3-15
	Geese of Medum, c. 2530 B.C., Egyptian painting	3-17
	Sesostris III, 1878 B.C. (Egyptian Museum), Egyptian sculpture	3-22
	Akhenaton, from a pillar statue in the Temple of Amen-Re, Karnak, c. 1375 B.C., Egyptian sculpture	3-36
	Second coffin of Tutankhamen, 1361–1352 B.C. (Egyptian Museum), Egyptian sculpture	3-39
	Death mask of Tutankhamen, innermost coffin, Egyptian sculpture	3-40
	Chest from Tutankhamen's tomb, Thebes, c. 1350 B.C., Egyptian painted chest	3-41
	Mentemhet the Governor, c. 650 B.C. (Egyptian Museum), Egyptian sculpture	3-44
Deir el-Bahri	Mortuary Temple of Queen Hatshepsut, c. 1450, Egyptian architecture	3-23
Edfu	Pylon Temple of Horus, c. 237–212 B.C., Egyptian architecture	3-27
Gizeh	Great Pyramids of Gizeh, c. 2530–2460 B.C., Egyptian architecture	3-7, 3-8, 3-11, 3-12
	The Great Sphinx, c. 2530 B.C., Egyptian sculpture	3-10, 3-11, p. 20
Hierakonpolis	*Men, Boats, Animals,* wall painting, c. 3500 B.C., Egyptian painting	3-1
Karnak	Temple of Amen-Re, begun c. 1500 B.C., Egyptian architecture	3-28, 3-29
Luxor	Temple of Amen-Mut-Khonsu, c. 1370–1280 B.C., Egyptian architecture	3-31
Saqqara	Stepped Pyramid of King Zoser, c. 2610 B.C., Egyptian architecture	3-6
	Hippopotamus Hunt, Tomb of Ti, c. 2400 B.C., Egyptian painting	3-16
Thebes	Tomb of Queen Nofretari, c. 1250 B.C., Egyptian painted sculpture	Intro. 12
	Tomb of Nakht, c. 1450 B.C., interior fresco, Egyptian painting	3-34

ENGLAND

Brighton	Nash, Royal Pavilion, 1815–1818, English architecture	21-3
Cambridge	Master Hugo, *Moses Expounding the Law*, early 12th century (Corpus Christi College), English manuscript	9-39
	The Eadwine Psalter, c. 1150 (Trinity College), English manuscript	9-41
Canterbury	William of Sens and William the Englishman, Canterbury Cathedral, 1179–1184, English architecture	10-40, 10-41
Chatsworth	Poussin, *Et in Arcadia Ego*, c. 1630 (Art gallery, Chatsworth House, Derbyshire), French painting	19-64
Durham	Durham Cathedral, begun c. 1093, English architecture	9-17, 9-18
Gloucester	Gloucester Cathedral, 12th to 15th centuries (choir, 1332–1557), English architecture	10-46
London	Chapel of Henry VII, 1503–1519 (Westminster Abbey), English architecture	10-47
	Jones, Banqueting House, Whitehall, 1619–1622, English architecture	19-75
	Wren, St. Paul's Cathedral, 1675–1710, English architecture	19-76
	Boyle and Kent, Chiswick House, near London, begun 1725, English architecture	20-5
	Barry and Pugin, Houses of Parliament, designed 1835, English architecture	21-2

British Library

Ornamental page from the *Book of Lindisfarne*, late 7th century, English manuscript	8-6
St. Matthew, from the *Book of Lindisfarne*, late 7th century, English manuscript	8-8

British Museum

Scenes of War, panel from the *Standard of Ur*, c. 2700 B.C., Sumerian mosaic	2-15
Ashurnasirpal II at War, Nimrud, c. 875 B.C., Assyrian sculpture	2-28
Ashurnasirpal II Drinking, Nimrud, c. 875 B.C., Assyrian sculpture	2-29
Ashurbanipal Hunting Lions, Nineveh, c. 650 B.C., Assyrian sculpture	2-30
Dying Lioness, Nineveh, c. 650 B.C., Assyrian sculpture	2-31
Fowling Scene, from the tomb of Nebamun (?), Thebes, c. 1450 B.C., Egyptian painting	3-33
Musicians and Dancers, from the tomb of Nebamun (?), Thebes, c. 1450 B.C., Egyptian painting	3-35, p.1
Psychostasis ("Soul-raising") *of Hu-Nefer,* Egyptian painting	3-43
Dionysos (Herakles?), from the east pediment of the Parthenon, Athens, 448–432 B.C., Greek sculpture	5-47
Three Goddesses, from the east pediment of the Parthenon, Greek sculpture	5-48
Lapith and Centaur, metope from the Parthenon, Greek sculpture	5-50
Horsemen, from the west frieze of the Parthenon, Greek sculpture	5-51
Mausolus, from the mausoleum at Halicarnassus, c. 355 B.C., Greek sculpture in Turkey	5-69
St. Michael the Archangel, leaf of a diptych, early 6th century	7-20
Purse cover from the Sutton Hoo ship burial, c. 655	8-2
Ku K'ai-chih (?), (c. A.D. 344–406), *Lady Feng and the Bear*, section of horizontal scroll *Admonitions of the Instructress to the Court Ladies*	12-12
Altar of the Hand, Benin sculpture	14-44
Areogun, door from the King's palace at Ikerre, 20th century, Yoruba carving	14-47
Kukailmoku, Hawaiian carving	14-57
Caradosso, medal showing Bramante's design for St. Peter's, 1506	17-8
Rembrandt, *The Three Crosses*, 1653, Dutch print	19-53

Courtauld Institute Galleries

Manet, *Bar at the Folies-Bergère*, 1882, French painting	21-41
Cézanne, *La Montagne Sainte-Victoire*, c. 1886–1888, French painting	21-66

National Gallery

Uccello, *The Battle of San Romano*, c. 1455, Italian painting	16-29
Leonardo, cartoon for *The Virgin and Child with St. Anne and the Infant St. John*, c. 1498, Italian drawing	17-2
Bronzino, *Venus, Cupid, Folly, and Time*, c. 1546, Italian painting	17-44
Jan van Eyck, *Man in a Red Turban*, 1433, Flemish painting	18-11
Jan van Eyck, *Giovanni Arnolfini and His Bride*, 1434, Flemish painting	18-12, 18-13
Holbein, *The French Ambassadors*, 1533, German painting	18-42
Holbein, *Christina of Denmark*, 1538, German painting	18-43

	Zurbarán, *St. Francis in Meditation, c.* 1639, Spanish painting	19-34
	Claude Lorraine, *The Marriage of Isaac and Rebekah (The Mill),* 1642, French painting	19-63
	Hogarth, *Breakfast Scene,* from *Marriage à la Mode, c.* 1745, English painting	20-20
	Reynolds, *Lord Heathfield,* 1787, English painting	20-34
	Constable, *The Haywain,* 1821, English painting	21-30

Tate Gallery

	Blake, *Pity, c.* 1795, English painting	20-42
	Tissot, *The Ball on Shipboard,* 1874, English painting	21-44
	Millais, *Ophelia,* 1852, English painting	21-48
	Burne-Jones, *King Cophetua and the Beggar Maid,* 1884, English painting	21-49
	Matisse, *Back I, c.* 1909, French sculpture	22-40
	Matisse, *Back IV, c.* 1929, French sculpture	22-41
	Nevelson, *An American Tribute to the British People,* 1960–1965, American sculpture	22-81

Victoria and Albert Museum

	Priestess Celebrating the Rites of Bacchus, leaf of an ivory diptych, Early Christian, *c.* A.D., 380–400, sculpture	7-19
	The Sacrifice of Iphigenia, panel from the *Veroli Casket,* Byzantine, 10th or 11th century, sculpture	7-64
	Carpet from the tomb-mosque of Shah Tahmasp at Ardebil, Iran, 1540, Persian textile	7-87

Wallace Collection

	Boucher, *Cupid a Captive,* 1754, French painting	20-15
	Fragonard, *The Swing,* 1766, French painting	20-16
Middlesex (county)	Adam, Etruscan Room, Osterley Park House, begun 1761, English architecture	20-24
Oxford	Piranesi, *Carceri 14, c.* 1750 (Ashmolean Museum), Italian print	20-43
Oxfordshire (county)	Vanbrugh, Blenheim Palace, 1705–1722, English architecture	20-4
Salisbury	Salisbury Cathedral, begun, *c.* 1220, English architecture	10-42 to 10-45
Salisbury Plain, Wiltshire	Stonehenge, *c.* 2000 B.C., prehistoric English architecture	1-15, 1-16
Sussex	*Kuan-Yin,* Early Ch'ing dynasty, Chinese sculpture	12-28
Twickenham	Walpole, Strawberry Hill, 1749–1777, English architecture	20-21
Windsor	Leonardo, *Embryo in the Womb,* 1510 (Royal Collection, Windsor Castle), Italian drawing	17-5
Worcestershire (county)	Miller, sham Gothic ruin, Hagley Park, 1747, English architecture	20-22
	Stuart, Doric portico, Hagley Park, 1758, English architecture	20-23

FRANCE

Aix-en-Provence	Ingres, *François Marius Granet,* 1807 (Musée Granet), French painting	21-23
Amiens	Amiens Cathedral, *c.* 1220–1236, French Gothic architecture	10-22 to 10-25
Angoulême	St. Pierre, 12th century, French Romanesque architecture	9-23
Ariège	*Bison with Superposed Arrows,* Niaux, *c.* 15,000–130,000 B.C., prehistoric French painting	1-7
	Sorcerer, Trois-Frères, *c.* 13,000–11,000 B.C., prehistoric French painting	1-9
Arles	St. Trophime, late 12th century, French Romanesque architecture	9-34
Autun	St. Lazare, *c.* 1130, French Romanesque architecture	9-30, 9-31
Bayeux	*Norman Cavalry Charging in the Battle of Hastings,* from the *Bayeux Tapestry,* 1070–1080, French textile	9-35
Beauvais	Beauvais Cathedral (choir, 1272; rebuilt after 1284), French Gothic architecture	10-29, 10-30
Blois	Mansart, Orléans wing of the Château de Blois, 1635–1638, French architecture	19-64
Bourges	Bourges Cathedral, 1195–1255, French Gothic architecture	10-19 to 10-21
Caen	St. Étienne, begun, *c.* 1067, French Romanesque architecture	9-14 to 9-16
Chambord	Château de Chambord, begun 1519, French Renaissance architecture	18-52
Chantilly	**Musée Condé**	
	The Limbourg Brothers, *Les Très Riches Heures du Duc de Berry,* 1413–1416, Flemish manuscript	18-4, 18-5
Chartres	**Chartres Cathedral**	
	West ("royal") portals, *c.* 1145–1170, French Gothic architecture	10-13, 10-14
	The "new" cathedral, begun 1194, French Gothic architecture	10-15 to 10-17
	Porch of the Confessors, *c.* 1220–1230, French Gothic architecture	10-31

	Good Samaritan window, early 13th century, French Gothic stained glass	10-35
	St. Theodore, south portal, *c.* 1215–1220, French Gothic sculpture	16-7
Colmar	Grünewald, *The Isenheim Altarpiece, c.* 1510–1515 (Musée Unterlinden), German painting in France	18-34, 18-35
Dijon	*St. George and the Dragon*, from the *Moralia in Job* manuscript, Romanesque, early 12th century (Bibliothèque Municipale), French manuscript	9-38
	Sluter, *The Well of Moses*, 1395–1406 (Chartreuse de Champmol)	18-1
	Broederlam, *The Presentation and the Flight into Egypt*, 1394–1399 (Musée des Beaux-Arts)	18-2
Dordogne (department)	Paleolithic cave paintings, Lascaux, 15,000–13,000 B.C., prehistoric painting	1-1, 1-3, 1-4, 1-6, 1-8
	Reindeer, Font-de-Gaume, *c.* 13,000–11,000 B.C.	1-10
	Relief Horse, Cap Blanc, *c.* 13,000–11,000 B.C., prehistoric sculpture	1-12
Fontainebleau	Rosso Fiorentino and Primaticcio, *Venus Reproving Love, c.* 1530–1540 (Gallery of Francis I), Italian painting in France	18-51
La Rochelle	Double-headed male figure, Easter Island, before 1860 (Museum of Natural History), sculpture	14-59
Laon	Laon Cathedral, *c.* 1160–1205, French Gothic architecture	10-5 to 10-8, 10-18
Lot (department)	*Spotted Horses and Negative Hand Imprints,* Pech-Merle, *c.* 15,000–13,000 B.C., Prehistoric painting	1-5
Lyons	Géricault, *Insane Woman (Envy),* 1822–1823 (Musée des Beaux Arts), French painting	21-17
Marseilles	Le Corbusier, Unité d'Habitation, 1947–1952, French architecture	22-104
	Preault, *Ophelia* (Musée de Longchamps), French painting	21-81
Moissac	St. Pierre, *c.* 1115–1135, French Romanesque architecture	9-27 to 9-29
Nimes	Pont du Gard, Roman aqueduct, 1st century B.C., Roman architecture in France	6-43
Paris	Abbey church of St. Denis, near Paris, 1140–1144, French Gothic architecture	10-1 to 10-3
	Notre Dame, 1163–1250, French Gothic architecture	10-9 to 10-12
	Jean de Chelles, rose window of the north transept, Notre Dame, 1240–1250, French Gothic stained glass	10-26, p. 310
	The Virgin of Paris, early 14th century (Notre Dame), French Gothic sculpture	10-39
	Sainte-Chapelle, 1243–1248 (rose window, 1485 or later), French Gothic architecture	10-27, 10-28
	Goujon, *Nymphs,* Fountain of the Innocents, 1548–1549, French sculpture	18-54
	Rembrandt, *Supper at Emmaus, c.* 1628–1630 (Musée Jacquemart-André), Dutch painting	19-47
	Hardouin-Mansart, Les Invalides (Église de Dôme), 1676–1706, French architecture	19-71, 19-72
	Boffrand, Salon de la Princesse, Hôtel de Soubise, 1737–1740, French architecture	20-6
	Soufflot, the Panthéon, 1755–1792, French architecture	20-25
	Vignon, La Madeleine, begun 1808, French architecture	21-1
	Garnier, the Opéra, 1861–1874, French architecture	21-4
	Rude, *"La Marseillaise,"* Arc de Triomphe, 1833–1836, French sculpture	21-7
	Manet, *Le Déjeuner sur l'herbe*, 1863 (Galerie du Jeu de Paume), French painting	21-39, 21-40
	Moreau, *Jupiter and Semele, c.* 1875 (Musée Gustave Moreau), French painting	21-72
	Labrouste, Bibliothèque Ste-Geneviève, 1843–1850, French architecture	21-85
	Picasso, *Bull's Head*, 1943 (Galerie Louise Leiris)	22-51
	Rogers and Piano, Pompidou Center, 1977, French architecture	22-117
	Bibliothèque Nationale	
	Villard de Honnecourt, *Lion Portrayed from Life, c.* 1230–1235 (Cabinet des Manuscripts), French Gothic drawing	Intro. 13
	Diptych of Anastasius, A.D. 517, Early Christian sculpture	7-21
	David Composing the Psalms, page from the *Paris Psalter, c.* 900, Late Byzantine manuscript	7-61
	Gospel Book of Archbishop Ebbo of Reims, c. 816–835, Migration manuscript	8-10
	Villard de Honnecourt, page from a notebook, *c.* 1240, French Gothic drawing	10-36
	Abraham and the Three Angels, from the *Psalter of St. Louis*, 1253–1270, French Gothic manuscript	10-37

Pucelle, page from the *Belleville Breviary, c.* 1325, French Medieval manuscript   18-3

Callot, etching from the *Miseries of War* series, 1621, French print   19-60

Louvre

Victory Stele of Naram-Sin, Akkad, *c.* 2300–2200 B.C., Akkadian sculpture   2-21

Gudea Worshipping, Telloh, *c.* 2100 B.C., Neo-Sumerian sculpture   2-22

Stele of Hammurabi, Susa, *c.* 1760 B.C., Babylonian sculpture   2-23

Winged human-headed bull, Khorsabad, *c.* 720 B.C., Assyrian sculpture   2-27

Lion from the Processional Way, Ishtar Gate, Babylon, *c.* 575 B.C., Neo-Babylonian sculpture   2-32

Statue of Queen Niparasu from Susa in Khuzistan, Ancient Iran, *c.* 1300 B.C., sculpture   2-34

Winged ibex, jar handle, Persia, 5th to 4th century B.C., Persian metalwork   2-40

Seti I Offering, Abydos, *c.* 1300 B.C., Egyptian sculpture   3-42

Euphronios, *Heracles Strangling Antaios,* Krater from Cerveteri, *c.* 510–500 B.C., Greek ceramic   5-9

Hera, from Samos, *c.* 560 B.C., Greek sculpture   5-14

Head of the Procession, from the east frieze of the Parthenon, Athens, 448–432 B.C., Greek sculpture   5-52

Niobid Painter, *Argonaut Krater, c.* 455–450 B.C., Greek ceramic   5-63

Nike of Samothrace, c. 190 B.C., Greek sculpture   5-76

Aphrodite of Melos, c. 150–100 B.C., Greek sculpture   5-83

The Harbaville Triptych, c. 950, Byzantine sculpture   7-65

Leonardo, *The Virgin of the Rocks, c.* 1485, Italian painting   17-1

Leonardo, *Mona Lisa, c.* 1503–1505, Italian painting   17-4

Raphael, *Baldassare Castiglione, c.* 1514, Italian painting   17-19

Michelangelo, *The Dying Slave,* 1513–1516, Italian sculpture   17-22

Michelangelo, *The Bound Slave,* 1513–1516, Italian sculpture   17-23

Cellini, *Diana of Fontainebleau,* 1543–1544, Italian sculpture   17-46

Giorgione, *Pastoral Symphony, c.* 1508, Italian painting   17-60

Titian, *Man with the Glove, c.* 1519 (?), Italian painting   17-64

Attributed to Enguerrand Quarton, *The Avignon Pietà, c.* 1455, French painting   18-25

Clouet, *Francis I, c.* 1525–1530, French painting   18-50

Lescot, Square Court of the Louvre, begun 1546, French architecture   18-53

Pilon, *Descent from the Cross,* bronze relief, 1583, French sculpture   18-55

Caravaggio, *Death of the Virgin,* 1605–1606, Italian painting   19-27

Van Dyck, *Charles I Dismounted, c.* 1635, Flemish painting   19-42

Rembrandt, *Supper at Emmaus, c.* 1648, Dutch painting   19-48

Le Nain, *Family of Country People, c.* 1640, French painting   19-59

Poussin, *Et in Arcadia Ego, c.* 1655 (?), French painting   19-61

Poussin, *The Burial of Phocion,* 1648, French painting   19-62

Perrault, Le Vau, and Le Brun, east façade of the Louvre, 1667–1670, French architecture   19-65

Puget, *Milo of Crotona,* 1671–1682, French sculpture   19-73

Rigaud, *Louis XIV,* 1701, French painting   20-1

Watteau, *L'Indifférent, c.* 1716, French painting   20-2

Watteau, *Return from Cythera,* 1717–1719, French painting   20-14

Quentin de la Tour, *Self-Portrait, c.* 1751, French painting   20-18

Chardin, *Grace at Table,* 1740, French painting   20-19

Houdon, *Diana,* 1790, French sculpture   20-29

Greuze, *The Return of the Prodigal Son,* 1777–1778, French painting   20-36

David, *Oath of the Horatii,* 1784, French painting   20-38

Barye, *Jaguar Devouring a Hare,* 1850–1851, French sculpture   21-8

Girodet-Trioson, *The Burial of Atala,* 1808, French painting   21-13

Gros, *Pest House at Jaffa,* 1804, French painting   21-14

Géricault, *Raft of the Medusa,* 1818–1819, French painting   21-15

Géricault, *Mounted Officer of the Imperial Guard,* 1812, French painting   21-16

Delacroix, *The Death of Sardanapalus,* 1826, French painting   21-18

Delacroix, *Liberty Leading the People,* 1830, French painting   21-19

Delacroix, *Tiger Hunt,* 1854, French painting   21-20

Ingres, *Oedipus and the Sphinx,* 1808, French painting   21-21

Ingres, *Grande Odalisque,* 1814, French painting   21-22

Ingres, *Paganini,* 1819, French painting — 21-24

Chassériau, *Esther Adorning Herself,* 1841, French painting — 21-26

Couture, *Romans of the Decadence,* 1847, French painting — 21-27

Millet, *The Gleaners,* 1857, French painting — 21-35

Courbet, *Burial at Ornans,* 1849, French painting — 21-38

Renoir, *Le Moulin de la Galette,* 1876, French painting — 21-57

Musée Guimet

Dance relief from Angkor Wat, Kampuchea, 12th century, Cambodian sculpture — 11-31

Prabhutaratna and Sakyamuni, Chinese, Northern and Southern dynasties, — 12-11
   c. A.D. 518, Chinese sculpture

Musée Rodin

Rodin, *The Kiss,* 1886–1898, French sculpture — 21-83

Rodin, *Balzac,* 1892–1897, French sculpture — 21-84

Poissy   Le Corbusier, Villa Savoye, 1929, French architecture — 22-61

Reims   **Reims Cathedral**

Central portal of the west façade, 1225–1290, French Gothic architecture — 10-32, 10-33

Crucifixion window, *c.* 1190, French Gothic stained glass — 10-34

Ronchamp   Le Corbusier, Notre Dame du Haut, 1950–1955, French architecture — 22-105, 22-106

Rouen   Façade of St. Maclou, 1500–1514, French Gothic architecture — 10-39

St. Germain-en-Laye   *Bison with Turned Head,* from La Madeleine, *c.* 11,000–9,000 B.C. — 1-11
   (Musée des Antiquités Nationales), prehistoric sculpture in France

Saint-Omer   Anonymous, *The Life and Miracles of St. Audomarus (Omer),* 11th century — 9-37
   (Bibliothèque Municipale), French Romanesque manuscript

Toulouse   St. Sernin, *c.* 1080–1120, French Romanesque architecture — 9-4 to 9-6

Christ in Majesty, late 11th century (in the ambulatory of St. Sernin), — 9-24
   French sculpture

Versailles   **Palace of Versailles**

The palace and surrounding park (park designed by Le Nôtre, 1661–1668), — 19-66, 19-67
   French architecture

Le Vau and Hardouin-Mansart, garden façade of the palace, 1669–1685, — 19-68
   French architecture

Hardouin-Mansart and Le Brun, Galerie des Glaces, *c.* 1680, French architecture — 19-69

Hardouin-Mansart, Royal Chapel, 1698–1710, French architecture — 19-70

Vézelay   *The Mission of the Apostles*, tympanum of the center portal of the narthex — 9-32, 9-33
   of La Madeleine, Vézelay, 1120–1132, French Romanesque sculpture

GERMANY

Aachen   The Palatine Chapel of Charlemagne, 792–805, Carolingian architecture — 8-16, 8-17

Bamberg   *The Bamberg Rider,* late 13th century (Bamberg Cathedral), German sculpture — 10-55

Neumann, pilgrimage church of Vierzehnheiligen, 1743–1772, German — 20-9 to 20-11
   architecture

Berlin   *Queen Nefertiti,* Tel el-Amarna, *c.* 1360 B.C. (Ägyptisches Museum, — 3-37
   West Berlin), Egyptian sculpture

Staatliche Museen (West Berlin)

Senmut with Princess Nefrua, Thebes, *c.* 1450 B.C., Egyptian sculpture — 3-32

King Smenkhkare and Meritaten (?), Tel el-Amarna, *c.* 1360 B.C., — 3-38
   Egyptian sculpture

Andokides Painter, *Herakles and Apollo Struggling for the Tripod*, — 5-8
   amphora *c.* 530 B.C., Greek ceramic

Echternach Master, *Doubting Thomas*, from the *Magdeburg Antependium*, — 8-26
   c. 970–990, Ivory sculpture

Gemäldegalerie, Staatliche Museen, Berlin-Dahlem (West Berlin)

Fouquet, *Étienne Chevalier and St. Stephen,* *c.* 1450, Flemish painting — 18-24

Dürer, *Hieronymus Holzschuher,* 1526, German painting — 18-39

Gossaert, *Neptune and Amphitrite, c.* 1516, Flemish painting — 18-45

Hals, *Malle Babbe, c.* 1650 (?), Dutch painting — 19-45

Georges De la Tour, *The Lamentation over St. Sebastian,* 1630s (copy ?), — 19-58
   French painting

Staatliche Museen, Antiken-Sammlung (Pergamon Museum), East Berlin
Reconstruction of the Ishtar Gate, Babylon, *c.* 575 B.C., Babylonian   2-33
   architecture
Altar of Zeus and Athena, Pergamon, *c.* 175 B.C., Greek sculpture in Asia Minor   5-78, 5-79
Model of the acropolis, Pergamon, Greek architecture in Asia Minor   5-97

Bremen   Mask, Sulka, 1900–1910, Melanesian sculpture   14-69
Cologne   Head of a crucifix, 1301 (St. Maria im Kapitol), German sculpture   10-56
    Cologne Cathedral, 1248–19th century, German Gothic architecture   10-48, 10-49, 10-57
    Lochner, *Madonna in the Rose Garden, c.* 1430–1435 (Wallraf-Richartz-   18-26
       Museum), German painting
    Barlach, *War Monument,* Gustrow Cathedral, 1927 (Schildergasse,   22-38
       Antoniterkirche, Cologne), German sculpture
Creglingen   Riemenschneider, *The Creglingen Altarpiece, c.* 1495–1499 (Parish church,   18-29
       Creglingen), German sculpture
Dessau (East Germany)   Gropius, shop block, the Bauhaus, 1925–1926, German architecture   22-63
Dresden (East Germany)   Antonello da Messina, *The Martyrdom of St. Sebastian, c.* 1475–1477   16-67
       (Gemäldegalerie, Abt. Alte Meister, Staatliche Kunstsammlungen, Dresden),
       Italian painting in Germany

Hamburg   **Kunsthalle, Hamburg**
    Runge, *Morning,* 1809, German painting   21-32
    Leibl, *Three Women in a Village Church,* 1878–1881, German painting   21-43
    Nolde, *St. Mary of Egypt Among Sinners,* 1912, Dutch painting   22-6

Hildesheim   Abbey church of St. Michael, 1001–1031 (restored), German architecture   8-22 to 8-24
    Adam and Eve Reproached by the Lord, 1015 (from the bronze doors of   8-25
       St. Michael's), Ottonian German architecture
Karlsruhe   Cranach, *The Judgment of Paris,* 1530 (Staatliche Kunsthalle, Karlsruhe),   18-33
       German painting
Lorsch   Torhalle (gatehouse) *c.* 800, German architecture   8-18
Marburg   Church of St. Elizabeth, 1233–1283, German architecture   10-50 to 10-52
Munich   Cuvilliés, Amalienburg, 1734–1739, French architecture in Germany   20-7, 20-8
    Otto, Olympic Stadium, 1971–1972, German architecture   22-112

    Alte Pinakothek
    Titian, *Christ Crowned with Thorns, c.* 1573–1575, Italian painting   17-65
    Pacher, *St. Wolfgang Forces the Devil to Hold His Prayerbook,* panel from   18-30
       the *Altar of the Fathers of the Church, c.* 1481, Swiss painting
    Altdorfer, *The Battle of Issus,* 1529, German painting   18-32
    Dürer, *The Four Apostles,* 1526, German painting   18-41
    Rubens, *The Rape of the Daughters of Leucippus,* 1617, Flemish painting   19-39
    Rubens, *The Lion Hunt,* 1617–1618, Flemish painting   19-40

    Bayerische Staatsbibliothek
    Cover of the *Codex Aureus of St. Emmeram,* Carolingian, *c.* 870, manuscript   8-12
    The Annunciation to the Shepherds, from the *Lectionary of Henry II,*   8-27
       1002–1014, Ottonian manuscript
    Otto III Enthroned, from the *Gospel Book of Otto III,* Reichenau, 997–1000,   8-28
       Ottonian manuscript

    Bayerische Staatsgemäldesammlungen
    Feuerbach, *Medea,* 1870, German painting   21-50

    Staatliche Antikensammlungen
    Exekias, *Dionysos in a Sailboat,* interior of an Attic black-figure kylix,   5-7
       c. 550–525 B.C., Greek ceramic
    Euthymides, *Revelers,* detail from an amphora, *c.* 510–500 B.C., Greek ceramic   5-10
    Kouros from Tenea, *c.* 570 B.C., Greek sculpture   5-15
    Fallen Warrior, from the Temple of Aphaia at Aegina, *c.* 490 B.C.,   5-31
       Greek sculpture
    Herakles, from the east pediment of the Temple of Aphaia at Aegina,   5-32
       c. 490 B.C., Greek sculpture
    Statuette of Young Woman, c. 420 B.C., Greek sculpture   5-60
    Boethos, *Boy Strangling a Goose,* 2nd century B.C., Greek sculpture   5-86

Naumburg   *Ekkehard* and *Uta, c.* 1250–1260 (Naumburg Cathedral), German sculpture   10-54
Rohr   Egid Quirin Asam, *Assumption of the Virgin,* 1723 (Monastery church   20-13
       at Rohr), German sculpture

Speyer	Speyer Cathedral, begun 1030, German Romanesque architecture	9-7 to 9-9
Trier	The Porta Nigra ("Black Gate"), *c.* A.D. 280–310, Roman architecture	6-80
	The Aula Palatina ("Audience Hall of the Palace"), *c.* 310 A.D., Roman architecture	6-81
Würzburg	Brygos Painter, *Revelers,* kylix from Vulci, *c.* 490 B.C. (Martin V. Wagner Museen der Universität, Würzburg), Greek ceramic	5-11

GREECE

Aegina	Remains of the Temple of Aphaia, *c.* 490 B.C., Greek architecture	5-30
Athens	Proto-Geometric amphora from Dipylon, 10th century B.C. (Keramikos Museum), Greek ceramic	5-1
	Monument of Lysicrates, 334 B.C., Greek architecture	5-74

The Acropolis

	The Acropolis (entire complex), Greek architecture	5-42, 5-43
	Iktinos and Kalikrates, the Parthenon, 448–432 B.C., Greek architecture	5-45, 5-46
	Mnesikles, the Propylaea, *c.* 437–432 B.C., Greek architecture	5-53
	Temple of Athena Nike, 427–424 B.C., Greek architecture	5-54
	The Erechtheum, 421–405 B.C., Greek architecture	5-55 to 5-57

Acropolis Museum

	Peplos Kore, c. 530 B.C., Greek sculpture	5-17
	Kore from Chios (?), *c.* 510 B.C., Greek sculpture	5-18
	Nike Fastening Her Sandal, from the Temple of Athena Nike, *c.* 410 B.C., Greek sculpture	5-59

National Museum

	Dagger blades from the royal tombs at Mycenae, *c.* 1600–1500 B.C., Aegean metalwork	4-28
	Funeral mask from the royal tombs at Mycenae, *c.* 1500 B.C., Aegean metalwork	4-29
	Cups with repoussé decoration (the *Vaphio Cups*), *c.* 1500 B.C., Aegean metalwork	4-30
	The Warrior Vase, from Mycenae, *c.* 1200 B.C., Aegean ceramic	4-31
	Dipylon Vase, Geometric amphora, 8th century B.C., Greek ceramic	5-2
	Geometric bronze warrior, late 8th century B.C., Greek sculpture	5-12
	Kroisos (Kouros from Anavysos), *c.* 540–515 B.C., Greek sculpture	5-16
	Grave Stele of Hegeso, from Dipylon cemetery, *c.* 410–400 B.C., Greek sculpture	5-58
	Warrior's Head, from the Temple of Athena Alea at Tegea, *c.* 350 B.C., Greek sculpture	5-68
	Antikythera Youth, late 4th century B.C., Greek sculpture	5-72
Corfu	Temple of Artemis, *c.* 600–580 B.C., Greek architecture	5-29
Daphne	*The Crucifixion*, mosaic, the monastery church at Daphne, 11th century, Byzantine architecture in Greece	7-55

Delphi	**Delphi Museum**	
	Treasury of the Siphnians, *c.* 530 B.C., Greek architecture	5-27, 5-28
	Charioteer, from the Sanctuary of Apollo at Delphi, *c.* 470 B.C., Greek sculpture	5-37
Didyma	Temple of Apollo (the Didymaion, near Miletus), begun 313 B.C., Greek architecture	5-88
Eleusis	*The Blinding of Polyphemos* and *Gorgons*, proto-Attic amphora, *c.* 675–650 B.C. (Eleusis Museum), Greek ceramic	5-4
Epidaurus	Corinthian capital, *c.* 350 B.C. (Epidaurus Museum), Greek architecture	5-73
	Theater, *c.* 350 B.C., Greek architecture	5-89, 5-90

Herakleion, Crete	**Archeological Museum**	
	Phaistos, Kamares pitcher, *c.* 1800–1700 B.C., Minoan ceramic	4-4
	La Parisienne, fresco, Knossos, *c.* 1500 B.C., Minoan painting	4-13
	Octopus Jar (amphora), Gournia, *c.* 1600 B.C., Minoan ceramic	4-17
	Three-handled jar with papyrus decoration, Knossos, *c.* 1500 B.C., Minoan ceramic	4-18
	The Harvester Vase (rhyton), Hagia Triada, *c.* 1500 B.C., Minoan ceramic	4-19, 4-20
	Snake Goddess, Knossos, *c.* 1600 B.C., Minoan sculpture	4-21

Hosios Loukas, Phocis	Church of the Katholikon, *c.* 1020, and Church of the Theotokos, *c.* 1040, Byzantine architecture	7-45, 7-46, 7-48
Knossos, Crete	Palace at Knossos, *c.* 1600–1400 B.C., Minoan architecture	4-5 to 4-9
	The Cupbearer, fresco, *c.* 1500 B.C., Minoan painting	4-11
	The Toreador Fresco, c. 1500 B.C., Minoan painting	4-12
Mycenae	The Lion Gate, *c.* 1300 B.C., Mycenaean architecture	4-25
	Treasury of Atreus, *c.* 1300 B.C., Mycenaean architecture	4-26, 4-27
Olympia	**Museum, Olympia**	
	Temple of Zeus, West Pediment reconstruction, 468–460 B.C., Greek architecture	5-39
	Apollo, from the west pediment of the Temple of Zeus at Olympia, 468–460 B.C., Greek sculpture	5-40
	Hippodameia and the Centaur, from the west pediment of the Temple of Zeus at Olympia, 468–460 B.C., Greek sculpture	5-41
	Praxiteles, *Hermes and Dionysos, c.* 340 B.C., Greek sculpture	5-65, 5-66
Pella	The *Lion Hunt* mosaic, *c.* 300 B.C., Macedonian mosaic	5-98
Thera	*Springtime Fresco*, Aegean painting	4-14
	Flotilla Fresco, Aegean painting	4-15
	Young Fisherman Fresco, Aegean painting	4-16
Thessaloniki	*Saint Onesiphorus and Saint Porphyrius*, detail of dome mosaic, Church of Saint George, late 5th century, Early Christian Greek mosaic	7-13
Tiryns	Citadel of Tiryns, *c.* 1400–1200 B.C., Mycenaean architecture	4-22 to 4-24
INDIA		
Agra	Taj Mahal, 1632–1654, Indian architecture	7-82
Ajanta	*Beautiful Bodhisattva Padmapani*, Cave I, *c.* A.D. 600–650, Indian painting	11-23
Bhuvanesvar, Orissa	Muktesvar Temple, *c.* A.D. 950, Indian architecture	11-20
Elephanta	Siva as Mahadeva, in rock-cut temple, 6th century A.D., Indian sculpture	11-15
Karli	Carved chaitya hall, *c.* A.D. 100, Indian architecture	11-7, 11-8
Khajuraho	Visvanatha Temple, *c.* A.D. 100, Indian architecture	11-21
Mahabalipuram	Rock-cut temples, 7th century A.D., Indian architecture	11-19
Muttra	Seated Buddha, Mathura, 2nd–3rd century A.D. (Archaeological Museum, Muttra), Indian sculpture	11-11
New Delhi	**National Museum**	
	Male nude, Harappa, 3rd–2nd millennium B.C., Indian sculpture	11-1
	Seals, Mohenjo-Daro, 3rd millennium B.C., Indian sculpture	11-2
Punjai, Tamil Nadu	Siva as Nataraja, Naltunai Isvaram Temple, *c.* A.D. 1000, Indian sculpture	11-22
Sanchi	The Great Stupa, completed 1st century A.D., Indian sculpture	11-5, 11-6
Sarnath	**Archaeological Museum**	
	Lion capital of column erected by Emperor Asoka, Pataliputra, 3rd century B.C., Indian architecture	11-3
	Seated Buddha Preaching the First Sermon, Sarnath, 5th century A.D., Indian sculpture	11-12
Udayagiri	*Boar Avatar of Vishnu*, Cave V at Udayagiri, *c.* A.D. 400, Indian sculpture	11-13
INDONESIA		
Borobudur, Java	Stupa, *c.* A.D. 800, Javanese architecture	11-26
IRAN		
Persepolis	Royal Audience Hall, *c.* 500 B.C., Persian architecture	2-35
	The palace complex, *c.* 500 B.C., Persian architecture	2-36
	Palace of Darius, *c.* 500 B.C., Persian architecture	2-38
	Subjects Bringing Gifts to the King, stairway to the Royal Audience Hall, *c.* 500 B.C., Persian sculpture	2-39
IRAQ		
Baghdad	**The Iraq Museum**	
	Female Head, Warka, *c.* 3500–3000 B.C., Sumerian sculpture	2-12
	Statuettes from the Abu Temple, Tell Asmar, *c.* 2700–2600 B.C., Sumerian sculpture	2-13, 2-14
	Head of an Akkadian Ruler, Nineveh, *c.* 2300–2200 B.C., Akkadian sculpture	2-19

Dura Europos	*Priests with Attendants, c.* 100–200 A.D.	7-23
Khorsabad	The citadel of Sargon II, *c.* 720 B.C., Assyrian architecture	2-23, 2-24
Samarra	The Great Mosque of Samarra, A.D. 848–852, Islamic architecture	7-66, 7-67
Ukhaydir	Islamic palace, late 8th century, Islamic architecture	7-72, 7-73
Ur	Ziggurat, *c.* 2100 B.C., Sumerian architecture	2-10, 2-11

ITALY

Arezzo	**San Francesco, Arezzo**	
	Piero della Francesca, *Annunciation, c.* 1455, Italian painting	16-34
	Piero della Francesca, *The Finding and Proving of the True Cross, c.* 1455, Italian painting	16-35
Assisi	Master of the St. Francis Cycle, *St. Francis Preaching to the Birds, c.* 1296 (?), (Upper church, San Francisco, Assisi), Italian painting	15-13
Bologna	Jacopo della Quercia, *The Expulsion from the Garden of Eden, c.* 1430 (San Petronio, main portal), Italian sculpture	16-3
Borgo San Sepolcro	Piero della Francesca, *Resurrection, c.* 1363 (Palazzo Communale), Italian painting	16-36
Caere	Necropolis, 5th–4th century B.C., Etruscan architecture	6-2
	Tomb of the Reliefs, 5th–4th century B.C., Etruscan architecture	6-3
Castelseprio	*The Angel Appearing to Joseph*, detail of wall painting, Santa Maria de Castelseprio, early 8th century, Byzantine painting in Italy	7-54
Chiusi	Canopic urn, second half of 7th century B.C. (Museo Etrusco, Chiusi), Etruscan ceramic	6-6
Florence	San Miniato al Monte, completed *c.* 1062, Italian architecture	9-21, 9-22
	Brunelleschi, Ospedale degli Innocenti, 1419–1424, Italian architecture	16-16
	Brunelleschi, Santo Spirito, 1436, Italian architecture	16-17, 16-18
	Michelozzo di Bartolommeo, Palazzo Medici–Riccardi, begun 1444, Italian architecture	16-23, 16-24
	Andrea del Castagno, *The Last Supper, c.* 1445–1450 (Sant' Apollonia), Italian painting	16-30
	Fra Angelico, *Annunciation, c.* 1440–1445 (San Marco, Florence), Italian painting	16-37
	Alberti, Palazzo Rucellai, *c.* 1455, Italian architecture	16-39
	Michelangelo, tomb of Giuliano de' Medici, 1519–1534 (New Sacristy, San Lorenzo), Italian sculpture	17-27
	Pontormo, *The Descent from the Cross,* 1525–1528 (Capponi Chapel, Santa Felicita), Italian painting	17-41
	Giovanni da Bologna, *Rape of the Sabine Women*, completed 1583 (Loggia dei Lanzi), Italian sculpture	17-47
	Cathedral of Florence (the Duomo)	
	The cathedral, begun 1296 by Arnolfo di Cambio; the campanile, designed 1334 by Giotto; the dome, by Brunelleschi, built 1420–1436, Italian architecture	10-58 to 10-60 16-15
	Andrea Pisano, south doors of the baptistry, 1330–1335, Italian sculpture	15-4, 15-5
	Ghiberti, east doors of the baptistry ("Gates of Paradise"), 1425–1452, Italian sculpture	16-10, 16-11
	Museo dell' Opera del Duomo	
	Donatello, *St. John the Evangelist,* 1412–1415, Italian sculpture	Intro. 9
	Donatello, *"Zuccone"* (prophet figure), 1423–1425, Italian sculpture	16-8
	Donatello, *Mary Magdalene, c.* 1454–1455, Italian sculpture	16-14
	Galeria Accademia	
	Michelangelo, *Unfinished Bound Slave,* 1519, Italian sculpture	Intro. 10
	Michelangelo, *David*, 1501–1504, Italian sculpture	17-20
	Laurentian Library (Biblioteca Medicea-Laurenziana)	
	The Scribe Ezra Rewriting the Sacred Records, from the *Codex Amiatinus*, Jarrow, early 8th century, Anglo-Saxon manuscript	8-7
	Michelangelo, vestibule of the library, begun 1524; stairway designed 1558–1559, Italian architecture	17-28
	Museo Archeologico	
	François Vase, from Chiusi, *c.* 575 B.C., Greek ceramic	5-6
	Chimera, from Arezzo, 5th to 4th century B.C., Etruscan sculpture	6-11

Museo Nazionale
Brunelleschi, *The Sacrifice of Isaac*, 1401–1402, Italian sculpture — 16-1
Ghiberti, *The Sacrifice of Isaac*, 1401–1402, Italian sculpture — 16-2
Donatello, *David*, c. 1430–1432, Italian sculpture — 16-12
Rossellino, *Matteo Palmieri*, 1468, Italian sculpture — 16-49
Verrocchio, *David*, c. 1465, Italian sculpture — 16-52
Pollaiuolo, *Herakles and Antaios*, c. 1475, Italian sculpture — 16-54

Or San Michele
Nanni di Banco, *Quattro Santi Coronati*, c. 1408–1414, Italian sculpture — 16-4
Donatello, *St. Mark*, 1411–1413, Italian sculpture — 16-5
Donatello, *St. George*, 1415–1417, Italian sculpture — 16-6
Luca della Robbia, *Madonna and Child*, c. 1455–1460, Italian sculpture — 16-51

Santa Croce
Giotto, *The Death of St. Francis*, c. 1320 (Bardi Chapel), Italian painting — 15-15, 15-16
Gaddi, *The Meeting of Joachim and Anna*, 1338 (Baroncelli Chapel), Italian painting — 15-18
Brunelleschi, Pazzi Chapel, begun c. 1440, Italian architecture — 16-19 to 16-21
Antonio Rossellino, tomb of Leonardo Bruni, c. 1445–1450, Italian sculpture — 16-48

Santa Maria del Carmine
Masaccio, *The Tribute Money*, c. 1427 (Brancacci Chapel), Italian painting — 16-26
Masaccio, *The Expulsion from Eden*, c. 1425 (Brancacci Chapel), Italian painting — 16-27

Santa Maria Novella
Masaccio, *The Holy Trinity*, 1428 (?), Italian painting — 16-28
Alberti, façade of the church, begun c. 1456, Italian architecture — 16-40
Ghirlandaio, *The Birth of the Virgin*, c. 1485–1490, Italian painting — 16-57

Galleria degli Uffizi
Cimabue, *Madonna Enthroned with Angels and Prophets*, c. 1280, Italian painting — 15-11
Giotto, *Madonna Enthroned*, c. 1310, Italian painting — 15-12
Simone Martini, *The Annunciation*, 1333, Italian painting — 15-19
Gentile da Fabriano, *The Adoration of the Magi*, 1423, Italian painting — 16-25
Andrea del Castagno, *Pippo Spano*, c. 1448, Italian painting — 16-31
Domenico Veneziano, *The St. Lucy Altarpiece*, c. 1445, Italian painting — 16-32
Fra Filippo Lippi, *Madonna and Child with Angels*, c. 1455, Italian painting — 16-38
Botticelli, *The Birth of Venus*, c. 1482, Italian painting — 16-60
Raphael, *Madonna with the Goldfinch*, 1505–1506, Italian painting — 17-16
Andrea del Sarto, *Madonna of the Harpies*, 1517, Italian painting — 17-37
Rosso Fiorentino, *Moses Defending the Daughters of Jethro*, 1523, Italian painting — 17-42
Parmigianino, *Madonna with the Long Neck*, c. 1535, Italian painting — 17-43
Titian, *Venus of Urbino*, 1538, Italian painting — 17-63
Hugo van der Goes, *The Portinari Altarpiece*, c. 1476, Flemish painting — 18-18, 18-19
Van Honthorst, *The Supper Party*, 1620, Dutch painting — 19-43
Vigée-Lebrun, *Self-Portrait*, 1790, French painting — 20-33

Herculaneum   First-style ("incrustation") wall painting from a Samnite house, 2nd century B.C., Roman painting — 6-26
Wall Mosaic in the House of Neptune and Amphitrite, Roman mosaic — 6-40
Mantua   Alberti, church of Sant' Andrea, designed c. 1470, Italian architecture — 16-42 to 16-44
Mantegna, Camera degli sposi (Room of the Newlyweds), 1474 (Ducal Palace), Italian painting — 16-64, 16-65
Giulio Romano, Palazzo del Tè, 1525–1535, Italian architecture — 17-48, 17-49
Romano, *Fall of the Giants*, 1532–1539, Sala dei Giganti, Italian painting — 17-50
Milan   Leonardo, *The Last Supper*, c. 1495–1498 (Santa Maria delle Grazie), Italian painting — Intro. 4, 17-3
The Paliotto (golden altar) early 9th century (Sant' Ambrogio), Early Medieval sculpture — 8-13
Sant' Ambrogio, late 11th to early 12th century, Italian architecture — 9-11 to 9-13
Milan Cathedral, begun 1386, Italian architecture — 10-62

Pinacoteca de Brera
Mantegna, *The Dead Christ*, c. 1501, Italian painting — 16-66
Raphael, *The Marriage of the Virgin*, 1504, Italian painting — 17-15

Monreale, Sicily	*The Pantocrator with the Virgin, Angels, and Saints,* apse mosaic, late 12th century, Byzantine mosaic	7-57
Naples	**Museo Nazionale**	
	Polykleitos, *Doryphoros, c.* 450 B.C. (Roman copy), Greek sculpture	5-61
	Third style ("ornate") wall painting, from a villa at Boscotrecase, near Pompeii, early 1st century A.D., Roman painting	6-31
	Still Life with Peaches, wall painting from Herculaneum, *c.* A.D. 50, Roman painting	6-34
	Genre scene (?) from the House of the Dioscuri, Pompeii, 1st century A.D., Roman painting	6-35
	Herakles and Telephos, wall painting from Herculaneum, *c.* A.D. 70, Roman painting	6-36
	Pastoral Scene, wall painting from Pompeii, 1st century A.D., Roman painting	6-37
	The Battle of Issus, mosaic from the House of the Faun, Pompeii, 1st century A.D., Roman mosaic	6-38
Orvieto	**Orvieto Cathedral**	
	Cathedral façade, begun, *c.* 1310, Italian architecture	10-56
	Signorelli, *The Damned Cast Into Hell,* 1499–1504 (San Brizio Chapel), Italian painting	16-61
Ostia	Floor mosaic from the Baths of Neptune, 2nd century, Roman mosaic	6-39
	Reconstruction of Roman insulae (apartment houses) from the early empire, Roman architecture	6-42
	Hadrian, portrait bust, *c.* A.D. 120 (Museo Ostiense), Roman sculpture	6-71
Padua	Donatello, *Gattamelata* (equestrian statue of Erasmo da Narni), *c.* 1445–1450 (Piazza del Santo), Italian sculpture	16-13
	Arena Chapel	
	Giotto, *Lamentation, c.* 1305, Italian painting	15-14
	Giotto, *The Meeting of Joachim and Anna, c.* 1305, Italian painting	15-17
Paestum	The "Basilica," *c.* 550 B.C., Greek architecture in Italy	5-22, 5-23
	Temple of Hera, *c.* 460 B.C., Greek architecture in Italy	5-23, 5-25, 5-26
Palestrina	Sanctuary of Fortuna Primigenia, *c.* 80 B.C., Roman architecture	6-18, 6-20
	Model of reconstructed Sanctuary of Fortuna Primigenia (Museo Archeologico, Palestrina), Roman architecture	6-19
Parma	Correggio, *The Assumption of the Virgin,* fresco, 1526–1530 (dome of Parma Cathedral), Italian painting	17-38, 17-39
Pescia	Berlinghieri, *St. Francis Altarpiece,* 1235 (San Francesco, Pescia), Italian painting	15-6, 15-7
Pisa	Traini (?), *The Triumph of Death, c.* 1350 (Campo Santo, Pisa), Italian painting	15-25
	Cathedral of Pisa	
	The cathedral group (baptistry, cathedral, and campanile), 1053–1272, Italian architecture	9-19, 9-20
	Nicola Pisano, pulpit of the baptistry, 1259–1269, Italian sculpture	15-1, 15-2
Pistoia	Giovanni Pisano, *The Annunciation and the Nativity,* 1297–1301 (pulpit of Sant' Andrea, Pistoia), Italian sculpture	15-3
Pompeii	Excavated portion of Pompeii, Roman architecture	6-21
	Forum of Pompeii, Roman architecture	6-22, 6-23
	The House of Pansa, 2nd century B.C., Roman architecture	6-24
	Atrium of the House of the Silver Wedding, 2nd century B.C., Roman architecture	6-25
	Second-style ("architectural") wall painting, Villa of the Mysteries, *c.* 50 B.C., Roman painting	6-28
	Fourth-style ("intricate") wall painting, Ixion Room, House of the Vetii, 1st century A.D., Roman painting	6-32
	Livia, c. A.D. 20 (Antiquario, Pompeii), Roman sculpture	6-68
Prato	Antonio da Sangallo, Santa Maria delle Carceri, 1485, Italian painting	16-45 to 16-47
Ravenna	**Mausoleum of Galla Placidia**	
	The Mausoleum, A.D. 425–450, Early Christian architecture	7-24, 7-25
	Christ as the Good Shepherd, mosaic, A.D. 425–450, Early Christian Mosaic	7-26

Sant' Apollinare in Classe
Sarcophagus of Archbishop Theodore, 7th century, Early Christian sculpture   7-22
The church, *c.* A.D. 533–549, Byzantine architecture in Italy   7-29
Apse mosaics, Byzantine mosaics in Italy   7-30

Sant' Apollinare Nuovo
Nave of the church, *c.* A.D. 504, Byzantine architecture   7-27
Miracle of the Loaves and Fishes, mosaic, *c.* 504, Byzantine mosaic in Italy   7-28

San Vitale
The church, *c.* A.D. 526–547, Byzantine architecture in Italy   7-31 to 7-34
Capital of a column, Byzantine architecture in Italy   7-35
Justinian and Attendants, apse mosaic, *c.* A.D. 547, Byzantine mosaic in Italy   7-36, 7-39
Theodora and Attendants, apse mosaic, *c.* A.D. 547, Byzantine mosaic in Italy   7-37
Christ Between Angels and Saints (The Second Coming), apse mosaic,   7-38
   c. A.D. 547, Byzantine mosaic in Italy

Reggio Calabria   *Riace Bronzes,* 460–450 B.C., Greek sculpture   5-33 to 5-36
Rimini   Alberti, San Francesco, Rimini, begun 1450, Italian architecture   16-41
Rome   *Head of a Roman, c.* 80 B.C. (Palazzo Torlonia), Roman sculpture   6-14
Temple of Fortuna Virilis, late 2nd century B.C., Roman architecture   6-16
Fourth-style wall painting, Domus Aurea of Nero, A.D. 60–67,   6-33
   Roman painting
Colosseum, A.D. 70–82, Roman architecture   6-45, 6-46
Pantheon, A.D. 118–125, Roman architecture   6-51, 6-52
Baths of Caracalla, *c.* A.D. 215, Roman architecture   6-55, 6-56
Ara Pacis Augustae, 13–9 B.C., Roman architecture   6-58 to 6-60
Arch of Titus, A.D. 81, Roman architecture   6-61 to 6-63
Column of Trajan, A.D. 113, Roman architecture   6-64, 6-65
Basilica of Constantine, *c.* A.D. 310–320, Roman architecture   6-85, 6-86
Arch of Constantine, A.D. 312–315, Roman architecture   6-89 to 6-91
Catacomb of Callixtus, 2nd century A.D., Early Christian architecture in Italy   7-1
Catacomb of Pamphilus, 3rd century A.D., Early Christian architecture in Italy   7-2
Catacomb of Saints Pietro and Marcellinus (painted ceiling), 4th century A.D.,   7-3
   Early Christian architecture in Italy
Santa Costanza (central-plan building with mosaics in the vault of the   7-7 to 7-9
   ambulatory), *c.* A.D. 350, Early Christian architecture in Italy
Vault mosaic, Mausoleum of the Julii, A.D. 250–275, Early Christian mosaic   7-10
Christ Enthroned in Majesty, with Saints, apse mosaic, Santa Pudenziana,   7-11
   A.D. 402–417, Early Christian mosaic in Italy
The Parting of Lot and Abraham, mosaic, Santa Maria Maggiore, *c.* A.D. 430,   7-12
   Early Christian mosaic in Italy
The Good Shepherd Sarcophagus, late 4th century A.D. (Museo del Laterano),   7-18
   Early Christian mosaic in Italy
Cavallini, *The Last Judgment,* fresco, Santa Cecilia in Trastevere, *c.* 1291,   15-10
   Italian painting
Bramante, the Tempietto, 1508, Italian architecture   17-6, 17-7
Antonio da Sangallo, Farnese Palace, *c.* 1541–1550 (top story of courtyard   17-12 to 17-14
   by Michelangelo, 1548), Italian architecture
Raphael, *Galatea,* fresco, 1513 (Villa Farnesina), Italian painting   17-18
Michelangelo, *Moses, c.* 1513–1515 (San Pietro in Vincoli), Italian sculpture   17-21
Giacomo della Porta, Il Gesù (façade), *c.* 1575–1584, Italian architecture   19-1
Giacomo da Vignola, Il Gesù (ground plan), *c.* 1575, Italian architecture   19-2
Maderno, Santa Susanna, 1597–1603, Italian architecture   19-5
Bernini, *The Ecstasy of St. Theresa,* 1645–1652. Cornaro Chapel,   19-11, p. 520
   Santa Maria della Vittoria, Italian Baroque sculpture
Bernini, Triton Fountain, Piazza Barberini, 1642–1643, Italian sculpture   19-12
Borromini, San Carlo alle Quattro Fontane, 1665–1676, Italian architecture   19-13, 19-14
Borromini, St. Ivo, begun 1642, Italian architecture   19-15 to 19-17
Bramante or Raphael, dome of Sant' Eligio degli Orifici, *c.* 1509,   19-20
   Italian architecture
Annibale Carracci, ceiling fresco in the Farnese Gallery, 1597–1601,   19-23
   Farnese Palace, Italian painting

Guido Reni, *Aurora*, ceiling fresco in the Casino Rospigliosi, 1613–1614, Italian painting — 19-24

Guercino, *Aurora,* ceiling fresco in the Villa Ludovisi, 1621–1623, Italian painting — 19-25

Caravaggio, *The Conversion of St. Paul, c.* 1601 (Santa Maria del Popolo), Italian painting — 19-26

Annibale Carracci, *Flight into Egypt*, 1603–1604 (Galleria Doria Pamphili), Italian painting — 19-30

Pozzo, *The Glorification of St. Ignatius*, ceiling fresco in the nave of Sant' Ignazio, 1691–1694, Italian painting — 19-32

Nervi, Palazzetto dello Sport, 1958, Italian architecture — 22-109

Capitoline Hill

Equestrian statue of Marcus Aurelius, *c.* A.D. 165, Roman sculpture — 6-72

Michelangelo, the Campidoglio (Capitoline Hill), including the Museo Capitolino, designed, *c.* 1537, Italian architecture — 17-29 to 17-31

Museo Capitolino

Dying Gaul, Pergamon, original *c.* 240 B.C. (Roman copy), Greek sculpture — 5-77

Eros and Psyche, c. 150 B.C., Greek sculpture — 5-85

She-Wolf of the Capitol, c. 500 B.C., Etruscan sculpture — 6-10

Portrait of a Lady, marble bust, *c.* A.D. 90, Roman sculpture — 6-70

Galleria Borghese

Titian, *Sacred and Profane Love, c.* 1515, Italian painting — 17-61

Bernini, *David*, 1623, Italian sculpture — 19-10

Museo Nazionale

Medallion of Hadrian, 2nd century A.D., Roman sculpture — 6-92

Gold coin with portrait of Maximin Daia, A.D. 308–314, Roman sculpture — 6-92

Ludovisi Battle Sarcophagus, 3rd century A.D., Early Christian sculpture — 7-17

Museo Nazionale Romano

Myron, *Discobolos*, original *c.* 450 B.C. (Roman copy), Greek sculpture — 5-38

Aphrodite of Cyrene, c. 100 B.C., Greek sculpture — 5-67

Apollonius (?), *Seated Boxer, c.* 50 B.C., Greek sculpture — 5-87

Garden Scene, detail of a wall painting from the House of Livia, Primaporta, late 1st century B.C., Roman painting — 6-30

Portrait bust of Vespasian, *c.* A.D. 75, Roman sculpture — 6-69

Museo Nazionale di Villa Giulia

Sarcophagus from Caere (Cerveteri), *c.* 520 B.C., Etruscan sculpture — 6-7

Apollo from Veii, *c.* 510 B.C., Etruscan sculpture — 6-8

Novius Plautius, *The Ficoroni Cist*, from Praeneste, late 4th century B.C., Etruscan metalwork — 6-13

Palazzo dei Conservatori

Marcus Aurelius Sacrificing, from an arch of Marcus Aurelius, late 2nd century A.D., Roman sculpture — 6-66

Constantine the Great, c. A.D. 330, Roman sculpture — 6-87

Santa Maria della Vittoria

Bernini, interior of the Cornaro Chapel, 1645–1652, Italian architecture — 19-11

Bernini, *The Ecstasy of St. Theresa*, Cornaro Chapel, 1645–1652, Italian sculpture — p. 520

St. Peter's

Bramante's plan for St. Peter's, 1505, Italian architecture — 17-7

Michelangelo, St. Peter's, 1546–1564, Italian architecture — 17-32 to 17-34

Dome of St. Peter's, completed by Giacomo della Porta, 1590, Italian architecture — 17-36, 19-3

Aerial view, Italian architecture — 19-3

Maderno, façade of St. Peter's, 1606–1612, Italian architecture — 19-4

Maderno, Santa Suzanna, façade, Italian architecture — 19-5

Bernini, piazza and colonnades, St. Peter's, Italian architecture — 19-3, 19-6

Bernini, Scala Regia in the Vatican, 1663–1666, Italian architecture — 19-7

Bernini, *baldacchino*, St. Peter's, 1624–1633, Italian architecture — 19-8

Bernini, *Cathedra Petri*, 1656–1666, Italian sculpture — 19-9

Sistine Chapel, Vatican
Perugino, *Christ Delivering the Keys of the Kingdom to St. Peter,* fresco,   16-62
    1481–1483, Italian painting
Michelangelo, interior of the Sistine Chapel, 1508–1512, Italian painting   17-24
Michelangelo, ceiling of the Sistine Chapel, 1508–1512, Italian painting   17-25
Michelangelo, *The Creation of Adam* (detail, ceiling of the Sistine Chapel),   17-26
    Italian painting
Michelangelo, *The Last Judgment* (including Michelangelo's "self-portrait"),   17-35, 17-36
    fresco, Sistine Chapel, 1534–1541, Italian painting

Vatican Library
Ulysses in the Land of the Lestrygonians, detail from the *Odyssey Landscape,*   6-29
    late 1st century B.C., Roman painting
The Vatican Vergil, early 5th century A.D., Early Christian manuscript   7-14

Vatican Museums
Phiale Painter, *Hermes Bringing the Infant Dionysos to Papposilenos,* krater   5-64
    from Vulci, . 440–435 B.C., Greek ceramic
Lysippos, *Apoxyomenos,* original *c.* 330 B.C. (Roman copy), Greek sculpture   5-70
Laocoön group, early 1st century B.C. (?), Greek sculpture   5-80
Mars from Todi, early 4th century B.C., Etruscan sculpture   6-9
Engraved back of mirror ("Calchas"), *c.* 400 B.C., Etruscan metalwork   6-12
Augustus of Primaporta, c. 20 B.C., Roman sculpture   6-57, 6-67
Caracalla, c. A.D. 215, Roman sculpture   6-73
Philip the Arab, A.D. 244–249, Roman sculpture   6-74
Domenichino, *The Last Communion of St. Jerome,* 1614, Italian painting   19-28

Vatican Palace
Raphael, *The School of Athens,* 1509–1511 (Stanza della Segnatura),   17-17, p. 526
    Italian painting
Bernini, Scala Regia, 1663–1666, Italian architecture   19-7

Rossano   *Pilate Demanding That the People Choose Between Jesus and Barabbas,* from   7-16
    The Rossano Gospels, early 6th century (Diocesan Museum, Archepiscopal
    Palace), book illumination

Sicily   **Piazza Armerina**
Plan of Roman villa, Roman architecture   6-82
Allegory of Africa, early 4th century, Roman mosaic   6-83
Young Women Exercising, early 4th century, Roman mosaic   6-84

Siena   Pietro Lorenzetti, *The Birth of the Virgin,* 1342 (Museo dell' Opera   15-21
    Metropolitane), Italian painting
Donatello, *The Feast of Herod, c.* 1425 (Baptistry, San Giovanni, Siena),   16-9
    Italian sculpture

Opera del Duomo
Duccio, *The Betrayal of Jesus,* from the back of the *Maestà Altarpiece,*   15-8
    1309–1311, Italian painting
Duccio, *The Annunciation of the Death of Mary,* from the *Maestà Altarpiece,*   15-9
    1309–1311, Italian painting

Palazzo Pubblico
Palazzo Pubblico, 1288–1309, Italian architecture   10-63
Simone Martini, *Guidoriccio da Fogliano,* fresco, 1328, Italian painting   15-20
Ambrogio Lorenzetti, *Good Government Enthroned,* fresco, 1339,   15-22
    Italian painting
Ambrogio Lorenzetti, *Peaceful City,* from the *Good Government* fresco, 1339,   15-23
    Italian painting
Ambrogio Lorenzetti, *Peaceful Country,* from the *Good Government* fresco,   15-24
    1339, Italian painting

Sperlonga   **Sperlonga Museum**
Agesander, Athenodorus, and Polydorus, *Odysseus' Helmsman Falling,*   5-81
    late 2nd century B.C., Greek sculpture
Agesander, Athenodorus, and Polydorus, *Head of Odysseus,* late 2nd   5-82
    century B.C., Greek sculpture

Stra	Tiepolo, *The Apotheosis of the Pisani Family,* 1761–1762, ceiling fresco in the Villa Pisani	20-12
Tarquinia	*Revelers,* Tomb of the Leopards, *c.* 470 B.C., Etruscan painting	6-4
	Woman of the Velcha Family, Tomb of Orcus (Hades), *c.* 470 B.C., Etruscan painting	6-5
Tivoli	Temple of the Sibyl, early 1st century painting B.C., Roman architecture	6-17
Todi	Santa Maria della Consolazione, begun 1508 (in the manner of Bramante), Italian architecture	17-9, 17-10
Turin	Guarini, Palazzo Carignano, 1679–1692, Italian architecture	19-18
	Guarini, dome of the Chapel of the Santa Sindone, 1667–1694, Italian architecture	19-19
	Juvara, the Superga, 1715–1731 (near Turin), Italian architecture	20-3
Urbino	Piero della Francesca, *The Flagellation of Christ, c.* 1455 (Palazzo Ducale, Galleria Nazionale delle Marche), Italian painting	16-33
Venice	*The Tetrarchs, c.* A.D. 305 (Piazza San Marco), Roman sculpture	6-88
	Verrocchio, *Bartolomeo Colleoni,* equestrian statue, *c.* 1483–1488 (Campo dei Santi Giovanni e Paolo), Italian sculpture	16-53
	Sansovino, the Zecca (Mint), 1535–1545, Italian architecture	17-51
	Sansovino, Library of San Marco, begun 1536, Italian architecture	17-51
	Palladio, San Giorgio Maggiore, 1565, Italian architecture	17-54, 17-55
	Bellini, *San Zaccaria Altarpiece,* 1505 (San Zaccaria), Italian painting	17-58
	Titian, *Madonna of the Pesaro Family*, 1519–1526 (Santa Maria dei Frari), Italian painting	17-62
	Tintoretto, *The Last Supper,* 1594 (San Giorgio Maggiore), Italian painting	17-67
	Longhena, Santa Maria della Salute, 1631–1648 (consecrated 1687), Italian architecture	19-21, 19-22
	Doge's Palace	
	Doge's Palace, *c.* 1345–1438, Italian architecture	10-64
	Veronese, *The Triumph of Venice, c.* 1585, Italian painting	17-69
	Galleria dell' Accademia	
	Bellini, *Madonna of the Trees, c.* 1487, Italian painting	17-56
	Bellini, *San Giobbe Altarpiece, c.* 1485, Italian painting	17-57
	Tintoretto, *The Miracle of the Slave,* 1548, Italian painting	17-66
	Veronese, *Christ in the House of Levi,* 1573, Italian painting	17-68
	St. Mark's	
	St. Mark's, begun 1063, Byzantine architecture in Italy	7-49 to 7-51
	The Passion, Resurrection, and Ascension of Christ, mosaics of vault and central dome, late 12th century, Byzantine mosaics	7-58
	Joseph in Egypt, mosaic in dome of the narthex, 1255–1260, Byzantine mosaic	7-59
Vicenza	Palladio, Villa Rotonda, *c.* 1566–1570, Italian architecture	17-52, 17-53
JAPAN		
Ise	Shoden (main building of the Ise Shrine), rebuilt every twenty years, reproducing third-century type, Japanese architecture	13-7
Kanagawa	Buson, *Enjoyment of Summer Scenery,* Tokugawa period, 1771 (Yasunari Kawabata Collection), Japanese painting	13-27
Kyoto	*The Sage Kuya Invoking the Amida Buddha,* Kamakura period, 13th century (Rokuharamitsu-ji Temple), Japanese sculpture	13-13
	Okyo, *Nature Studies,* Tokugawa period, 18th century (Nishimura Collection), Japanese painting	13-28
	Katsura Palace	
	Gardens, the Shokintei, Japanese architecture	13-16
	First room of the Shokintei, Japanese architecture	13-17
	Pond and garden, Shokintei, Japanese architecture	13-18
	Eastern façade, Japanese architecture	13-22
	Palanquin Entry, Japanese architecture	13-23
	Interior, Japanese architecture	13-24
Nagoya	Takayoshi, *The Tale of Genji* (scroll), late Heian period, 12th century (Tokugawa Museum), Japanese painting	13-8
Nara	*The Flying Storehouse,* from the *Shigisan Engi* (Legends of Mount Shigi), Fujiwara period, late 12th century (Chogosonshi-ji), Japanese painting	13-10

Horyu-ji
Tori Busshi, *Shaka Triad*, Asuka period, A.D. 623 (Horyu-ji Temple),   13-2
   Japanese sculpture
Miroku, Asuka period, mid-7th century (Chugu-ji Nunnery), Japanese sculpture   13-3
Amida Triad, from the *Shrine of Lady Tachibana*, Nara period, early 8th   13-4
   century (Horyu-ji Temple), Japanese sculpture
Tamamushi Shrine, Asuka period, 7th century (Horyu-ji Museum),   13-5
   Japanese painting
Kondo (Golden Hall), Asuka period, 7th century, Japanese architecture   13-6

Tokyo   **Hatakeyama Memorial Museum**
Tea ceremony water jar, Momoyama period, late 16th century, Japanese ceramic   13-19

Tokyo National Museum
Liang K'ai, *The Sixth Ch'an Patriarch Chopping Bamboo*, Southern Sung   12-20
   dynasty, 13th century, Chinese painting
Sesshu, *Landscape*, from a hanging scroll, Ashikaga period, 1495,   13-15
   Japanese painting
Uji Bridge, six-fold screen, Momoyama period, 16th–17th century,   13-20
   Japanese painting
Tohaku, *Pine Trees*, six-fold screen, Momoyama period, 16th–17th century,   13-21
   Japanese painting
Korin, *White Plum Blossoms*, screen, Tokugawa period, late 17th to early   13-26
   18th century, Japanese painting

Uji   Hoodo (Phoenix Hall) Byodoin temple, Heian period, 11th century,   13-12
   Japanese architecture
Yamaguchi   Animal scroll, attributed to Toba Sojo, later Heian period, late 12th century   13-11
   (Kozan-ji), Japanese drawing

JORDAN

Jericho   Proto-Neolithic fortifications, 8000–7000 B.C., architecture   2-1
Khirbat al-Mafjar   Islamic floor mosaic, palace at Khirbat al-Mafjar, second quarter of 8th century   7-76
Mshatta   Islamic stone frieze, palace at Mshatta, *c.* A.D. 743   7-74, 7-75
Petra   Al-Khazneh ("The Treasury"), Rock-cut mausoleum, 2nd century,   6-79
   Roman architecture

KAMPUCHEA (CAMBODIA)

Angkor   Overall plan of site, 12th and 13th centuries, Cambodian architecture   11-29
Angkor Thom   Bayon, 12th and 13th centuries, Cambodian sculpture and architecture   11-32, 11-33,
   p. 412
Angkor Wat   Aerial view, Cambodian architecture   11-30
Pnom Penh   *Harihara*, Prasat Andet, 7th century (Musée Albert Sarraut), Cambodian   11-28
   sculpture

MEXICO

Chalcacingo, Morelos   Relief sculpture, Olmec, *c.* 1100–800 B.C., Mexican sculpture   14-2
Chichén Itzá   Ruins of a Mayan city, Mexican architecture   14-4
La Venta   *Colossal head*, Olmec, 1500–800 B.C., Mexican sculpture   14-1
Mexico City   *Coatlicue*, goddess of earth and death, Aztec, 15th century (Museo Nacional   14-10
   de Antropologia), Mexican sculpture
Quiriguá   *Great Dragon,* Maya, 6th century, Mexican sculpture   14-6
Teotihuacán   Temple of Quetzalcóatl, 3rd century, Mexican architecture   14-9
Uaxactún   Ruins of a Mayan temple group, Mexican architecture   14-5

NETHERLANDS

Amsterdam   Spirit figure, Papuan Gulf, New Guinea (Tropenmuseum)   14-66
Rembrandt, *Syndics of the Cloth Guild*, 1662 (Rijksmuseum), Dutch painting   19-52
Ezinge   Foundations of an Iron Age house, Iron age architecture in Netherlands   8-11
Haarlem   Hals, *Assembly of Officers and Subalterns of the Civic Guard (Archers of*   19-46
   St. Adrian), c. 1633 (Frans Halsmuseum), Dutch painting
The Hague   Kalf, *Still Life,* 1659 (Royal Picture Gallery/Mauritshuis), Dutch painting   19-56
Van Ruisdael, *View of Haarlem from the Dunes at Overveen, c.* 1670   19-57
   (Royal Picture Gallery/Mauritshuis), Dutch painting
Otterloo   Redon, *The Cyclops,* 1898 (Kroeller-Moeller Rijksmuseum), French painting   21-73
Paolozzi, *Medea,* 1964 (Kroeller-Moeller Rijksmuseum), Dutch sculpture   22-79

Utrecht	*The Utrecht Psalter, c.* 830 (University Library), Medieval manuscript	8-11
	Rietveldt, Schroeder House, 1924, Dutch architecture	22-60
NIGERIA		
Jos	Head, 5th century B.C. to 2nd century A.D. (National Jos Museum), Nok sculpture	14-41
Lagos	*Queen Mother Head*, early 16th century (National Museum), Benin sculpture	14-43
Ndiama Obube	Mbari House, Ibo sculpture	14-49
NORWAY		
Oslo	Animal head from the Oseberg ship burial, *c.* 825 (University Museum of National Antiquities), Migration sculpture	8-3
	Munch, *The Scream*, 1893 (Oslo Kommunes Kuntsamlinger Munch-Museet), Norwegian painting	21-76
Urnes	Stave church ornament *c.* 800, porch of stave church, architectural ornament	8-5
PERU		
Cuzco	Temple of the Sun, Inca, 15th century (now church of Santo Domingo), Peruvian architecture	14-17
POLAND		
Kraków	Stoss, *The Death and Assumption of the Virgin,* 1477–1489 (Church of St. Mary), German sculpture	18-28
SCOTLAND		
Edinburgh	Gainsborough, *The Honorable Mrs. Graham*, 1775 (National Gallery of Scotland), English painting	20-31
Glasgow	Rosa, *St. John the Baptist in the Wilderness, c.* 1640 (Glasgow Art Gallery), Italian painting	19-31
	Degas, *Ballet Rehearsal (Adagio),* 1876 (Glasgow Art Gallery), French painting	21-59
SPAIN		
Barcelona	Gaudí, Casa Milá, 1907, Spanish architecture	22-56
Castellón	*Marching Warriors*, Gasulla gorge, *c.* 8000–3000 B.C., prehistoric painting in Spain	1-14
Cordoba	Mosque at Cordoba, Islamic, 8th to 10th century, Islamic architecture	7-68 to 7-71
Granada	The Alhambra, 1354–1391, Islamic architecture	7-78, 7-79
	Pedro Machuca, courtyard of the palace of Charles V, *c.* 1526–1568, Spanish architecture	18-57
Madrid	**Museo del Prado**	
	Rogier van der Weyden, *The Escorial Deposition, c.* 1435, Flemish painting	18-14
	Bosch, *The Garden of Earthly Delights, c.* 1500, Flemish painting	18-22, 18-23
	Patinir, *Landscape with St. Jerome, c.* 1520, Dutch painting	18-47
	Juan de Herrera, the Escorial, *c.* 1563–1584, Spanish architecture	18-58 to 18-60
	Ribera, *The Martyrdom of St. Bartholomew, c.* 1639, Spanish painting	19-33
	Velázquez, *Los Borrachos,* 1628, Spanish painting	19-35
	Velázquez, *Las Meninas,* 1656, Spanish painting	19-37
	Goya, *The Dream of Reason*, from *Los Caprichos, c.* 1794–1799, Spanish painting	20-44
	Goya, *The Family of Charles IV,* 1800, Spanish painting	21-9
	Goya, *The Third of May, 1808,* 1814, Spanish painting	21-10
	Goya, *Saturn Devouring His Children,* 1819–1823, Spanish painting	21-12
	Picasso, *Guernica,* 1937 Spanish painting	22-16
Tahull	*Adoration of the Magi,* 11th century (Santa Maria, Tahull, Catalonia), Spanish painting	9-36
Toledo	El Greco, *The Burial of Count Orgaz,* 1586 (Santo Tomé), Spanish painting	18-61
Valladolid	San Gregorio, portal, *c.* 1498, Spanish architecture	18-56
SRI LANKA (CEYLON)		
Polonnaruwa	Buddha from Gal Vihara, near Polonnaruwa, 11th–12th century A.D., sculpture	11-25
SWEDEN	**Moderna Museet**	
	Gonzalez, *Woman Combing Her Hair, c.* 1930–1933, Spanish sculpture in the U.S.	22-46
	Tatlin, *Monument to the Third International,* 1919–1920, Russian sculpture	22-47
	Rauschenberg, *Monogram,* 1959, American painting	22-88

SWITZERLAND

Basel	Malanggan tableau, painted bamboo, New Ireland (Museum für Völkerkunde), Melanesian woodcarving	14-69
	Canoe-prow figure, Solomon Islands, Melanesia, 19th to 20th century (Museum für Völkerkunde und Schweizerisches Museum für Volkskunde), Melanesian decorative art	14-70

Kunstmuseum

Kokoschka, *The Bride of the Wind,* 1914, Austrian painting	22-5
Mondrian, *Composition in Blue, Yellow, and Black,* 1936, Dutch painting	22-20

Bern	Klee, *Death and Fire*, 1940 (Paul Klee-Stiftung), Swiss painting	22-31
Geneva	Witz, *The Miraculous Draught of Fish,* 1444 (Musée d'Art et d'Histoire), German painting	18-27
Lugano	Ghirlandaio, *Giovanna Tornabuoni* (?), 1488 (Sammlung Thyssen-Bornemisza), Italian painting	16-58

SYRIA

Dura-Europos	*Priests with Attendant*, detail of a mural, Temple of the Palmyrene Gods, 2nd–3rd century A.D., Near Eastern painting in Syria	7-21

TURKEY

Bogazköy, Anatolia	Lion Gate, *c.* 1400 B.C., Hittite architecture	2-24
Catal Hüyük, Anatolia	Çatal Hüyük, excavated Neolithic site, architecture	2-3, 2-4
	Seated Goddess, c. 5900 B.C., Anatolian sculpture	2-5
	Deer Hunt, wall painting, Level III, *c.* 5750 B.C., Anatolian painting	2-6, 2-7
	Landscape with Volcanic Eruption (?), detail of a wall painting, Level VII, *c.* 6150 B.C., Anatolian painting	2-8
Edirne	Sinan, Mosque of Selim II (Selimiye Cami), 1569–1575, Islamic architecture	7-83 to 7-86
Istanbul	Anthemius and Isidorus, Hagia Sophia, A.D. 532–537, Byzantine architecture	7-41 to 7-44
	The Harrowing of Hell, fresco, Mosque of the Ka'riye, *c.* 1310–1320, Byzantine painting	7-60
Priene	Excavations of Priene, 4th century B.C., Greek architecture in Asia minor	5-79
	Partially restored Hellenistic house (House XXXIII), Greek architecture in Asia Minor	5-82

UNITED STATES

Adams County, OH	Serpent Mound (North American Indian, prehistoric era)	14-22
Andover, MA	Calder, *Horizontal Spines*, 1942 (Addison Gallery of American Art, Phillips Academy), American sculpture	22-49
Bear Run, PA	Wright, Kaufmann House ("Falling Water"), 1936–1939, American architecture	22-62
Berkeley, CA	Shaman mask representing a sea mammal, before 1900, (Lowie Museum), Eskimo carving	14-19
	Hofmann, *Effervescence*, 1944 (University Art Museum), German painting	22-69
Bloomfield Hills, MI	Webster, False Face mask, Iroquois, 1937 (Cranbrook Institute of Science), American Indian carving	14-39
Boston, MA	Rubens, *Thomas Howard, Earl of Arundel, c.* 1630 (Isabella Stewart Gardner Museum), Flemish painting	19-41

Museum of Fine Arts

Monet, *Rouen Cathedral, c.* 1880, French painting	Intro. 5
Mantiklos "Apollo," Thebes, *c.* 680 B.C., Greek sculpture	5-13
Ma Yuan, *Bare Willows and Distant Mountains,* Southern Sung dynasty, 13th century, Chinese painting	12-19
The Burning of the Sanjo Palace, Kamakura period, 13th century, Japanese painting	13-14
Hokusai, *The Great Wave*, from *Thirty-six Views of Mount Fuji,* Tokugawa period, early 19th century, Japanese woodcut	13-30
Dürer, *The Fall of Man (Adam and Eve),* 1504, German print	18-37
El Greco, *Fray Felix Hortensio Paravicino,* 1609, Spanish painting	18-62
Turner, *The Slave Ship,* 1840, English painting	21-29
Sargent, *The Daughters of Edward Darley Boit,* 1882, American painting	21-46

Buffalo, NY	Sullivan, Guaranty (Prudential) Building, 1894–1895, American architecture	21-89

Albright-Knox Gallery

Mummy Portrait of a Man, Faiyum, 2nd century A.D., Roman painting in Egypt	6-41
Gauguin, *Spirit of the Dead Watching,* 1892, French painting	21-70
Lachaise, *Standing Woman,* 1912–1927, French sculpture	22-37

Cambridge, MA	*District God*, Cook Islands (Peabody Museum, Harvard University), Polynesian sculpture	14-58
	Fogg Art Museum, Harvard University	
	Picasso, *Bathers,* 1918 Spanish painting in France	Intro. 3
	T'ang tomb figurine (horse), 7th–9th century, Chinese sculpture	12-17
	Dürer, *Melencolia I,* 1514, German print	18-40
Charlottesville, VA	Jefferson, Monticello, 1770–1806, American Neoclassical architecture	20-26
Chicago, IL	Cylinder seal, Ur, *c.* 2700 B.C. (The Oriental Institute, University of Chicago), Sumerian sculpture	2-18
	Sullivan, the Carson, Pirie, Scott Building, 1899–1904, American architecture	21-90
	Wright, Robie House, 1907–1909, American architecture	22-57, 22-58
	Art Institute of Chicago	
	Messenger and runner figures, Mochica, Peru, 5th–6th century A.D., Peruvian sculpture	14-13
	Puvis de Chavannes, *The Sacred Grove,* 1884, French painting	21-51
	Harunobu, *The Evening Glow of Andon,* 1765, Japanese woodcut	21-60
	Degas, *The Morning Bath,* 1883, French pastel painting	21-62
	Cassatt, *The Bath, c.* 1892, American painting	21-63
	Seurat, *Sunday Afternoon on the Island of La Grande Jatte,* 1884–1886, French painting	21-64
	Toulouse-Lautrec, *At the Moulin Rouge,* 1892, French painting	21-71
Cincinnati, OH	Ritual cauldron from Luristan, Iran, 8th century B.C. (Cincinnati Art Museum), Persian metalwork	2-41
Cleveland, OH	**The Cleveland Museum of Art**	
	Tung Ch'i-ch'ang, *Autumn Mountains,* horiziontal scroll, Ming dynasty, early 17th century, Chinese painting	12-25
	Haniwa figures (horse and peasant), Japan, 5th–6th century A.D., Japanese sculpture	13-1
	Ryder, *Death on a Pale Horse, c.* 1910, American painting	21-78
Denver, CO	Mask, Kwakiutl, *c.* 1890	14-31
Detroit, MI	**The Detroit Institue of the Arts**	
	Gentileschi, *Judith and Maidservant with the Head of Holofernes, c.* 1625, Italian painting	19-29
	Fuseli, *The Nightmare,* 1781, Swiss painting in England	20-41
	Moore, *Reclining Figure*, 1939, English sculpture	22-53
Dinwoody, WY	Human figures engraved on a sandstone cliff, attributed to prehistoric Shoshone, American Indian sculpture	14-24
Hanover, NH	Orozco, *Hispano-America, c.* 1933 (Baker Memorial Library, Dartmouth College), Mexican painting in the U.S.	22-32
Houston, TX	Johnson, Pennzoil Place, American architecture	22-118
Kansas City, MO	**Nelson Gallery-Atkins Museum**	
	Pi, ritual disk, Late Chou dynasty, 5th–3rd century B.C., Chinese jade carving	12-3
	T'ang tomb figurine (dancer), 7th–9th century, Chinese sculpture	12-17
Los Angeles, CA	"The Drinker," seated shaman figure from Colima, Mexico (collection of Proctor Stafford), Mexican sculpture	14-3
	Pissarro, *Place du Théâtre Français*, 1895 (Los Angeles County Museum of Art), French painting	21-56
Malibu, CA	Lysippos (?), *Athlete (The Getty Bronze),* late 4th century (J. Paul Getty Museum), Greek sculpture	5-71
Mesa Verde National Park, CO	Cliff Palace, Pueblo, *c.* A.D. 1100, American Indian architecture	14-26
Minneapolis, MN	Davis, *Colonial Cubism,* 1954, American painting	22-75
	Birkerts, Federal Reserve Bank, 1972–1973, American architecture	22-113
New Haven, CN	**Yale University Art Gallery**	
	Kagle (mask), Dan, African sculpture	14-53
	Pollaiuolo, *Hercules and Deianera, c.* 1470, Italian painting	16-56
	Corot, *The Harbor of La Rochelle,* 1851, French painting	21-34
	Van Gogh, *The Night Café,* 1888, Dutch painting	21-68
	Schwitters, *Merz Picture 19,* 1920, German college painting	22-23
	Lipchitz, *Man with Mandolin,* 1917, French sculpture	22-42

New Orleans, LA	Moore, Piazza d'Italia, American architecture	22-121, 22-122
New York, NY	Tao-Chi, *Landscape*, Ch'ing dynasty, late 17th century (C.C. Wang Collection) Chinese painting	12-26
	Goya, *Tampoco*, etching from the *Disasters of War*, 1810 (New York Public Library), Spanish print	21-11
	Cole, *The Course of Empire: Desolation*, 1836 (New York Historical Society), English painting in the U.S.	21-31
	Mies van der Rohe, Seagram Building, 1956–1958, German architecture in the U.S.	22-67

American Museum of Natural History

| Portrait jar, Mochica, Peru, 5th–6th century A.D., Peruvian ceramic | 14-12 |
| Wood helmet, Tlingit, Northwest Coast, American Indian carving | 14-32 |

Solomon R. Guggenheim Museum

Kandinsky, *Improvisation 28*, 1912, Russian painting	22-10
Picasso, *Accordionist*, 1911 Spanish painting	22-13
Wright, Solomon R. Guggenheim Museum, 1943–1959, American architecture	22-107, 22-108

Metropolitan Museum of Art

Rodin, *The Thinker*, 1880, French sculpture	Intro. 2
Model of hypostyle hall from the Temple of Amen-Re, Karnak, Egypt, architecture	3-30
Geometric Dipylon krater, 8th century B.C., Greek ceramic	5-3
Old Market Woman, 2nd century B.C., Hellenistic Greek sculpture	5-84
Second-style ("architectural") wall painting from the Villa Boscoreale, near Pompeii, 1st century B.C., Roman painting	6-27
Aqa Mirak, *Laila and Majnun in Love at School*, from a manuscript of the Khamsa of Nizami, 1524–1525, Persian book illumination	7-88
Frankish ornaments, 5th–6th century	8-1
Han Kan, *Horse*, T'ang dynasty, eighth century, Chinese drawing	12-16
Kiyotada, *Dancing Kabuki Actor*, Tokugawa period, *c.* 1725, Japanese print	13-26
Textile, Coastal Tiahuanaco style, *c.* A.D. 800, Peruvian textile	14-16
Iphri figure, Ijo people, Nigeria, 20th century sculpture	14-45
Mask, Dan, Liberia, 19th to 20th century, African sculpture	14-52
Wild bush spirit, Baule people, Ivory Coast, sculpture	14-56
Ancestral poles, Asmat, New Guinea, 1960, New Guinea sculpture	14-67
Skull, Iatmul, New Guinea, sculpture	14-68
Pollaiuolo, *Battle of the Ten Nudes*, *c.* 1465, Italian print	16-55
Bronzino, *Portrait of a Young Man*, *c.* 1550, Italian painting	17-45
Campin (Master of Flémalle), *The Mérode Altarpiece*, *c.* 1425–1428, Flemish painting	18-6
Christus, *The Legend of Saints Eligius and Godeberta*, 1449, Flemish painting	18-16
Schongauer, *St. Anthony Tormented by the Demons*, *c.* 1480–1490, German print	18-31
Dürer, *The Four Horsemen of the Apocalypse*, *c.* 1498, German print	18-36
Velázquez, *Juan de Pareja*, 1649–1650, Spanish painting	19-36
Vermeer, *Young Woman with Water Jug*, *c.* 1665, Dutch painting	19-54, 19-55
Clodion, *Nymph and Satyr*, *c.* 1775, French sculpture	20-28
Daumier, *The Third-Class Carriage*, *c.* 1862, French painting	21-37
Bonheur, *The Horse Fair*, 1853, French painting	21-53
Bastien-Lepage, *Joan of Arc*, 1880, French painting	21-54
Monet, *Rouen Cathedral*, 1894, French painting	21-55
Carpeaux, *Ugolino and His Children*, 1865–1867, French sculpture	21-80
Picasso, *Portrait of Gertrude Stein*, 1906 Spanish painting in France	22-11

Museum of Modern Art

Van Gogh, *Starry Night*, 1889, Dutch painting	21-69
Rousseau, *The Sleeping Gypsy*, 1897, French painting	21-77
Derain, *London Bridge*, 1906, French painting	22-2
Beckman, *Departure*, triptych, 1932–35, German painting	22-7
Grosz, *Punishment*, 1934, German painting	22-8
Picasso, *Les Demoiselles d'Avignon*, 1907, Spanish painting in France	22-12
Picasso, *Three Musicians*, 1921, Spanish painting in France	22-15
Braque, *The Table*, 1928, French painting	22-17
Malevich, *Suprematist Composition: White on White*, *c.* 1918, Russian painting	22-22
Duchamp, *To be looked at (from the otherside of the glass), with one eye, close to, for almost an hour*, 1918, French painting	22-24

Ernst, *Two Children Are Threatened by a Nightingale,* 1924, German painting 22-26, p. 802

Miró, *Painting,* 1933, Spanish painting 22-27

Dali, *The Persistence of Memory,* 1931, Spanish painting 22-28

Klee, *Twittering Machine,* 1922, Swiss painting 22-30

Shahn, *Handball,* 1939, American painting 22-33

Maillol, *Mediterranean,* 1901, French sculpture 22-35

Lehmbruck, *Standing Youth,* 1913, German sculpture 22-36

Barlach, *Head,* 1927, German sculpture 22-39

Archipenko, *Woman Combing Her Hair,* 1915, Russian sculpture 22-43

Boccioni, *Unique Forms of Continuity in Space,* 1913, Italian sculpture 22-44

Brancusi, *Bird in Space,* 1927, Romanian sculpture 22-45

Duchamp, *Bicycle Wheel,* 1951 (third version after lost original of 1913), 22-50
French sculpture

Ray, *Gift, c.* 1958 (replica after destroyed original of 1921), American sculpture 22-52

Giacometti, *City Square (La Place),* 1948, Swiss sculpture 22-54

Bacon, *Number VII from Eight Studies for a Portrait,* 1953, Irish painting 22-68

De Kooning, *Woman I,* 1950–1952, American painting 22-72

Wyeth, *Christina's World,* 1948, American painting 22-74

Newman, *Vir Heroicus Sublimis,* 1950–1951, American painting 22-76

Riley, *Current,* 1964, English painting 22-78

Museum of the American Indian

Incised shell gorget from Sumner County, Tennessee, Missippian culture, 14-21
c. A.D. 1200–1500, American Indian shell carving

Kachina spirit mask, Hopi, late 1890s, American Indian sculpture 14-30

Whitney Museum of American Art

Rothko, *Four Darks on Red,* 1958, American painting 22-73

Philadelphia, PA   Soundbox of a harp, Ur, *c.* 2600 B.C. (University Museum, University of 2-16, 2-17
Pennsylvania), Sumerian musical instrument

Eakins, *The Gross Clinic,* 1875 (Jefferson Medical College), American painting 21-42

Homer, *The Fox Hunt,* 1893 (Pennsylvania Academy of the Fine Arts), 21-47
American painting

Howe and Lescaze, Philadelphia Savings Fund Society Building, 1931–1932, 22-65
American architecture

Oldenburg, *Clothespin,* 1977 (Centre Square), American sculpture 22-100

Philadelphia Museum of Art

Daumier, *Rue Transnonian,* 1834, French print 21-36

Léger, *The City,* 1919, French painting 22-18

Duchamp, *Nude Descending a Staircase #2,* 1912, French sculpture 22-19

Phoenix, AZ   Gérôme, *Thumbs Down! (Pollice Verso), c.* 1859 (Phoenix Art Museum), 21-28
French painting

Pittsburgh, PA   Rouault, *The Old King,* 1916–1938 (Museum of Art, Carnegie Insitute), 22-4
French painting

Portland, OR   T'ang tomb figurine (peddler), 7th–9th century (Portland Art Museum), 12-17
Chinese sculpture

Richmond, VA   Jefferson, State Capitol, designed 1785–1789, American Neoclassical 20-27
architecture

Kauffmann, *Cornelia, Mother of the Gracchi,* 1785 *(Museum of Fine Arts),* 20-37
Swiss painting

Salem, MA   Door lintel, Maori (Peabody Museum of Salem), New Zealand, Maori 14-61
architecture

Salt Lake, UT   Smithson, *Spiral Jetty,* 1970, American sculpture 22-84

San Francisco, CA   **Asian Art Museum of San Francisco**

Sakyamuni Buddha, Northern and Southern dynasties, A.D. 338, 12-9
Chinese sculpture

Mei-p'ing vase, Sung dynasty, Chinese ceramic 12-21

Santa Barbara, CA   Cave painting, probably Chumash, North American Indian painting 14-23

Seattle, WA   Sotatsu and Koetsu, *Deer and Calligraphy,* Tokugawa period, early 17th 13-25
century (Seattle Art Museum), Japanese scroll painting

Vail, CO   Venturi, Brant–Johnson House, American architecture 22-119, 22-120

Washington, D.C.   Temple mural of warriors surrounding captives on a terraced platform, Maya, 14-8
Bonampak, Mexico, *c.* 6th century (copy, Carnegie Institute, Washington, D.C.)

	Delacroix, *Paganini, c.* 1832 (The Phillips Collection), French painting	21-25
	Saint-Gaudens, *Adams Memorial,* 1891 (Rock Creek Cemetery), American sculpture	21-79
	National Gallery of Art	
	Monet, *Rouen Cathedral, c.* 1880, French painting	Intro. 5
	Pannini, *Interior of the Pantheon, c.* 1750, Italian painting of Roman architecture	6-53
	Desiderio da Settignano, *Bust of a Little Boy, c.* 1455, Italian sculpture	16-50
	Bellini, *Feast of the Gods,* 1514, Italian painting	17-59
	Rogier van der Weyden, *Portrait of a Lady, c.* 1455, Flemish painting	18-15
	Hals, *Balthasar Coymans,* 1645, Dutch painting	19-44
	Rembrandt, *Self-Portrait, c.* 1660, Dutch painting	19-51
	Houdon, *Count Cagliostro,* (Giuseppe Balsamo), 1771–1789, French sculpture	20-30
	Gainsborough, *Mrs. Richard Brinsley Sheridan, c.* 1785, English painting	20-32
	Cézanne, *Still Life, c.* 1890, French painting	21-65
	Pei, National Gallery Addition, 1978, American architecture	22-115, 22-116
	Smithsonian Institution	
	Greenough, George Washington, 1832–1841, American sculpture	21-6
	Freer Gallery of Art, Smithsonian Institution	
	Kuang (ritual vessel), Shang dynasty, 12th century B.C., Chinese bronze	12-1
	Yu (ritual vessel) Early Chou dynasty, *c.* 10th century B.C., Chinese bronze	12-2
	Whistler, Peacock Room, home of F. R. Leyland, 1876–1877	21-91
	Hirshhorn Museum and Sculpture Garden, Smithsonian Institution	
	Rodin, *Burghers of Calais,* 1886, French sculpture	21-82
	Hopper, *Eleven A.M.,* 1926, American painting	22-34
Williamstown, MA	Bouguereau, *Nymphs and Satyr,* 1873 (Clark Institute), French painting	21-52
U.S.S.R. (Soviet Union)		
Leningrad	**Hermitage Museum**	
	Rembrandt, *The Return of the Prodigal Son, c.* 1665, Dutch painting	19-49
	Matisse, *Red Room (Harmony in Red),* 1908–1909, French painting	22-3
Moscow	Cathedral of the Annunciation, 1482–1490, Late Byzantine architecture	7-53
	The Vladimir Madonna, 12th century (State Historical Museum), Late Byzantine painting	7-62
	Tretyakov Gallery	
	Rublëv, *The Old Testament Trinity Prefiguring the Incarnation, c.* 1410, Byzantine painting	7-63
	Repin, *A Religious Procession in the Kursk District, c.* 1880, Russian painting	21-45
Vladimir	St. Dmitri at Vladimir, 1194–1197, Byzantine architecture	7-52
YUGOSLAVIA		
Nerezi	Lamentation over the Dead Christ, 1164, Byzantine wall painting	7-56
Pella	*Hunter, c.* 300 B.C., Greek mosaic	5-98
Split	Palace of Diocletian, A.D. 300–305, Roman architecture	6-75 to 6-77

Picture Credits

page

82 top	Hirmer Fotoarchiv, Munich
82 bottom	Hirmer Fotoarchiv, Munich
83 right	Archives Photographiques
84 left	Staatliche Antikensammlungen und Glypothek, Munich. Photo: F. Kaufmann
84 right	Hirmer Fotoarchiv, Munich
85	Bildarchiv Preussischer Kulturbesitz, Ägyptisches Museum, Berlin
86 left	Alinari/Art Resource
86 right	Anderson/Giraudon/Art Resource
119 left	Board of Trinity College, Dublin
119 right	Giraudon/Art Resource
120 left	Bulloz
120 right	Alinari/Art Resource
121 left	MAS
122 left	Giraudon/Art Resource
162 left	The Art Institute of Chicago
162 right	Courtesy of the Cultural Relics Bureau, Beijing, and The Metropolitan Museum of Art, New York
163 left	The Metropolitan Museum of Art, New York, Gift of John D. Rockefeller, Jr., 1941
163 right	From *Japanese Prints: Hokusai and Hiroshige in the Collection of Louis V. Ledoux.* Copyright 1951 © 1979 by Princeton University Press
164	Reproduced by courtesy of the Trustees of The British Museum
165	The Art Institute of Chicago, Lucy Maud Buckingham Collection
166 left	Raghubir Singh/Woodfin Camp and Associates
166 right	© Museum Rietberg Zürich
254 left	National Gallery of Art, Washington, Andrew W. Mellon Collection
254 right	Cliché des Musées Nationaux, Paris
255 right	Scala/Art Resource
256 top	National Gallery, London
256 bottom	Alinari/Art Resource
257 left	The Metropolitan Museum of Art, New York
257 right	Alinari/Art Resource
258 left	Scala/Art Resource
258 right	Alinari/Art Resource
302 left	The Solomon R. Guggenheim Museum, New York. Photo: Robert E. Mates
302 right	Karl Ströher Collection, Hessiches Landesmuseum, Darmstadt
303 left	© Bruno Jarret, Musée Rodin, Paris
303 right	Alinari/Art Resource
304 left	Collection, The Museum of Modern Art, New York
304 right	The Solomon R. Guggenheim Museum, New York
305 top	The St. Louis Art Museum
305 bottom	The Metropolitan Museum of Art, New York, Bequest of Mrs. H. O. Havemeyer, 1929, The H. O. Havemeyer Collection
306 left	Reproduced with permission of AT&T
306 right	Courtesy of the Australian Information Service
307 left	The Museum of Modern Art, New York, Bequest of David M. Levy
307 right	The Metropolitan Museum of Art, New York